face it
with Love

---

the guide to conquering fear

Charmaine —

May God ever open your eyes to just how much He loves you !

FACEIT, LLC Publishing
PO Box 7511
Gainesville, GA 30504

face it

with Love

---

the guide to conquering fear

by

KIM MOORE

Table of Contents

Acknowledgements

Wherever we are, whatever we accomplish and in all that we possess, people have played a role. There is no one or no thing that is self-made. Everything happens in and through relationship.

My life and this book are no different. It is virtually impossible to thank all that have contributed. Many of these people are acknowledged on the pages that follow.

However, there is one in particular. This one was given to me for the day of adversity. First, she was a daughter in spirit. Many years later she became a friend and then an advocate. In 2014, we partnered to form FACEIT, LLC. Today, we are activating God's people to live free and fearless.

Amy for your love, support and sacrifice my whole heart overflows with thanksgiving.

Introduction

In June of 2013, I was soaking in my bathtub, which I had repurposed into a hot tub. My body had fully surrendered to the heat when I heard God say, "Make a list, and call those pastors' wives that you know personally. Ask them whether or not they trust you to deliver a message at an upcoming women's meeting." Immediately, I objected. My past rushed to my aid. Growing up, I was strongly discouraged from inviting myself to another's house to play, eat, or sleep. It was considered impolite. Rather, I was taught to wait until I was invited. I frowned upon kids, and even ministers, inviting themselves places. Despite thinking it rude, a part of me enjoyed the ability of others to display such frankness—*just not enough to do it!*

The truth is that there is a fear of rejection cleverly hidden beneath my desire to be polite. I fear that the very hint of inadequacy would be grounds for refusal. In his E-book, *The 14 Silent Struggles – You Thought No One Else Understood*, Andy Mort sums up my experience best when describing the "Imposter Syndrome." Andy writes, "It feels like you're somewhere you aren't equipped to be; everyone else knows what they're doing, and you are punching above your weight in a place you don't belong."

Often, I have felt this way when it comes to ministry. Even though I am very confident that God has given me wisdom and revelation from the gospel of Jesus Christ, I have felt insecure and susceptible to the taunts of the adverse accusations that I am an *imposter*—that is, *one who pretends to be someone else in order to deceive others, especially for dishonest gain.*

The fear I experienced was real. My protest to God's request was earnest, albeit learned. There I sat in my repurposed bathtub. No sooner had I let go of my complaint that the hot water again had its way, relaxing my muscles. Then, I clearly heard these words, "Face Your Fear: Fulfill Your Destiny." My soul wrapped itself around these words before I could object. Six simple words: one huge assignment. And then, the still small voice repeated His request. *"Make a list and call those pastors' wives that you know personally. Ask them whether or not they trust you to deliver a message at an upcoming women's meeting."*

This time, I agreed. Still, I was afraid. What made the fear more terrorizing was that God did not promise me everything was going to turn out to my liking. He didn't tell me that the women would say yes. Rather, He said that if I got in the room with that which I feared, I would fulfill my destiny. Fulfilling my destiny did not depend on the approval of these women. All of them could have refused my request, and I still would have fulfilled my God-given assignment!

Why did I have such fear? This was my community. Loosely, we held together through a common desire to minister to God's people. We shared ministry overseers, attended annual retreats, and joined together for infrequent breakfasts or lunches. We supported one another's ministry, as well as were able. I was familiar with these women. They were familiar with me. Yet, I feared rejection. They gave me no reason to fear. I brought it to the assignment all by myself. And now, I would have to face it!

Making the list was the easy part. I came up with a list of about ten names. I successfully connected with seven pastors' wives, while playing phone tag with three others. Trembling, I made the first call hoping to get voice-mail. Instead, she picked up right away. I asked for a time I could speak with her about something God placed on my heart. She said, "Let's talk right now!" I was not prepared for this response. With stuttering speech, I asked her whether or not she would trust me to speak at an upcoming women's meeting. Now, imagine me stammering as I requested an opportunity to speak to a group of women. I don't know of any that speak for a living that stutter! Yet, here I am.

I told her of the fear I experienced in calling her at the risk of being perceived as an imposter, and a minister at that! It is interesting that despite the fact that she knew me, heard me speak, and has often validated the gift and anointing God has given me to speak, I still contended with fear! No reassurance offered abated the fear of being an imposter. Not only was I afraid of rejection, but I was also afraid of being perceived as ill equipped, fake, and self-serving. I felt all of that, even though none of it was true.

Fortunately, this Pastor's wife, along with the six others I contacted, knew me. They too, had already heard me speak.

All seven enthusiastically said, "Yes!" One said that God had brought me to her mind to speak in the couple of months preceding my request. Another said that she had always desired that I come, but wasn't sure of the best format. Still another said that she believed this was only the beginning of what God was about to do and that I should come immediately! Within the next couple of months, I spoke to the women in each of these places. Still, even if these women all had refused my request, I would have fulfilled my destiny. God said that if I faced my fear, I would fulfill my destiny. When I initiated the request, despite feeling inadequate, phony, and self-promoting, I completed my assignment. I asked. Whether I was accepted, or refused, my satisfaction had to rest in answering God's request. This time, the fact that I was met with such enthusiasm was the icing on the cake. And while almost everybody likes icing, sometimes the cake has to be enough.

I remember the time I needed to have a sensitive conversation with my husband. My heart's desire was to have a meaningful and productive conversation. I took care to find the best time, as well as to manage my words and demeanor. Despite my preparation and optimism, I still feared his response. The discussion ended abruptly when, after registering objection, my husband left the house.

I was crushed. I lay on my bed and cried. I asked the Lord what I could do to mend things. Softly, I heard God say, "Make his favorite meal." That meant barbecue chicken in the slow cooker with cabbage, and potatoes. I went to the store, got what I needed, and prepared the meal. I made it many times before. So, it was easy.

Upon texting my husband to let him know what I made, he quickly let me know that he wasn't hungry and did not know when he would be home. I was devastated! I ran back to my bedroom, flung myself across the bed, and cried a completely new set of tears. Here is the dialogue between God and me that followed:

God: *Who told you to make his favorite meal?*
Me: *You did.*
God: *And I thank you for making me a meal. I am well pleased.*
Me: *But it didn't mend things between us.*
God: *Outcomes belong to me. It is enough that you made the meal. It was not a waste.*

The Christ life is about obedience to God. Responding to God had to be enough for me. This is especially so, since I didn't get the outcome I desired. We can do the right things, the right way, at the right time, with the right people, and the right motive. But this does not always guarantee that we will get the right or desired outcome. Outcomes belong to God! Paul makes this clear in I Corinthians 3:7. He writes, "So then, neither he who plants is anything, nor he who waters, but God who gives the increase. God determines the outcome of a thing!" This is freeing. All we have to do is our part.

And sometimes our part is simply doing the right thing for the sake of doing it. Knowing we cannot control outcomes liberates us to focus on what we are doing presently. For instance, God's will is always to heal us. How God accomplishes His will varies from situation to situation. Sometimes, He heals through the restoration of health in this life. At other times, He heals through death. Why does God choose one method for this one and another for that one? Who knows? But we can know with certainty that God knows what is best for us. Moreover, He works all things together for the good of those that love Him!

I remember Julisa. She was diagnosed with stage 4-breast cancer. Back in 2011, Julisa was given 12 to 14 months to live. I remember her fear and her prayer. Julisa feared not being around for her 3 young children. The thought frightened her more than death. In spite of that tremendous fear, her prayer went something like this: "Lord, I know it is your will to heal me. And I trust you will do this. Thank you for healing me." Julisa continues to live and defied the doctor's prediction. She is healed. What stood out against the backdrop of the fear of not being present for her kids was Julisa's love for God. She was fully persuaded that God would heal her body. But Julisa left it up to God whether He would do so in this life and fulfill her desire, or whether He would do so by removing her from her body via death. Julisa admits that, "Sitting in the room with Jesus and cancer has been easier some days than others." Still, she clings to the belief that the outcome belongs to God.

And then, there is Sharon. I also had the privilege to experience her journey through breast cancer. What is remarkable is that she also believed God would heal her, and left the method up to God. Today, Sharon travels across the country to share her story and encourage others who are battling the disease.

But there are countless others that love God and also

believed God would heal them. And He did. They experienced healing when God removed them from bodies plagued with cancer. Death was the method God chose. We may never know why. However, we cannot say that they had less faith than Julisa or Sharon. Perhaps they had more. What we can say is that God has been faithful in His healing. And whether through life or death, how He chooses to heal remains His prerogative. That's because the outcome belongs to God. Perhaps we might experience far less stress and greater joy if we grasp this one fact: the final outcome of a thing belongs to God. If an outcome seems inconsistent with what we expect from God, then it could be that God has not rendered a final decision on the matter. In this case, it is important to continue believing. We must continue to participate in God's word what we know to be true and see what God will do for us!

Recently, I learned of a woman that was healed of cancer. She remained cancer free for five years before it reappeared. The second time, God healed her through death. A cancer diagnosis evokes a fear of death in nearly everyone. Despite medical strides, some still die. Whether we live or die may matter less than how we respond to the circumstances in which we find ourselves. The Christian life is about yielding to a supremely loving God. Sometimes, we refuse this supremely loving God because we are afraid. Like me, some fear rejection. Others fear abandonment. Still others fear poverty. And then some fear sickness and disease. Many more fear dying. There is an endless list of other things that people fear.

As I am writing this book, I am realizing a new fear. That is, the fear of commanding others. I have led by example, guided others through counseling, and influenced others through teaching. But I have not commanded others. Let me explain. Leading not only involves serving by example, but also providing a foundation of trust, building on a connection, and moving people to action. All of these are important.

But leading also requires giving direction, making hard decisions, and accepting the outcome of those decisions. At various times, I have had wonderfully brilliant people around me to help implement the vision God has given me. They have been competent in their areas of expertise and cheerfully volunteered their time for my cause. I chose to lean on their expertise at times when I knew God was telling me to do otherwise. I neither felt qualified, nor secure enough with God, to object. Honestly, I did not believe God would back my redirecting those more skilled than I. Each time I over-relied on the competence and expertise of others to make decisions that God intended me to make, the projects were pro-longed. I struggled. The competent became weary and eventually chose other projects.

Although not something I enjoy, leading does involve telling others what to do—*even when they have more knowledge and skill than we do.* Sometimes that means taking risks without a favorable guaranteed outcome. But the outcome belongs to God. Making decisions and directing people belongs to the leader.

Immediately, what comes to mind is the centurion's response to Jesus offering to come to his home and heal his servant. The entire story is found in Matthew 8:5-13. The centurion says this to Jesus in verse 8 and 9,

> "Lord, I am not worthy that You should come under my roof.
> But only speak a word, and my servant will be healed. For I
> also am a man under authority, having soldiers under me. And
> I say to this *one*, 'Go,' and he goes; and to another, 'Come,' and
> he comes; and to my servant, 'Do this,' and he does it."

Jesus marveled, acknowledging the greatness of the centurion's faith. Jesus told the Centurion, "Go your way; and as you have believed, so let it be done for you." And his servant was healed.

Commanding is telling others what to do and knowing they will do it. Of this, I have been afraid. I always believed that commanding meant being in charge and highly visible. Jesus and the centurion had a different understanding. Both were subservient to others. Remember what the centurion said, "For I, also, am a man under authority."

Jesus and the centurion were "servants" that had been given command of others. They neither saw themselves, nor behaved as if they were "number one." In fact, Jesus said that He did not come to be served, but rather to serve under the command of His Father.

Part of my challenge was that I was still bound by humanity's inherent tendency to want to be "number one." I had not yet experienced the freedom that comes from recognizing that I am not in charge. On my own, I rightfully thought that I did not have what it took to direct others. In John 5:19, Jesus told His disciples the following: "I tell you the truth; the Son can do nothing by himself. He does only what he sees the Father doing. Whatever the Father does, the Son also does." Jesus meant it literally when He told Thomas in John 14:10, "The words that I speak to you I do not speak on My own authority; but the Father who dwells in Me does the works." Paul agrees in II Corinthians 5:19, saying, "God was in Christ reconciling the world to Himself."

It was God first working in Christ, rather than Christ initiating the work Himself. Jesus participated with God! But God did the work. Maybe instead of asking God what might we do for Him today, we should ask God what work He would like to do through us today, and then we can simply participate.

If Jesus, the Son of God, did not have what it took, why should we be so foolish to think that we do. On my own, I was insecure. I was striving to be "number one," when all God asks is that I follow, yield, and respond to Him. I did not need more self-confidence. I had enough. It got me here, to this place of *insecurity*. I needed more confidence in the God that gives me assignments. There's a farewell I have enjoyed using at the end of letters that now has added meaning. It reads like this, "Serving at the pleasure of His command." I am "number two," and I am happy to be so.

I am beginning to experience the freedom and joy of being number two! I no longer fear making decisions and directing others, because prayerfully they reflect God's agenda, and the outcome of my actions belongs to Him. In the event that I make mistakes, and I surely will, I can know that even these were built into His plan for my life. And He wastes nothing! He works all together for the good of those that love Him. I can lend my entire being to God's initiatives because I don't have to be "number one." I don't have to be "right." I don't have to be "first," "the best," or even "the most." I just have to be me.

This book is not about any one fear, nor is it solely about me. Rather, it is about receiving love, growing bold, and conquering fear. All of us contend with fear. Except for Jesus Christ, all have been defeated by fear. Regardless of the fear, the antidote is love. It is always love.

FACE IT is something each of us has the opportunity to do everyday. Each day, we have opportunities to accept or reject perceptions of people, situations, and opinions of others that are shrouded in fear. Or, we can simply respond with love. *Face It with Love: The Guide to Conquering Fear* is about seeing and developing new ways of responding to the fear that blocks God's blessings to us, as well as a way to recognize the benefits of these blessings.

The outcomes belong to God. Blessings and benefits are His to distribute. But entering and remaining in God's process is ours to decide. We do not have to work up the courage to enter or remain in the process when we become afraid. Instead, God pours courage into our hearts for us to receive.[1]

His love commands our devotion and inspires submission. God's love makes us bold. Love motivates us to do the unimaginable, whether it is mundane or monumental. That's because God's love is the only thing that trumps fear. And His love is best expressed through community. Today, it's your turn. It's my turn. It's your turn. It's our turn to demonstrate God's love in both the small and large things, in both need and abundance, between fellow Christians and those who do not share our faith, at home and abroad. This requires that we FACE whatever and whoever stands in the way. By facing it, we become God's tangible love on Earth. It's time for that love to shine! You know it as well as I. Eleanor Roosevelt urges us onward with these words: "You gain strength, courage, and confidence by every experience in which you really stop to look fear in the face. You are able to say to yourself, 'I have lived through this horror. I can take the next thing that comes along.' You must do the thing you think you cannot do."[2]

CHAPTER 1

The Key

"You want me to give her a key?" the guy asked.

"I want you to give her a possibility. And that's what a key represents, an open door, a chance."[3]

We all need a chance at a fulfilling life. Without such possibility, we hope in vain. Everybody needs a chance! Otherwise, we merely exist, but do not live to the fullest.

Life is beautiful. It can also be ugly. Life is supposed to be about love and relationships, not fear and isolation. It's supposed to be about the duet of connection and separation. The irreconcilable differences between them are responsible for some of our greatest achievements. It is also the culprit for much of the tension we experience inside and out—*both personally and relationally*. This tension exists in the most educated and relationally healthy, as well as the uneducated and relationally unhealthy. It exists in rich and poor. The quality of our lives and relationships has to do with how well we manage the tension.

This book is not about how to do that. However, it is about an underlying factor that contributes to this tension.

And it is this underlying factor that threatens balance and harmony. It also hinders many of us from experiencing life to the fullest. So, what is our best chance and hope for knowing a more abundant life? What is the door through which we can pass to experience deeper, more robust, and loving relationships? How can this happen when we are all so wonderfully and dreadfully different? And then to think God made each of us this way! All of us are as distinct as our individual fingerprints, including identical twins. Each one of us is God's unrepeatable miracle and an intentional expression of our Creator. But also, sin left us deeply wounded and with some amazing survival skills that are counterproductive to enjoying life in grace with God and others. We are perfect and without flaw in Christ. However, while in these earthly bodies, we must contend with our flesh that is anti-Christ.

When magnified, we are as different as individual grains of sand. The countless shapes, sizes, and colors in a fist full of sand are nothing short of miraculous. Still take a walk along any sandy beach and the sand looks and feels like one unified masterpiece appearing relatively the same color! When enlarged, it's hard to believe the sheer number of entirely completely separate pieces of sand present so unified. Sand is one. It is also many granules. We are like that. We can be like that. Whether we are speaking about marriage, a family, the Body of Christ, a company, or community, we are like sand. We can be like sand. We must be whole and wholly separate. That is, we must own and develop that which makes us unique. We also must accept and nurture that which makes us the same. As we do, God knits us together. He is making us into one fine specimen, that is, the Bride of Christ.

It's through love and relationships that we contribute to developing the family of God, and in turn, we build the Kingdom of God. The family of God loosely consists of all those that accept Christ as their Savior and Lord. The Kingdom of God is righteousness, joy, and peace in the Holy Spirit. We develop the family as we develop disciples. We build the Kingdom as we stand right with Christ, bringing His reign to our own hearts and minds first and then to the relationships that concern us. Moreover, we build the Kingdom, as the joy and peace belonging to Christ rules each one of us. As Christians, we share the DNA of Christ. Within our born-again DNA is all the potential of Christ.

It's in our spiritual DNA to be someone amazing, do something astounding, and connect deeply with others! It's in us to let go of something we value in order to acquire something we perceive to be of greater value. It's in us to be significant in the circles of people that God has given us to influence. Therefore, influence we must. The fact that we are still alive is proof that our highest and best use has yet to be realized! We have yet to amaze the people to whom we have been assigned!

Today, God continues to perform the work He began in you. You are reading these words (and hopefully the words that follow) at this exact moment in time because you have yet to achieve your God-given dreams and experience satisfaction in relationships with those you love and care about most. Whether we are speaking about the purpose for which God created you, or the relationships that matter most to you, your hopes and dreams reside on the other side of fear. Reading further, you will discover that this is not by some fluke! Rather, it is intentional.

The key to personal and relational fulfillment is facing that which we fear. The bigger the stage upon which we face fear the greater our reward. Although every stage seems big and every room seems small when fear is present. Fear has a foreboding presence wherever it is experienced.

Still, God decided that facing their fear would result in His people developing the substance and stamina of Jesus Christ. God is using this little understood principle today. And it is the key to meaningful relationships and work. Paul writes the principle this way: "So I find that, as a rule, when I want to do what is good, evil is right there with me."[4] Recently, a pastor suggested that most Christians have or will struggle with fear, especially given all that's occurring in the world now.

Fear has robbed so many of the joy and privilege of having someone to love, something to do, and something for which to hope. Adam and Eve sinned. Jesus died for their sin and for every other sin known to mankind. But Jesus did not just die for the sin we committed. He actually became the sin we committed! Let us appreciate that it is one thing to *do* something for another, and it's another thing to *become* something on behalf of another. Think about it this way. The chicken offers eggs to our breakfast. We have bacon because the pig became our breakfast. It is not hard to see the worth of each contribution.

By becoming sin for us, Jesus gave us the opportunity and an open door to experience a real and intimate relationship with our Creator. Jesus' act of humility restored us to God. To God, we are as though we had not sinned. And we that receive the complete work of Christ are free from sin. Apostle Michael Leavell offers, "We do not struggle with sin, [but] rather [with] the temptation to sin."[5] Temptation is not sin. Occasionally, we do lose to temptation and sin. When we do, we have an advocate and a high priest. We can confess our sin and find forgiveness, grace, and hope in our time of need. I don't mean to oversimplify this. Godly sorrow produces discipline, desire, and a zeal for God and anger toward sin. Godly sorrow produces a testimony by taking what the enemy intended to destroy you and using it to build the Kingdom!

Sometimes there are consequences when we sin that we must painstakingly work through. However, remember that sin has already been punished. So, while the consequences may feel like God is punishing us, He's not. To do so would mean we are being tried and punished twice for the same crime! God doesn't belabor our sins! We shouldn't either—not the sins of others, nor our own! Still, many people do. Fear hides, resides, and fuels temptation and sin. And this is something to consider when we are tempted and give in to sin.

Unfortunately, we often focus first and almost exclusively on the sin committed. People leave us feeling no more liberated than when they came to us! Unknowingly, we contribute to others' recurrent sin. This leaves many well-intentioned Christians doubtful that real change is possible. For some, freedom from sin might seem possible for others, but not for them.

It's what God focuses on first that has become the game-changer for so many others, including me. When Adam and Eve sinned, they both knew it and God already knew it! He did not begin by asking Adam and Eve about their sin. That would have been a dead-end question! It neither helped Adam or Eve, nor improved their relationship with God. Instead, knowing that Adam and Eve had sinned, God asked, "Where are you?" By virtue of Adam's answer, God might have also asked, "What are you thinking?" Both of these open-ended questions support real dialogue. Both help, rather than hinder, the one that desires freedom.

Surprisingly, Adam's answer revealed a bigger problem than sin. Adam's response to God asking, "Where are you?" was, "I heard Your voice in the garden, and I was afraid because I was naked; and I hid myself." In this one sentence, we learned Adam's location physically, mentally, emotionally and spiritually. Physical location: Garden (of Eden). Mental location: trying to fix his condition. Emotional location: afraid. Spiritual location: separated from God. Like Adam, we try to fix what we have done ourselves and apart from God. And since we can't fix it, we hide it because we are afraid of being punished. Our biggest problem is not sin. As previously stated, sin already has been fully addressed by the sacrifice of Jesus Christ. Our biggest problem is fear! Fear prompted Adam and Eve to cover and hide. Fear prompted Adam and Eve to make a costume in preparation for audience with God.

Fear also undermined Adam and Eve's relationship by changing it from one based on love and trust to one based on fear and suspicion. Fear obstructed their pathway to rule, subdue, and replenish the earth. Fear affected their ability to work together toward a common goal. For Adam and Eve, fear was the real culprit. Fear affects our ability to engage in healthy, meaningful, and fulfilling relationships. It also interferes with our ability to fulfill our God-given purpose. Adam and Eve discovered this very thing.

Writing this book made it indelibly clear to myself and others that facing that which we fear is the greatest singular obstacle to experiencing fulfillment, both personally and relationally. When fear shuts us down or causes us to behave erratically, neither money, nor time can bail us out. Consider the man that had money and time, but was immobilized by fear in Matthew 25:24-26:

> Then he who had received the one talent came and said, 'Lord, I knew you to be a hard man, reaping where you have not sown, and gathering where you have not scattered seed. And I was afraid, and went and hid your talent in the ground. Look, there you have what is yours.'
>
> But his lord answered and said to him, 'You wicked and lazy servant, you knew that I reap where I have not sown, and gather where I have not scattered seed.

Oftentimes, I have thought if only I had the money, the time, or the right people I would be able to—*you fill in the blank!* Perhaps you have felt this way, too. Fear is no respecter of resources. The things and experiences we desire most are on the other side of fear. Fear cannot be bribed. It has one objective. I like the way Jesus sums it up: "The thief's purpose is to steal and kill and destroy."[6]

On the other hand, Jesus came that we might have a rich and rewarding life. He planned for our lives and relationships to be exciting, robust, and full of adventure! So, you might be fresh off an amazing conquest and ready to experience God on a completely new level. Or, you might be in the throes of defeat and with great effort drag yourself to these words. Regardless, one thing is for sure. This is your time. This is your now. This is your moment. What separates this moment from past moments is that you are here in it, not there. What connects this moment to your future is that you are here in it, not there. Therefore, what you do now matters, perhaps more than ever. When your past, present, and future are all in the same place, needless to say, it is tense. But this is the only place that long-lasting victories are won! We need more victories among God's people. We need your personal victories and we need relationship victories. This is the way we influence the arena to which God assigns us.

Lack of money hasn't done us in, nor has a lack of relationships. It's not even a lack of opportunity in many cases. It's fear: plain and simple. Fear separates us from resources, people, and opportunities. Fear's objective is to isolate us from that which we require to relate well with others and to pursue our purpose. Until we face fear, we can have only pseudo-hope of the kind of Godly experiences we crave in life and relationships.

The fear you refuse to face is the key that unlocks new opportunities, opens doors, and offers you the possibility of experiencing God's rich and satisfying life for yourself and with others! Life is about love, relationships, and conquests. And the key to fulfilling relationships and dreams is getting in the room with that which you fear!

CHAPTER 2

Moses' Key

If I were to ask you to name Moses' single greatest accomplishment, what would you say? If you are like most people, you would say that he delivered the children of Israel from Egypt. Most of us have heard the story so many times that we don't consider any other possibility. I mean what could possibly rival bringing a nation of people out of bondage? It's understandable that Moses is best remembered for delivering God's people from Pharaoh. But what if this achievement was the result of something even bigger? What if Israel's deliverance from Egypt was the result of something else? What if, in the wisdom of God, Israel's deliverance was tied to Moses overcoming his fear? I mean, what if Moses' prize for facing his fear was the freedom of a nation. What if a nation of people came crashing through the doors of freedom because one man dared to get in the room and contend with his fear? Maybe it was in facing his fear that Moses fulfilled his destiny.

"ORDINARY MAN CONFRONTS KING: WINS FREEDOM FOR HIS NATION!" This makes for a great headline. It's punchy, grabs attention, and easily peaks our interest. Nearly everyone has been in a fight! Most of us desire to win. And if we have ever fought in a fight with someone or something we perceive as being bigger than ourselves, we're hooked. We want to find out how this ordinary man won. That's what a subtitle does for us. It elaborates on the headline and is usually short, potent, and to the point. If I were to give the above headline a subtitle, it would read: **Moses Faces Fear and Fulfills His Destiny.**

This is a great place to pick up Moses' story. But first, I should say that I really like Moses, and it's not because of his most famous accomplishment. Aside from Moses being honest, helpful, and expressing genuine love for God and His people, it's his lesser-known accomplishment that inspires me.

We first meet Moses in Exodus 1. He was born during the time when God's people were enslaved in Egypt. Joseph had died and a new Pharaoh rose to power. The new Pharaoh didn't know Joseph. The Hebrew people no longer enjoyed the favor of the Pharaoh. Despite oppression, God's people multiplied in number. To stave off fear of retaliation, Pharaoh ordered the death of all male children born to Hebrew women, of which Moses was one.

Moses' mother and sister Miriam saved Moses by placing him in a basket and floating it in the Nile River. Pharaoh's daughter found him, adopted him, named him "Moses," and raised him in the palace of the Pharaoh himself. As Moses reached adulthood, empathy for the plight of his people heightened. One day, he observed an Egyptian beating a Hebrew slave. Moses interceded, killed the Egyptian, and tasted the reality of deliverance for the first time. In a similar incident, this time involving two Hebrew brothers, Moses unsuccessfully intervened. One of the brothers hassled Moses and suggested that he would kill one of them as he did the Egyptian. It was then that Moses realized that killing the Egyptian was public knowledge. Moses was afraid.[7]And sure enough, Pharaoh knew it and sought to kill Moses. He fled from the 'face' of Pharaoh.[8]

Moses ran away to the land of Midian. We find him at the well where shepherds water their sheep. Jethro's daughters are at the well shepherding his flocks when other shepherds prevent them access to the water. Moses interrupts the shepherds to gain access for Jethro's daughters. For the second time Moses recognizes the power of delivering someone from the hands of another. Again, Moses experienced his God-given purpose and desire. A spark was lit. But it wouldn't be for another 40 years before Moses turned aside to see the bush on fire without being consumed.

You and I also have God-given dreams and desires. Like Moses, we have probably already experienced the power as a result of engaging those desires. Years ago, I remember conducting training sessions for employees working in the field of developmental disabilities. The first time I put the script down and just began to teach conversationally, the response was amazing. I was asked if I spoke on any other topics outside the field. Another person asked if I was a motivational speaker. Still, another asked whether or not I was a minister. The questions were interesting, given that most of the content had to do with Medicaid policy and requirements, which left little room for personal interpretation and was, by many accounts, boring. But I was in demand. I felt powerful, important, and effective. However, it would still be many years before I would become a full-time writer and speaker.

Earlier on in his adult life, which likely began at a far younger age than our own, Moses experienced the power of freeing some people from the grips of others. Earlier in my own adult life, I experienced the power of releasing people through speaking. And much earlier than that, writing became the place I went to commune with my heart. I am almost certain that if you haven't already, you will very soon encounter an opportunity that will resonate loudly with something on the inside of you. Or, perhaps you already have and just haven't realized it. It could be that as you read these words, that very experience flashes across your mind. If God wants us to participate with the dream He has given, then He must awaken it within us somehow. Likely, He has already introduced you to the dream He dreams with you, or the qualities you find desirable in a marriage partner. You may not realize it immediately. But perhaps you will recall the power, joy, and fulfillment experienced when engaging in that activity or relating to the person with those attributes.

For others, that awakening may come through a painful experience. For these, it may not be a taste of power, but rather powerlessness and sadness that instigates the desire to make things better for others. For example, after watching his brother suffer with adverse effects from the use of multiple medications, a teenager decided to become a pharmacist who specialized in researching drug interactions.

And consider how God shared His desire with Adam concerning a mate. God brought the animals (male and female) to Adam to see what he would call them. And whatever Adam called them that became their name. Now imagine that you and I watched as one hundred animals came to us in twos. And we were given the responsibility of naming each pair. What desire is likely to arise in us? What question are we likely to ask? That's right, "Where's my other?" Adam was one. There was no other. Adam likely experienced longing for another, one like himself. God awakened this desire in Adam. God's dream had become Adam's desire.

Whatever is relevant to God's dreams for us, He must awaken a desire for it within us. We must acquire a taste for the dreams and relationships that God desires to share with us. If we do not, we will not have a compelling reason to pursue it relentlessly. For Adam, it was upon being presented animals in reproductive pairs. For my young friend, it was watching a sibling suffer adverse effects of medication. For me, it was the joy in training others. And for Moses, it was experiencing the power of setting another free. Whatever God desires to express through us, He must first impress upon us.

Moses was first impressed when he delivered the Hebrew from the Egyptian. He was again impressed at the well upon interceding with the male shepherds on behalf of the female shepherds.

And he was massively impressed when he saw a flaming bush that was not consumed by the fire. What happened afterwards begins the story of Moses' lesser-known accomplishment that I find absolutely remarkable. So many messages have been offered concerning the fact that the bush burned, albeit was not consumed. I am throwing this in the mix. First, Moses stopped to consider the phenomenon. Certainly, he had observed other bushes on fire, and he may have even set some on fire. But, this one was different. Although it burned, the fire did not destroy it—*as fires typically do.* Could it be that an incensed, albeit immature Moses, was initially consumed by his desire to free God's people? Could it be that the Moses that stopped to contemplate the bush on fire, yet not destroyed, was actually seeing himself? What I mean is could this be the visual God gave Moses to carry with him on the orders he was about to receive? Moses was well acquainted with his human mortality. But now maybe God was introducing Moses to his Divine immortality. And where he was going, Moses would certainly need to know God was with Him!

That's because God requested Moses to return to the 'face' of his fear in order to deliver His people. You will recall that Moses ran from the 'face' of Pharaoh because he threatened to kill Moses and he feared death. It is easy to miss the first half of Exodus 3:10 because the second part sounds so much more glorious, " . . . bring my people out of Egypt." God desired to bring His people out of bondage to a good and large land, to a land flowing with milk and honey. And Moses got the assignment! Wow!

But it's what came before in Exodus 3:10 that caused a man consumed by the desire to liberate God's people to stumble. God said to Moses, "I am sending you to Pharaoh . . ." Not Pharaoh! Certainly not Pharaoh, the one that threatened to kill Moses! Seriously, God? The verse in its entirety reads this way:

> Now go, for I am sending you to Pharaoh. You must lead my people Israel out of Egypt.[9]

God was sending Moses to a person, rather than a nation. And that person held the key to the open door of freedom for a nation. Remember, Moses ran from this man because he feared losing his life. To Moses, Pharaoh was the threat of death personified. God was sending Moses to face death. He would have to face this fear to fulfill his destiny. In fact, the only way Moses could fulfill his dream to liberate God's people was to confront that which he feared. Moses would have to face death in order to overcome the fear of death.

Wait a minute. That's like God saying to me in 1982, " . . . Strengthen the weak hands, and make firm the feeble knees. Say to those who are fearful-hearted, 'Be strong, and do not fear! Behold, your God will come with vengeance, with the recompense of God; He will come and save you' " Then and sometimes even now, my own hands feel weak, my own knees feel feeble, and I, too experience fear! Don't get me wrong; since I first encountered Christ, I have had a deep desire to tell everyone and anyone that would listen about God. That desire has not waned over the years. It has intensified. And fear has kept pace!

That's because I was also insecure. I was so insecure it was debilitating. The only voice I could muster the courage to use was on paper. Paper accepted my words without question. No matter how many misspellings, or how flawed the grammar, paper always received my words. Written words became the truest expression of my heart. On paper, I was honest. I was raw. Paper was unconditionally accepting. It told me that I was okay. But sharing my thoughts with those that mattered most was difficult. To think of having to share thoughts with a room full of people I didn't know was impossible. It wasn't that I did not know what I desired to say, or that saying it was difficult. The potential adverse response to my thoughts loomed larger than actually speaking them. I was afraid of saying the wrong thing and of the possible repercussions. The Bible has a word for this. It's called fear. Jesus had something to say about this. In Matthew 10:28, after telling the disciples to speak what they hear from Him (and even shout it), Jesus encourages them further, saying, "Do not fear those who kill the body but cannot kill the soul. But rather, fear Him who is able to destroy both soul and body in hell."

I was so insecure that I would outwardly please others and inwardly rebel because I was afraid of rejection. Whether it is rejection or abandonment, fear keeps us quiet when we ought to speak up. Fear keeps us sitting down when we ought to stand up. It keeps us hidden when God wants to show us off. Single-handedly, fear derails dreams and undermines relationships.

The only way to overcome fear and experience a rich and rewarding life is to get in the room with that which we fear. And that room lies within us. Facing fear requires that we get to the heart of the matter. Here's what I mean. Read over the chart below and see what many say they fear versus what is actually feared.

Diagram 1: What We Really Fear

WE SAY WE ARE AFRAID OF	WHAT WE REALLY MEAN IS THAT WE ARE AFRAID OF
1. **Heights**	Falling
2. **Water**	Drowning
3. **The Dark**	What might be lurking in the dark
4. **Sickness and Disease**	Dying
5. **Commitment**	Responsibility
6. **Trusting Others**	Abuse, neglect, exploitation
7. **Public Speaking**	Rejection
8. **Loving**	Being loved in return
9. **Fighting**	Losing
10. **Giving**	Lack

Do any of these fears ring true with you? One or more are likely to resonate with each of us. That's because we were born into sin and fear of punishment was a consequence. In Genesis 3:10 it was a fear of punishment from God that prompted Adam and Eve to hide. And, while Jesus' dying on the cross destroyed sin, fear, and our tendency to hide, many of us have not learned how to behave within this truth. The ability to living truthfully requires more than praying and believing something true. It requires love, courage, and relationships. This is why so many of our confessions are empty and our lives lack the richness and fullness that God intended. The Christ-life is meant to be experienced in the community of God, the Holy Spirit, and fellow believers. Herein lies our greatest possibility for true and lasting transformation and deep, loving relationships with others.

By misnaming that which we fear, overcoming the fear is hopeless. Managing a fear of heights by not climbing up the 102 floors of New York's Empire State Building does not address the fear of falling. Until one is in a situation in which they risk falling, they will continue to fear falling. We call this getting in the room with that which we fear.

Similarly, staying away from water will not resolve the fear of drowning. It is only when one is in the water that they can overcome the fear of drowning. I remember taking a group of ladies on my boat one summer. None of them could swim and wore lifejackets. All feared drowning. I stopped the boat in the middle of the lake and jumped in. I invited the ladies to join me. It took about 30 minutes for the three ladies to muster the courage to enter the water from the steps. Once in the water, we played and talked for a while. I showed them that where their feet went, their body would follow. Also, I showed them how to tread water as we played. Through it all, they were increasingly able to relax. I applauded their bravery.

Still, I knew the lifejackets were their security. And I wanted them to experience true freedom from the fear of drowning. That meant one thing—taking off the lifejackets. I was willing to take the risk with them. As a former water safety instructor, lifeguard, and competitive swimmer, I pushed the envelope by asking each of them, one at a time, to remove the lifejacket and tread water with me. You can imagine the looks I got! "You aren't serious!" said one. Another said, "I 'm scared." I asked each to trust me. Each took a turn by removing her lifejacket, floating, and treading water unaided. They could have not accomplished this on their own. Fear was present. But love was also present. And perfect love drives away fear! That day these ladies minds were changed. They were in water and they did not drown, as they feared. With love's assurance of safety, they were able to overcome their fear of drowning.

Overcoming fear requires more than faith. It requires love and support from others. It requires community. Moses learned this too.

face it *with Love*

CHAPTER 3

The Backstory is the Real Story

God loves the idea of delivering His people! In this world, I think few things excite God more than to rescue His children, that they might experience freedom. Paul shares this enthusiasm in his first letter written to the Galatian Church,

> Jesus gave his life for our sins, just as God our Father planned, in order to rescue us from this evil world in which we live.[10]

Six times in the Old Testament, Father God raised up a man to deliver His children. All were deeply flawed. Still, God used them anyway! Moses was one of them. Insecure and fearing for his life, Moses ran from Pharaoh to the land of Midian. The story picks up in Exodus 2 with Moses sitting beside a well. We are told the priest of Midian has seen the daughters that shepherded their father's flock. It was their routine to water the flock from the well where Moses sat. But on this occasion, other shepherds were there and chased the shepherdesses away.

Moses responded, as if rescuing people were an innate trait. And likely, it was a characteristic distinct to Moses, which God was grooming within him. Exodus 2:17 and 18 (NLT) reads, "So, Moses jumped up and rescued the girls from the shepherds. Then he drew water for their flocks."

Indeed, Moses had at least two other recorded rescue attempts. One rescue was successful. The other failed. This time he succeeded. And it was a good thing too. Moses' confidence suffered from the previous failed attempt to intervene between brothers. He needed a confidence boost. This served nicely! The fact that it was women that Moses rescued likely spiked his confidence in the same way spiking the punch with alcohol is intended to covertly get a party started. Moses was pumped! But it didn't end there. The daughters' father insisted they invite Moses to dine in their home with them. They did and Moses accepted the invitation. Moses ended up remaining with Jethro and his family, shepherding the flock for about forty years.

During that time, he married Zipporah, one of Jethro's daughters. Moses ran from fear of Pharaoh into the arms of love! And it was all by God's design! The Hebrew meaning of Zipporah is "bird." It is commonly accepted that birds symbolize freedom and eternity. Birds are unfettered by gravity and soar high above earthly constraints. They are beautiful to watch. Unaided, our bodies are incapable of reaching such heights while maintaining such poise. For this reason, birds easily summon our fascination and win our admiration!

In the Bible, birds are classified as clean or unclean. Consider them both in Genesis 8:6-9.

After another forty days, Noah opened the window he had
made in the boat and released a raven. The bird flew back
and forth until the floodwaters on the earth had dried up.
He also released a dove to see if the water had receded and
it could find dry ground. But the dove could find no place
to land because the water still covered the ground. So, it
returned to the boat, and Noah held out his hand and drew
the dove back inside.

One difference between the two kinds of birds can been seen in
their behavior. Like the raven, dirty birds tend to be self-regulating
and reliant. While doves and other clean birds are self-regulating,
they are community minded. The raven experienced freedom and
never returned to the ark, preferring rather to rely upon itself. The
dove on the other hand, upon finding no dry land returned to the
ark and Noah's outstretched hand. They were in it together. When
we carefully study Zipporah, whose name means, "bird," we find a
woman that was both autonomous and communal. She used her
freedom to self-govern to benefit the community. One particular
incident comes to mind that seems to underscore this notion.
When Moses finally heads to Egypt with his wife and sons to
rescue God's people, one night, the Lord confronts Moses and
tries to kill him.[11] While the Bible does not give exact reason for
God's anger toward Moses, we might reasonably guess based on
Zipporah's actions. Exodus 4:26 says that she took a flint and cut
off her son's foreskin. Perhaps Moses failure to adhere to the law
of circumcision on the 8th day after a male infant's birth incited
God. Zipporah used her independence abating God's anger to the
benefit of her family and the entire community of Israel. That
woman was Moses' wife.

So, fear forced Moses' insecurity to the surface. He responded by running. But as God would have it, Moses ran into love. Love had a name. This time it was Jethro, a father. A father's love revitalized Moses. A father's love provided Moses freedom and bestowed upon him a future. His provision had a name. This time it was Zipporah. But God didn't stop building Moses' character and confidence by revitalizing, releasing, and giving him a future. God gave Moses stamina. Sons represent strength and permanence of the bloodline. Moses named his first son, Gershom "for he said, 'I have been in a foreign land.'"[12] Moses gained confidence in an unfamiliar place, with unfamiliar people who loved him. But it was in receiving that love and acceptance (symbolized by offspring) that inspired his confidence and built his strength. Moses named his second son, "Eliezer," which means "God is my help." God is the essence of strength. Through the naming of his sons, we can see Moses gaining confidence by transferring his focus from people to God—from those he can see to Him that he can't see. Where Moses perhaps could not see God before, we can conclude he is beginning to see God now!

That's what love does. It helps us to see what is not readily observable. This kind of seeing most often happens in a community of people joined by some purpose. It can happen among a group of soccer moms, a family, a small church group, a group of co-workers, or a few friends living life together. It can happen among a coed group, a multi-generational group, a mixed culture group, or an economically diverse group. The thing that's important is that the group is held together by external or internal purpose. Soccer, little league, cheerleading, and other sports' moms and dads are externally held together because their children play sports together. And a small church group or friends are held together by shared values. Commitment is needed regardless of what holds the group together.

Moses held himself together with Jethro's family. All saw him, as he did them. Jethro and Zipporah saw beyond Moses exterior to the man that would later be known as the deliverer of God's people. They loved Moses by speaking to that man! That's what God's love does. It speaks to your uniqueness, always aiming at your heart. God's love is more concerned about who you are, rather than what you do. Jethro and Zipporah loved Moses passionately. They rekindled desire inside of Moses. And it took a long time.

Sometimes the healing and restoration we need on the inside does not come about because we ignore our responsibility to participate in the process. While time doesn't change anything, change does require time. It takes many new experiences over time to root and ground us into a new way of thinking. It took Moses 40 years! Relationship hopping, whether from person to person, church to church, or job to job, hinders the real and lasting changes we desire for others and ourselves. That's not to say some relationships don't need to end. They do. Dr. Henry Cloud has written an excellent book about such relationships. It's called, "Necessary Endings."[13] In it he says,

> Your business and your life will change when you really, really get it that some people are not going to change, no matter what you do, and that still others have a vested interest in being destructive.

To some degree, nearly all people have the potential to change. The fact that some people realize this potential and others do not may have a lot to do with the choices we make. Cloud adds, "All of your precious resources—time, energy, talent, passion, money—should only go to the buds of your life or your business that are the best, are fixable, and are indispensable."[14]

Though we will all experience the need to end a relationship at some time in our lives, it's the long lasting healthy ones that offer the best possibility for growing confidence and courage. We need both to fulfill our dreams and enjoy life to the fullest. Moses' development was arrested and his destiny placed on hold when he ran in fear of Pharaoh. Life, hope, and courage slowly seeped back into him as he gave and received love from Jethro's family.

I remember when I first returned to church after being separated from my husband in July 2013. It had been months. After visiting many churches, I happened upon Joy Christian Center in Buford, Georgia. I found myself returning Sunday after Sunday. The love I experienced was overwhelming. The events landing me at this Church did not seem nearly as important as the fact that I was there. People were more concerned about validating my identity in Christ than trying to figure out what had happened to me and/or what I had done. Pastors Michael and Michelle were devoted to God and it was apparent. They were genuine. They asked nothing of me and offered me everything— time, resources, and unconditional love. I found their humility rare and admirable. I felt like they were in my distress right along with me, yet a step (or three or five), ahead of me. There was something different about Pastors Michael and Michelle. I wanted to follow them. I did and I gained much needed strength. Shortly after being there, I remember asking God what He would have me do. Clearly, I heard God say, "Love My people." That seemed too easy, so I waited for Him to tell me more. But each time I went back to God, He simply said, "Love My people." For the next 18 months that's exactly what I did. I visited the sick. I prayed for different ones. I sent note cards and gift cards, and I gave gifts. Intentionally, I sought out those needing encouragement. I loved and do love God's people at Joy. Life, hope, and courage began flowing into me again.

My heart is forever knitted together with this community of believers. Joy was one of the communities God used to heal my wounds and speak to my uniqueness. Another community was formed by my now son-in-law, Phillip, and one of my spiritual daughters, friend, and now FACEIT business partner, Amy. Both entered the very painful experience of my separation from my husband, affirmed me, and leant hands and resources that enabled me to move beyond crisis. Through Phillip and Amy, Joy Church, and my family and friends, God poured His love and compassion into this bruised reed and smoking flax. Every day, I am getting stronger and more confident.

After we have been crushed, humiliated and embarrassed, it is good that we heal and regain our strength. It was a good thing for Moses. And it would prove beneficial to an entire nation of people. It is good for me too and for those that stand to benefit from my life. And it is good for you to heal, to be restored, and to be strengthened. Whatever God has assigned us to do, will inevitably root out any tendency to accomplish it by our own efforts. It comes as a devastating blow to our pride, often directly related to the area of our assignment. For a very long time, my passion has been relationships. I am a counselor. I have written books, taught classes, and even spoken as a general session speaker at major conferences on marriage. What a blow to my ego to experience the demise of my own marriage. How humiliating! I have no words. This wasn't supposed to happen. But it did.

Like Moses, the love I received from God through community was essential. Love inspires courage. Moses would need a great deal of courage to face the man he ran from in fear. But first, Moses would have to face himself. To enter God's delight in delivering a nation of people from Pharaoh would require Moses to look at the man in the mirror.

CHAPTER 4

The Man in the Mirror

Love single-handedly inspires courage to face that which is difficult, dreadful, and potentially damaging or destructive. If we are to have a chance at a rich, fulfilling life including open and honest relationships with family and friends, we must face that which we fear. It is only through facing our fears that we can achieve our God-given dreams. We must do this by ourselves and with others. We also must do this *for* others and ourselves.

When what is occurring outside of us seems dreadful, it is a whole lot easier to speak up about it, rather than what's happening inside. Like the time a friend disclosed that each time a certain person spoke up, she became irritated. She admitted to having a word for this person: arrogant. My friend said she was shocked when God calmly said to her that the woman was only doing what He had asked. The woman was declaring God's word aloud. The woman was speaking up and out. She was confident. My friend was irritated because the woman was doing something that God had asked my friend to do. I know this because we have often talked about her belief and desire that God would have her speak publicly. And she was not doing so. When asked why, my friend confessed to being afraid. So, the real problem was not what the woman was doing. It was what my friend was not doing that caused her anguish. She feared the rejection that might follow speaking up.

I am thankful she trusted me enough to invite me into the room with her fear. I loved her. She knew it. And so sharing this space with her gave me the opportunity to encourage her. Here's what I said to her. *"God asked you to speak. He did not give you responsibility to decide the outcome. He has kept this authority for Himself. Therefore, speak, and leave the outcome to God. You might very well be rejected. But your success does not depend on whether or not you are accepted. Rather, you are successful because you have spoken!"* God's response to Cain's irritation with Abel reinforces this idea.

> So, the Lord said to Cain, "Why are you angry? And why has your countenance fallen? If you do well, will you not be accepted? And if you do not do well, sin lies at the door. And its desire is for you, but you should rule over it."[15]

Unlike my friend, Cain was unwilling to look in the mirror and admit his need to be accepted. Instead, he condemned his brother to appease his feelings of rejection. Cain eventually killed Abel. It is almost always easier to put another person down than to deal with what is really going on within ourselves. But only when we do this can the love of God heal, restore, and empower us to behave differently.

Both Cain and my friend needed to feel acceptance. She experienced love and gained, acceptance. Cain refused love and forfeited acceptance. They both feared rejection. My friend began to speak publicly and was fulfilled. Cain killed his brother and never experienced the acceptance he so desperately needed and desired. I John 3:11-12 reads,

> This is the message you have heard from the beginning: WE SHOULD LOVE ONE ANOTHER. We must not be like Cain, who belonged to the evil one and killed his brother. And why did he kill him? Because Cain had been doing what was evil, and his brother had been doing what was righteous.

Why is love so important? For many reasons, though one reason in particular is that only love can overcome fear. There is no other force powerful enough on the face of the earth, or in the heavens, capable of annihilating fear! Whether our goal is fulfillment in our relationships or achieving our God-given purpose, one thing is certain: fear stands in the way. It's supposed to! That's just the nature of fear. And facing it is the best and perhaps the only possibility we have to experience that which we truly desire. Our truest desires are imbedded deep within us. So are the things that harass and hinder us from realizing those desires. Probably, this is why God has a tendency to work on us from the inside out, using people and circumstances to thrust our hearts to the surface.

God uses people in many ways to accomplish His purpose in our lives. Concerning the Lord, Paul writes in II Corinthians

3:18 (NKJV), "But we all, with unveiled face, beholding as in a mirror the glory of the Lord, are being transformed into the same image from glory to glory, just as by the Spirit of the Lord."

God uses people in many ways to accomplish His purpose in our lives. Individuals and communities give us an opportunity to see ourselves. They act like mirrors to us. Not only do others help us see who we are, but also they show us who we are not. When we are bent on learning, everyone becomes instructor. People give us an opportunity to understand what's happening inside of us. Consider the relationship between an eagle and a snake. Both are predatory animals. When the eagle uses his talons and takes the snake up in the sky, the snake understands his weakness. In relationship to the eagle, whose habitat includes the sky, the snake realizes its lack of orientation, stability, and power. Perhaps all the snake can think about is being back on the ground. When the eagle sets it free and the snake finally lands, it is either dead or severely disoriented. In any case, he becomes food for the eagle. But had this relationship played out on the ground, the eagle might be at a severe disadvantage given the agility and striking ability of the snake. On the ground, the eagle would quickly come to terms with its lack of mobility and strength. Each reminds the other both what is and what it is not.

But these are animals and we are people. Loving and unloving people make requests and demands of us that can challenge us. We can only respond with what is in us, whether good or bad. In Matthew 12:34 (and again in Luke 6:45), Jesus said that it was out of the abundance of our heart that we speak. In other words, the well from which we think, act, and behave is located deep within us. In the same verses, Jesus said that it's not what goes in us that defiles him, rather what comes from a man. It's not the requests or demands made of us that reveal completely who we are. How we respond may tell even more about us. Again and again, Jesus' responses to loving and unloving people distinguished Himself as the *Son of the Living God*. While attending a wedding with His mother and His disciples, Jesus' mother commented that the wedding guests had no more wine. In John 2:4, Jesus responded by saying, "What does this have to do with me?" Ignoring him, His mother told the servants to do whatever Jesus said. They did. Through the servants, Jesus turned six pots of water into wine, thereby proving He was the Son of God.

And on many other occasions when loving and unloving people made requests that sometimes challenged Him, He distinguished Himself. Religious, albeit unloving, Pharisees and Sadducees challenged Him. His responses not only distinguished Himself as the Son of God, but also proved that they were not. The people who help us are the people who are determined to become the people God intends them to be—*people full of love, truth, grace, and power*. God's aim is a people that are growing fearless because there is nothing they value more than an intimate relationship with Him, through His Son Jesus Christ.

Concerning Jesus our Lord, Paul writes in II Corinthians 3:18 (NKJV), "But we all, with unveiled face, beholding as in a mirror the glory of the Lord, are being transformed into the same image from glory to glory, just as by the Spirit of the Lord."

When we look at Jesus and relate to Him, it's like looking in a mirror. Through Jesus, we can see whom God is making of us and we can see where we are still not very much like Him at all. When we interact with others, we can see just how much love and integrity we possess. We find out other things too, like how much keeping our word matters to us, how patient or impatient we are, how kind or unkind we are, or how merciful or judgmental we are. These are valuable insights to the one desiring to reflect Christ in all and to all.

Fear tempts us to reject the very information that could change the trajectory of our lives for good and improve the quality of our lives and relationships. After tempting us, fear quickly supplies a costume for us to hide under. And then the charade begins. Some hide behind money, position, or notable people. Others hide behind illicit drug use, sexual perversion, or other forms of pleasure. Still, others hide behind education, work, welfare, sickness, and the pulpit, *even God's Word*. The number of costumes is virtually endless. Anything can become a costume. All have paraded around in costume, believing they go undetected. But God, our loved ones, and those that truly know Christ are not fooled by our appearance. At one time or another, we are all like the child sitting in the middle of the floor, covered by a blanket hollering to very attentive parents, "You can't see me?" *Really?"*

We might fool everyone else, though I don't think that's entirely true either. But there is nothing hidden from God's sight! All things are naked and open to Him whom we must give account.[16] Psalm 139:11 states that even the night is light to God.

God is interested in loving our hearts so well that we grow bold, conquer fear, and love others. But first, He has to get to our hearts. So, He tells Samuel the Prophet, "Don't judge by his appearance or height, for I have rejected him. The Lord doesn't see things the way you see them. People judge by outward appearance, but the Lord looks at the heart."[17] The Prophet Jeremiah goes further in saying, "I, the Lord, search the heart; I test the mind, even to give every man according to his ways, according to the fruit of his doings."

While God does not need to, I believe He exposes the heart by testing the mind for our sake. Maybe it is so that we can see the guts - the real reason why so many of us are hindered in experiencing joy in relationships and in pursuing our life's purpose. Could unexposed, unprocessed hearts undermine the helpfulness of all the wonderful materials available to us? So much is written in support of our strengths that aptly encourages godly character. Yet, here we are: stuck. God got it right! He always gets it right! And He also got it right with Moses.

Consider God's conversation with Moses. This exchange began forty years after Moses had been fully welcomed into the love of Jethro's family and community. Moses' hope had been renewed. His mind was free from the emotional defeat he suffered when running in fear for his life. He was mentally and emotionally available again. Moses had the stamina to endure a solid round of testing of the mind that would result in the discovery of his heart. God awaited Moses' arrival to that very day. Fear caused Moses to run from Pharaoh. Fear would stand in the way of rescuing Israel. God knew this and planned to address it!

We have to ask ourselves how many times Moses saw a burning bush? How many times might he have ignited a bush to burn stubble from the field? I doubt seeing a burning bush was new to Moses. However, this time it was different. Moses saw something different. He stared at the burning bush to see that it was not being consumed. And that was nothing short of miraculous!

God was able to capture Moses' attention because love prepared him for the encounter. Love gave Moses hope. It built him up. He was available. He was free to see that although the tree burned, it was not consumed. Sometimes we can't see because, like Moses, we have run away from or failed at the thing that's supposed to be our mission! Moses was supposed to rescue people, many people! Yet, he failed to deliver two people. It's like the carpenter who beautifies everyone else's home, while his own home lies in shambles. Or, like the investment banker who makes a lot of money for others and files bankruptcy. Or like me, successfully averting many divorces, while suffering the undoing of my own marriage. Whatever your desire or God-given dream may be, it is highly probable that, like Moses and many others, you will fail before you succeed. You may feel pain and hardship before the pleasure and ease God intends. It has been this way for centuries. That's because the truth is this: every God-given relationship, dream, or purpose rests on the other side of fear. And we typically lose our first few bouts with fear. It doesn't make us any weaker than we are already. It proves that we are human.

We all need revelation, or a Divine spark after we have been derailed. Moses got his through the burning bush. Moses' curiosity let God know he was ready for more and that he could handle more confrontation than before. But also, the imagery of the bush defying the power of fire would be a strong and useful reminder to Moses upon facing Pharaoh.

It reminds me of the three men that were thrown in the fiery furnace. The King was so furious by their refusal to worship him that he heated the furnace seven times hotter than usual. It was so hot that the soldiers that cast the three men into the furnace were killed instantly. But the same fire had no power over Shadrach, Meshach, and Abed-Nego. Upon looking into the furnace, the King was surprised at seeing four men in the fire. And here's the best part, in the King's own words,

> Blessed be the God of Shadrach, Meshach and Abed-Nego, who sent His Angel and delivered His servants who trusted in Him and they frustrated the king's word and yielded their bodies, that they should not serve nor worship any god except their own God! Therefore, I make a decree that any people, nation, or language that speaks anything amiss against the God of Shadrach, Meshach and Abed-Nego shall be cut in pieces, and their houses shall be made an ash heap; because there is no other God who can deliver like this.[18]

These three men faced the fear of death. I am certain none of them wanted to die. However, astonishingly, they were not motivated by a desire to live. They were motivated by love and their devotion to God, and they trusted Him with the outcome. Their position was simple. They told the King,

Our God whom we serve is able to deliver us from the
burning fiery furnace, and He will deliver us from your hand,
O king. But if not, let it be known to you O king, that we
do not serve your gods, nor will we worship the gold image
which you have set up.

God was well able to deliver the men in this life, but even if
He didn't they had no intention of worshipping the King's gods.
The three men trusted God with the outcome of the matter.
Regardless of how it turned out, they already won! Paul attests
when he told the Philippians, "For to me, to live is Christ, and to
die is gain."[19]

Although the story of these three men took places hundreds
of years after Moses' death, it is still useful to us. Their love and
devotion to God governed their behavior. It was important to each
to make it clear that they worshipped God. And if their worship
resulted in death, they were willing to die. Although they were
certain God could deliver them in life, they also understood God
could just as well deliver them from the king through death. So,
they didn't try to control the outcome. Facing fear doesn't mean the
outcome is always naturally desirable. However, it does mean that
we willingly take our place in front of fear and let God determine
the outcome. He loves us best and knows what is best for us and
all others involved. The three Jewish men didn't second-guess
God. We would do well not to either. Still, we do. Moses did.

Moses' Turn

And now it was Moses' turn. God and Moses shared the
dream to set the Israelites free from Egyptian bondage. But

Moses was afraid.

Diagram 2: Moses' Fears

MOSES' FEAR	PROOF OF THIS FEAR
Fear of Death	*Ex. 2:14, 15:* Then Moses was afraid, thinking, "Everyone knows what I did." [15] And sure enough, Pharaoh heard what had happened, and he tried to kill Moses. But Moses fled from Pharaoh and went to live in the land of Midian.
Fear of Authority Fear of Confrontation	*Ex. 3:10:* "Who am I to appear before Pharaoh? Who am I to lead the people of Israel out of Egypt?
Fear of Being Alone/ Unsupported	*Ex. 3:13:* "If I go to the people of Israel and tell them, 'The God of your ancestors has sent me to you,' they will ask me, 'What is his name?' Then what should I tell them?"
Fear of Rejection Fear of Not Being Heard	*Ex. 4:1:* But Moses protested again, "What if they won't believe me or listen to me? What if they say, 'The Lord never appeared to you'?"
Fear of Public Speaking	*Ex. 4:10:* But Moses pleaded with the Lord, "O Lord, I'm not very good with words. I never have been, and I'm not now, even though you have spoken to me. I get tongue-tied, and my words get tangled."
Fear of Inadequacy	*Ex. 4:13:* But Moses again pleaded, "Lord, please! Send anyone else."

Yes, this is the same man we credit and salute as a hero for delivering God's people! Although I think God delivered His people, it was the man Moses he used to accomplish His will. Moses willingly got in the room with that which he feared and trusted God with the outcome! He is rightfully a hero. Moses is a hero because he overcame the villain of fear. It resulted in a nation of people crashing through the doors behind him! It's what Moses overcame that won the freedom for God's people.

Of what are you afraid? Rejection? Abandonment? Inadequacy? Falling? Drowning? Are you afraid of being judged, or possibly, of what's in the dark? It doesn't matter whether we are speaking about a relationship, a desire, dream, or a specific assignment from God; fear will be present. Fear is unavoidable. All these things matter to God. More importantly, you matter to God. He loves you. And fear is the principal enemy of love. Paul makes it clear that when we would do good, evil is present with us. For now, when love is present, fear is there also. There is no escaping fear without confrontation. Facing fear is the only way to fulfill our hopes and dreams. The things we want and desire most are tied to the thing of which we are most afraid.

This was the case with Moses. He had to be torn on the inside. On the one hand, he was extremely passionate about the condition of the Israelites. He must have dreamed about providing them relief from bondage and suffering. On the other hand, he was afraid to die, afraid of authority, afraid of confrontation, afraid of rejection, afraid of not being heard, afraid of speaking up, and afraid that he would not measure up. Can you relate to any of these fears?

Moses was so afraid that he condemned the man God wanted to use. As expressed in Diagram 2, Moses protested his competence. Unless Moses developed a deeper trust in the God he believed in, his destiny would remain just outside of his arm's reach. Moses took flight from fear and landed in the arms of a loving family and community. There, he received love and learned to give love. All of his hope was renewed and his strength was restored. Then, Moses saw a burning bush that was not consumed. At the bush, God spoke to Moses. Diagram 3 begins with God distinguishing Himself to Moses. And then He begins to talk about His anguish concerning the Israelites' condition. God not only had Moses' attention; He had his heart.

When fear defeats us, perhaps we need love and someone to speak to our heart before addressing our behavior. Maybe we need to experience love so we can participate whole-heartedly in the process of achieving our dreams and destiny. Moses did. And when Moses stopped and was drawn to the burning bush, God knew it was His opportunity. Illustrated in Diagram 3, here's how the conversation went.

Diagram 3: Conversation Between God and Moses

GOD SPEAKS	MOSES' RESPONSE	MOSES' FEAR
"Moses, Moses!" **(Exodus 3:4)**	"Here I am."	
"Do not come any closer," the Lord warned. "Take off your sandals, for you are standing on holy ground. I am the God of your father—the God of Abraham, the God of Isaac, and the God of Jacob."	When Moses heard this, he covered his face because he was afraid to look at God. **(Ex. 3:6)**	Fear of Judgment
"I have certainly seen the oppression of my people in Egypt. I have heard their cries of distress because of their harsh slave drivers. Yes, I am aware of their suffering. Now go, for I am sending you to Pharaoh. You must lead my people Israel out of Egypt." **(Ex. 3:7,10)**	"Who am I to appear before Pharaoh? Who am I to lead the people of Israel out of Egypt?" **(Ex. 3:11)**	Fear of Authority/ Confrontation
"I will be with you. And this is your sign that I am the one who has sent you: When you have brought the people out of Egypt, you will worship God at this very mountain." **(Ex. 3:12)**	"If I go to the people of Israel and tell them, 'The God of your ancestors has sent me to you,' they will ask me, 'What is his name?' Then what should I tell them?" **(Ex. 3:13)**	Fear of Being Alone/ Unsupported
"I AM WHO I AM. Say this to the people of Israel: I am has sent me to you." God also said to Moses, "Say this to the people of Israel: Yahweh, the God of your ancestors—the God of Abraham, the God of Isaac, and the God of Jacob—has sent me to you. **(Ex. 3:14, 15)**	Moses was silent.	None Noted
God gave Moses two signs to convince the Elders of Moses' authority: the staff becoming a snake and his hand becoming as white as snow. **(Ex. 4:2-7)** In verse 9, God gave Moses a 3rd sign to convince the Elders of his authority: turning water into blood.	But Moses pleaded with the Lord, "O Lord, I'm not very good with words. I never have been, and I'm not now, even though you have spoken to me. I get tongue-tied, and my words get tangled." **(Ex. 4:10)**	Fear of Public Speaking

GOD SPEAKS	MOSES' RESPONSE	MOSES' FEAR
"Now go and call together all the elders of Israel. Tell them, 'Yahweh, the God of your ancestors—the God of Abraham, Isaac, and Jacob—has appeared to me. He told me, 'I have been watching closely, and I see how the Egyptians are treating you. I have promised to rescue you from your oppression in Egypt. I will lead you to a land flowing with milk and honey—the land where the Canaanites, Hittites, Amorites, Perizzites, Hivites, and Jebusites now live.' The elders of Israel will accept your message." **(Ex. 3:16-18)**	"What if they won't believe me or listen to me? What if they say, 'The Lord never appeared to you'?" **(Ex. 4:1)**	Fear of Rejection/ Not Being Heard
"Who makes a person's mouth? Who decides whether people speak or do not speak, hear or do not hear, see or do not see? Is it not I, the Lord? 12 Now go! I will be with you as you speak, and I will instruct you in what to say." **(Ex. 4:11, 12)**	"Lord, please! Send anyone else." **(Ex. 4:13)**	Fear of Inadequacy
Then the Lord became angry with Moses. "All right," he said. "What about your brother, Aaron the Levite? I know he speaks well. And look! He is on his way to meet you now. He will be delighted to see you. 15 Talk to him, and put the words in his mouth. I will be with both of you as you speak, and I will instruct you both in what to do. 16 Aaron will be your spokesman to the people. He will be your mouthpiece, and you will stand in the place of God for him, telling him what to say. 17 And take your shepherd's staff with you, and use it to perform the miraculous signs I have shown you." **(Ex. 4:14-17)** Before Moses left Midian, the Lord said to him, "Return to Egypt, for all those who wanted to kill you have died." (Ex. 4:19)	So, Moses went back home to Jethro, his father-in-law. "Please let me return to my relatives in Egypt," Moses said. "I don't even know if they are still alive." **(Ex. 4:18)**	Fear of God

Get Out

First, note that even though God and Moses shared the desire to deliver the Israelites from the Egyptians, God sent Moses to Pharaoh in order that he may bring the children of Israel out. Moses had already tried to change the condition of God's people from inside. At best, he might improve conditions for the Israelites; however, an entire economy was built and sustained by them. The Egyptians profited from slave labor. That they would develop the altruism to free God's people without force was highly unlikely. And, however caring and kind, Moses contributed to the system that oppressed God's people.

While it is clear that in other instances God used men and women to influence the system of which they were a part, in this case, God delivered Moses from the system he would eventually confront.[20] Whether or not we choose to work within a relationship, church, or job, or separate ourselves to influence change is a matter between the individual and God. God has a reliable history in accomplishing His will. He has never failed. That we implement His will His way is secondary only to knowing His will. One of the best questions we can ask God is how He would have us respond to people and circumstances. The right response for one may be the wrong response for another. For Moses, leaving the system was best. He proved unable to stand up to Pharaoh. Thus, Moses ran. I like how Paul sums up staying or going when challenged. I Corinthians 10:13 reads, "The temptations in your life are no different from what others experience. And God is faithful. He will not allow the temptation to be more than you can stand. When you are tempted, he will show you a way out so that you can endure."

In other words, we have either the grace to stay, or the opportunity to go. As it was with Moses, what we do is ultimately between God and us. To assist us when needed, God provides wisdom through pastors, counselors, mentors, family members, and friends to help us make these decisions.

Go Back

Secondly, Moses would have to go back from whence he came. He ran from fear. Now God required him to return to it. And while the Pharaoh and all the people that sought to kill Moses were dead (Ex. 4:19), the new Pharaoh would become the face of fear with which Moses would have to contend. Fear is spirit and, therefore, requires a body to legally conduct business in the earth. That's because the earth was given to human beings to rule.[21] Any spirit without a human body is operating illegally in the earth. This includes the Holy Spirit. We will discuss this further in Chapter 6.

Get Up

In going back to face the new Pharaoh, God offered Moses the opportunity to rise above fear. But first, he would have to face it. Moses was now prepared to do what he was unable to years before. He could do so because he had received 40 years of love, encouragement, and life experience in the family and community of Jethro and Zipporah. John informs us that mature love drives out fear because fear is accompanied by the thoughts of pain and punishment. And he that fears pain and punishment is neither free, nor available to fully and completely engage his desire or purpose.[22]

Why Harden Pharaoh's Heart?

Here is something else I find interesting. If it was God's will to deliver His people, and Pharaoh was initially willing, why did God harden Pharaoh's heart?[23] After the second plague of frogs, Pharaoh conceded to letting the people go.[24] It doesn't seem to make sense that he would change his mind. Either Pharaoh's willingness to let God's people go after the first plague was a fraud to get rid of the frogs and God knew it, or Moses needed to cut his teeth on nine objections to let God's people go. To "cut your teeth" means to acquire or develop a new skill through an experience. Moses was learning how to use his voice, confront authority, and find confidence in God alone. For Moses, and oftentimes for us, this is "on the job" training! With each plague decreed, Moses grew in faith and stature. His voice changed, something we typically associate with maturity. His spirit of intent grew undeniable. He was not leaving the room of fear without God's people! And by the 10th plague, he was done. Those that have children can relate.

Let's suppose you have a child named Jonathan Wainwright Matthews. Your child is upstairs and you request he come to you downstairs. You may start like this, "Johnny, honey please come here." He doesn't respond so you politely summon little Johnny again. He still doesn't answer. So you call him again, "John, come here." When that doesn't work, your tone changes.

Emphatically, you say, "Jonathan, Jonathan Wainwright . . . Jonathan Wainwright Matthews come here now!" By the 4th or 5th time, your entire disposition has changed. You are firm, matter of fact, and fully expect your son to show up. The degree of seriousness escalates. It's not friendly or cordial anymore. You spirit of intent is undeniable. Johnny, John, and Jonathan would do well to come now.

So could the ten plagues be a combination of God being glorified in the midst of His people, an address of Pharaoh's stubbornness, Moses' catalyst to develop new skills and the confidence to go along with them. Moreover, could the repetitive experiences we have be partly for the benefit of others, partly to develop a skill or confidence within ourselves, and partly for God's glory?

When facing fear, we need skill and confidence. They must be developed. That's because when we fear there is a tendency to hold back, or return to what is familiar—even though it means facing re-enslavement. After the Israelites were freed from Egypt, they wandered in circles for 40 years. Here's the reason. If the people are faced with a battle, they might change their minds and return to Egypt.[25]

In other words, fear of fighting and facing war may cause them to return to Egypt and give up their freedom. Another reason for their 40-year wilderness experience could be that many were unresponsive and rebelled against God. Numbers 32:13 states that all of these people died in the wilderness. An entire generation died.

The wilderness is commonly considered to be an empty place. It is certainly not a place that one would choose to set up their dream home, or any home at all, except perhaps John the Baptist. Without the creature comforts of that day, there was plenty of time to receive love, grow bold, and conquer fear of war. And the Bible let's us know they did just that as they entered the Promised Land and defeated the armies.

The love and kindness exchanged between Jethro and Zipporah's family and Moses over many years restored Moses' hopes, and dreams. Love enabled him to believe again. Love inspired Moses to enter the room with that which he feared and risk destruction. But instead, he won the freedom of a nation of people! What might love inspire us to do?

CHAPTER 5

The Influence of Love

Both Moses and Esther were raised in captivity. However, Moses was raised in the palace. Esther was not. The King's daughter adopted orphan Moses. An uncle adopted orphan Esther. Moses received an education available only to the wealthy. Esther did not.

Esther's father died during her mother's pregnancy, and her mother died during childbirth.[26] Therefore, Mordecai adopted his young cousin. He loved Esther as a daughter and raised her as such. While some commentaries suggest that Esther became Mordecai's wife, the Bible simply does not support this. That she was brought to the palace as a candidate suitable for marriage to the King implies that she was a virgin and further discredits the idea that Mordecai and Esther were married. What we do know is that Mordecai's love prepared a woman to act bravely in a time of great national need.

Mordecai's love and devotion to God and strident faith appears similar to Daniel, Shadrach, Meshach, and Abed-Nego, who were also captives in Babylon. Likewise, in some sort of government service, Mordecai's allegiance to God did not waiver. Over the years, Esther experienced Mordecai's loyalty and obedience to God at the expense of himself. She was in fact a recipient of God's love through Mordecai. When reading the Book of Esther, one cannot help but notice her poise, patience, wisdom, humility, and graciousness.

Mordecai loved Esther. Fatherly love was apparent in at least five things Mordecai did for Esther. First, Mordecai took on Esther as his own flesh and blood.[27] Although she was not from the seed of his loins, Mordecai loved Esther by choosing her. Deep down inside all of us, children and adults, men and women, we all desire to be chosen. We need a sense of belonging to develop the confidence required to face our fears. Esther belonged. She had a family and a community. Mordecai made sure of this.

Secondly, he loved Esther by affirming her beauty and balancing it with the inward beauty of a meek and quiet spirit. It was no secret that Esther was physically beautiful. The Bible says so. Esther won the admiration of all that saw her, including the King.[28] Esther was outwardly stunning and inwardly substantive. She was Jewish at heart and identified with her people in captivity, as did Moses. With nothing to prove and everything to lose, Esther did not reveal her nationality as Mordecai had instructed.

A third way a father shows love for his children is by telling them who they are, and this is precisely what Mordecai did. Esther knew she was Jewish. Her heritage was Jewish. She was raised Jewish. The people she loved were Jewish. In all ways, she identified as Jewish. Mordecai was responsible for instilling faith and religious practices into Esther's life. Mordecai was so successful in ensuring Esther's indelible love for God and His people that he told her not to reveal her true identity upon entering the palace.[29]

But this was also a way of protecting Esther. Love protects. The fourth way Mordecai protected Esther was by instructing her to be quiet until speaking became necessary. But Mordecai also concerned himself with Esther's well being. According to Esther 2:11, every day Mordecai, who was already enlisted in the King's service, walked in front of the courtyard of the harem to learn how Esther was doing. Whatever influence Mordecai had, it is apparent that it would be used to aid and protect Esther. That's just what love does.

Lastly, love releases that which it loves. Mordecai released Esther to the King. But he also released her by recognizing her free will. Mordecai requested Esther to approach the King and disclose Haman's plot to kill the their people, that is, the Jewish people. No doubt, Mordecai had an optimistic end in mind. However, after speaking his desire to Esther and responding to her concern, Mordecai left the decision to her. He did not try to control the outcome. Esther was free to choose how she would respond to the threat of the annihilation of her people.

Concerning the threat, the discourse between Mordecai and Esther went like this (See Diagram 4). However, right before this Mordecai learned of the disgruntlement of two of the King's eunuchs. They sought to kill the King. Mordecai alerted Esther, who in turn informed the King. The two men were executed. And now Mordecai had angered Haman, who was second in command to the King. By refusing to bow to Haman, Mordecai incurred not only Haman's wrath but also a promise to destroy his people—the Jewish people. Mordecai prayed and fasted. But also, all the Jews in the provinces where the decree to massacre the Jews was sent joined Mordecai.[30]

When Esther got wind of Mordecai's behavior, she was distraught. She sought to comfort Mordecai by sending him clothes in exchange for his sackcloth, but he refused. Esther sent Hathach, one of the King's attendants assigned to her, to learn why Mordecai was so distressed. Mordecai told Hathach all that had transpired between him and Haman. He showed the King's decree acting on Haman's behalf to kill all the Jews in the provinces listed. In Diagram 4, Hathach gave Mordecai's words to Esther and here is her response.

Diagram 4: Discourse Between Mordecai and Esther

MORDECAI'S SPEAKS	ESTHER'S RESPONSE	ESTHER'S FEAR
Mordecai told him the whole story, including the exact amount of money Haman had promised to pay into the royal treasury for the destruction of the Jews. 8 Mordecai gave Hathach a copy of the decree issued in Susa that called for the death of all Jews. He asked Hathach to show it to Esther and explain the situation to her. He also asked Hathach to direct her to go to the king to beg for mercy and plead for her people. **(Es. 4:7, 8 NLT))**	"All the king's officials and even the people in the provinces know that anyone who appears before the king in his inner court without being invited is doomed to die unless the king holds out his gold scepter. And the king has not called for me to come to him for thirty days." **(Es. 4:11 NLT)**	Fear of Death
"Don't think for a moment that because you're in the palace you will escape when all other Jews are killed. 14 If you keep quiet at a time like this, deliverance and relief for the Jews will arise from some other place, but you and your relatives will die. Who knows if perhaps you were made queen for just such a time as this?" (Es. 4:13, 14 NLT)	"Go and gather together all the Jews of Susa and fast for me. Do not eat or drink for three days, night or day. My maids and I will do the same. And then, though it is against the law, I will go in to see the king. If I must die, I must die." Es. 4:15, 16 NLT)	Fear of Death

face it *with Love*

Esther did approach the King. On the third day of the fast, Esther dressed in her royal robes and stood in the entranceway of the King's inner court. The King was facing the entrance and welcomed Esther by extending the golden scepter. The King asked what Esther desired, offering her up to half the kingdom before she responded. Through a series of invitations to banquets, two of which included Haman, the King granted Esther's request. The latter banquet included the King and Haman only. During this banquet, Esther exposed Haman's plot to destroy the Jews. The King was enraged by Haman's insult to Queen Esther. He ordered that Haman be impaled on the 75-foot high sharp pole he devised to kill Mordecai!

But the Jews were still in peril. So, Esther approached the King who again extended the golden scepter. Here's what the King said to Esther,

> I have given Esther the property of Haman, and he has been impaled on a pole because he tried to destroy the Jews. Now go ahead and send a message to the Jews in the king's name, telling them whatever you want, and seal it with the king's signet ring. But remember that whatever has already been written in the king's name and sealed with his signet ring can never be revoked.[31]

With Mordecai's help, a decree was written under the King's signature that gave all the Jews the authority to unite to defend their lives. They were allowed to kill anyone of any nationality or province who might attack them or their children and wives, and to take the property of their enemies.

Many feared the Jews and converted in order to save themselves from being destroyed. On the day the King's two decrees went into effect, the Jews overpowered their enemies. The Bible records it this way in Esther 9:2-4,

> The Jews gathered in their cities throughout all the king's provinces to attack anyone who tried to harm them. But no one could make a stand against them, for everyone was afraid of them. And all the nobles of the provinces, the highest officers, the governors, and the royal officials helped the Jews for fear of Mordecai. For Mordecai had been promoted in the king's palace, and his fame spread throughout all the provinces as he became more and more powerful.

Love matters! In fact, love is not only necessary when facing fear. It is the only thing powerful enough to override fear. Mordecai loved Esther as a father loved a daughter. He instilled in Esther love and devotion to her faith and her people. She was a confident woman, unaffected by her beauty, and clearly not motivated by wealth, fame, or fortune. Love made her bold and courageous.

But she was also human. She was mortal. Of her own admission, Esther feared mortality. Of her own volition, she risked the possibility of dying by approaching the King, uninvited. Uncertain of the outcome, Esther stood in the entranceway of the King's inner court and faced this fear. She won, not because she lived. Like Moses, Esther won because she entered the room with someone that had the ability to end her life. Like Moses, Esther faced fear and won the life of a nation of people! Esther is a national hero because, like Moses, she received unconditional love from Mordecai, his family, and their community and that love inspired bravery!

face it *with Love*

It is so easy to give people acclaim for accomplishments that are easily seen. But I suggest that the real applause ought go to Moses for facing fear. And praise to Esther for facing the fear of death by risking her life for the life of her people.

And if facing fear weren't essential to fulfilling dreams, whether personally or relationally, then perhaps the Bible would rest with these examples. But it doesn't.

CHAPTER 6

You Can Run, But You Cannot Hide

Solomon writes in Ecclesiastes 10:19, "Money answers everything." Money certainly helps! Having enough money allows for access to the best doctors, the best treatments, the best schools and country clubs, the best attorneys, etc. But money cannot heal us, make us learn, make us enjoy those extra blessings, or necessarily cause us to prevail despite having the best attorney. And although money can delay our appointment with fear, it does not enable us to elude fear forever. You may hide from fear, but fear will seek you out. Eventually, fear will find you and not just once. Job was wealthy. Tragedy struck.. During the calamity, Job admits, "For the thing I greatly feared has come upon me, and what I dreaded has happened to me."[32]

Money did not give Job a pass on facing fear. Like us, Job's destiny stood on the other side of fear. Job actually experienced that which he feared. After his bout with fear, it appeared all was lost for good. That is, until we read Job 42:10, 12, 13, 16,

And the LORD restored Job's losses when he prayed for his friends.

Now the LORD blessed the latter *days* of Job more than his beginning; for he had fourteen thousand sheep, six thousand camels, one thousand yoke of oxen, and one thousand female donkeys. He also had seven sons and three daughters.

After this, Job lived one hundred and forty years, and saw his children and grandchildren *for* four generations.

Since Job said that which he feared happened, we can know specifically what Job feared by what was taken from him.

Diagram 5: Job's Fears (Job 1:13-19, 2:1-7)

WHAT WAS TAKEN FROM HIM	WHAT JOB FEARED
Livestock	Loss of Possessions
Employees / Business	Loss of Income
Sons and Daughters	Loss of Family
Houses	Loss of Property
Health	Loss of Life

As wealthy as he was, Job feared many of the same things we all fear. And Job served God! Still his external success and devoted service to God did not permit him to side-step fear. And neither will our apparent successes, nor our service to God, spare us from having to face that which we fear. With money, we might run from fear, but we cannot truly and safely hide.

The Disciples' Fear

Before tucking themselves away in the upper room due to fear; the disciples preached, cast out demons, healed the sick, and baptized new believers.33 Despite their success and service to God, they feared what the Jewish religious leaders might do to them. John 20:19 reads,

> Then, the same day at evening, being the first day of the week, when the doors were shut where the disciples were assembled, for fear of the Jews

What could they have possibly feared? For three years, they lived and worked alongside the Son of God. I think the discourse between Peter and Jesus subsequent to Jesus foretelling them of going to Jerusalem, suffering many things, and dying captures what they all feared. See Diagram 6.

Diagram 6: What the Disciples Feared

JESUS	PETER	DISCIPLES' FEAR
From that time Jesus began to show to His disciples that He must go to Jerusalem, and suffer many things from the elders and chief priests and scribes, and be killed, and be raised the third day." **(Matt. 16:21 NKJV)**	"Far be it from You, Lord; this shall not happen to You!" **(Matt. 16:22 NKJV)**	Fear of Loss of a Loved One
"Get behind Me, Satan! You are an offense to Me, for you are not mindful of the things of God, but the things of men." **(Matt. 16:23)** Then Jesus said to His disciples, "If anyone desires to come after Me, let him deny himself, and take up his cross, and follow Me. For whoever desires to save his life will lose it, but whoever loses his life for My sake will find it. For what profit is it to a man if he gains the whole world, and loses his own soul? Or what will a man give in exchange for his soul? For the Son of Man will come in the glory of His Father with His angels, and then He will reward each according to his works. "Assuredly, I say to you, there are some standing here who shall not taste death till they see the Son of Man coming in His kingdom." **(Matt. 16:24-28 NKJV)**		Fear of Dying/ Death

And how did Jesus address the disciples' fear? John records it this way. "Peace to you! As the Father has sent Me, I also send you." And when He had said this, He breathed on them, and said to them, "Receive the Holy Spirit. If you forgive the *sins* of any, they are forgiven them; if you retain the sins of any, they are retained."

He gives them peace. He breathes on them and encourages them to receive the Holy Spirit. And then tells them that if they release the Jewish religious leaders, they will be free to fulfill their purpose. Notice, Jesus gives them something. He didn't just say, "Don't be afraid." He quieted them with peace, making it easy for them to receive His Spirit. And may I gently remind you that Love is Spirit. Then it is not a stretch to say that Jesus breathed loved on His disciples. Love releases others from the pain they cause us. Jesus didn't ask the disciples to release the Jews until He gave them something with which to release them. Overcoming fear requires love. Jesus gave them love. When we are afraid, we will first need love if we hope to overcome the fear.

Earlier in John 13:34, Jesus speaks these words to His disciples, "A new commandment I give to you, that you love one another; as I have loved you, that you also love one another." And again in John 15:12, Jesus repeats himself, "This is My commandment, that you love one another as I have loved you." Just before this, in John 15:9, we read Jesus' words to the disciples, "As the Father loved Me, I also have loved you; abide in My love." And speaking to His Father in John 17:23, Jesus acknowledges His Father's love., " . . . You loved Me before the foundation of the world." As my dear brother, Pastor

Marlow often says, "Love rolls down hill." —citing I John 4:19, "We love Him because He first loved us."

Fear calls love out. It demands love. And love expels fear. But love does not always prevent evil from having its way with us. The apostles knew the love of God that expelled fear. When one recognizes fear and acts anyway, some pretty amazing things can happen. Just consider the Acts of the Apostles. They performed miracles, cast out demons, were outspoken about their faith, healed the sick, raised the dead, and built a powerful corporate body of believers that also did the same.

But also, some pretty grievous things can happen when love allows. Some of the apostles were stoned, beaten, imprisoned, starved, shipwrecked, and in other ways tortured. All were persecuted. Paul writes of his experiences in I Corinthians 11:24-28:

> From the Jews five times I received forty stripes minus one. Three times I was beaten with rods; once I was stoned; three times I was shipwrecked; a night and a day I have been in the deep; *in* journeys often, *in* perils of waters, *in* perils of robbers, *in* perils of *my own* countrymen, *in* perils of the Gentiles, *in* perils in the city, *in* perils in the wilderness, *in* perils in the sea, *in* perils among false brethren; in weariness and toil, in sleeplessness often, in hunger and thirst, in fasting often, in cold and nakedness—besides al the other things that come upon me daily.

In all, Paul ends by conveying, ". . . my deep concern for all the churches." Paul's love for God's people screams loudest. He suffers for the sake of those of us that believe because of his example. It was his love for God and for God's people that motivated him to face the loss of possessions, loss of family and friends, loss of sleep, and loss of food, and to endure beatings and confinement. Love inspired Paul.

As Christians, we will suffer at one time or another, and all who live godly will suffer persecution.[34] However, we may not suffer to the extreme of Paul, the other apostles, or even our brothers and sisters around the world.

Facing fear means risking the loss of something or someone we hold dear. And while some fears seem to loom larger than others, no fear is small to the person facing it. The fear of what's in the dark is, to a child, as big and real as the fear of sickness and disease is to an adult. Fear is not measured by the size of what we face. It is measured by our internal fortitude or lack thereof to what we face. We are not necessarily weak because we have conceded to fear. We very well may be weak because we did not!

Jesus Attests

Moses, Esther, Job, and the Disciples all contended with fear and caved in before conquering it. And even if I could only write about these former champions of love that overcame fear: it would be enough to say that, more than any other singular thing or person, facing our fears is the key to fulfilling our God-given desires and dreams.

But also, Jesus faced and overcame fear to fulfill His destiny on earth. To say that Jesus, the Son of man, was also a champion of love that overcame fear seals the deal. Jesus is the champion of champions of love! He never lost to fear. He never folded! My goodness, His forbearance was amazing, and His victory remarkable!

One championship moment occurred in the Garden Of Gethsemane. The entire account is recorded in Matthew 26:36-56. Now, we have to know that fear was present. We know this because Jesus was grappling to embrace the highest act of love, that is, self-sacrifice.[35] His decision would result in an overthrow of the government, *or not*. Isaiah prophesied the outcome of Jesus' decision when he said, "For a child is born to us, a son is given to us. The government will rest on his shoulders. And he will be called: Wonderful Counselor, Mighty God, Everlasting Father, and Prince of Peace."[36]

We know because the opposite of love is fear. Perfect love casts out fear. If so, then fear, instead of hate, is love's archrival. We know the spirit of fear was in the Garden of Gethsemane because Paul stated that evil is present whenever one wills to do well.[37] Certainly, Jesus showing such great love for us while we displayed total disregard for Him is at least good. But it is so much more than good. It is a way of expressing a deep love. Good and evil were together in the Garden, as were love and fear. We know that fear was present because, upon entering the Garden, the first thing Jesus acknowledged was temptation. Not even Jesus could hide and avoid an encounter with fear. Twice Jesus responded by instructing His disciples to pray, in case they enter temptation.[38] In case? Jesus did. Are we greater than our Lord? So, I take this to mean that in the case that we have entered temptation our prayers will prevail for us. Jesus had to choose love over a very formidable adversary.

Jesus was in the fight of His life. His entire body was involved. The fight was taking its toll on Jesus. Luke, the Physician describes

Jesus' condition: "And being in agony, He prayed more earnestly. Then His sweat became like great drops of blood falling down to the ground."[39]

Just before this, Luke said that an Angel from heaven appeared to Jesus to strengthen his body.[40] Jesus affirms His need in Matthew 26:41 and Mark 14:38. Jesus says that His spirit is willing indeed, but His flesh is weak. Jesus is not weak because fear defeated Him, but rather from defending His position. Paul attempts to capture the intensity of Jesus' Garden experience by scolding fellow Christians; comparing it to the anguish they were experiencing. Paul writes, "For consider Him who endured such hostility from sinners against Himself, lest you become weary and discouraged in your souls. You have not yet resisted to bloodshed, striving against sin."[41]

Jesus also stared fear in the face when he was confronted by Pilate. Pilate listened to the Jewish religious leaders and became "more afraid."[42] He was already afraid because Jesus was innocent. But Pilate became more afraid at the Jews' insistence that Jesus must die. Pilate was the face of fear. Fear went back and confronted Jesus again concerning His origin. But Jesus said nothing. A fearful, enraged Pilate responded to Jesus' silence saying, "Are you not speaking to me? Do you not know that I have power to crucify You, and power to release You?"[43]

We can interpret this in one of two ways. Fearful and desperate, Pilate might be admonishing Jesus to give him something to work with in order to set him free. Or, Pilate could be enjoying the feeling of power that fear arouses in others. Either way, Jesus' response to fear was both firm and loving. Here's what Jesus said to Pilate in John 1:11: "You could have no power at all against Me unless it had been given you from above. Therefore, the one who delivered Me to you has the greater sin."

First, love instructs Pilate. Jesus recognized the bind Pilate was in. He comforts Pilate as well as anyone could, saying essentially what you Pilate had was given to him. Pilate wasn't solely at fault. Knowing Pilate was conflicted and afraid, this was the best olive branch Jesus could offer. Jesus said that King Herod committed the greater sin by returning Him (Jesus) to Pontius Pilate. Luke 23:11 reads, "Then Herod, with his men of war, treated Him with contempt and mocked Him, arrayed Him in a gorgeous robe, and sent Him back to Pilate."

Then this champion of love spoke truth. Though the deck of cards seemed stacked against Him, Jesus didn't fold. Here's the truth Jesus' spoke in John 2:19: "Destroy this temple, and in three days, I will raise it up."

The ultimate outcome was pre-determined. Without any trouble, Jesus won. And though, to many, it appeared He had lost, it would be temporary—just seconds in the midst of eternity. For though His body was destroyed, He would rise from the dead. Jesus confronted fear with love and truth. The spiritual condition of His soul was healthy. His cause was godly. And His community up to the point of His betrayal was strong.

Jesus' destiny lay on the other side of fear. Like those champions of love having gone before Him, Jesus would take His turn to face fear. Jesus won not because His body was spared. It was not. He won because He got in the room and came face to face with fear and trusted God with the outcome. Whatever temporary loss Jesus experienced, it ushered in something greater! We, the Church, are the greater good that came from Jesus' death! Jesus faced fear and won the freedom of a nation of people! We are the joy set on the other side of fear. Jesus stood face to face with fear, enduring the cross, and despising the shame. And in doing so, He won our freedom!

When champions of love get in the room and face fear, they risk, and in some cases experience initial loss. But that doesn't matter so much to champions of love because they know that they ultimately will win. Champions of love understand that, "Light affliction, which is but for a moment, is working for us a far more exceeding *and* eternal weight of glory, while we do not look at the things which are seen, but at the things which are not seen. For the things that are seen *are* temporary, but the things, which are not seen, are eternal."[44]

For they consider, "The sufferings of this present time (this present life) are not worth being compared with the glory that is about to be revealed to us *and* in us *and* for us *and* conferred on us!"[45]

Today, more than ever we need champions of love. Neither money, nor possessions, neither education, nor race or gender, can successfully compete with the spirit (and culture) of fear in marriages, families, churches, communities, our nation, and even the world. Fear is spirit; therefore, Spirit must overthrow fear. In Romans 8:2, Paul says it is the life-giving Spirit that has freed us from Satan's power. To overcome fear, we need to know the spiritual condition of our soul, the cause for which we contend, and the quality of the community from which we find support.

face it *with Love*

CHAPTER 7

Face Your Fear

Many have used the letters that make up the word 'fear' to convey its meaning: *false evidence appearing real*. It sounds witty. But what happens when your past serves up evidence that what you presently fear is real and can happen? Is it still witty when someone proves, from similar circumstances, that what you fear can happen? And what happens when your physical body begins to adversely react to fear? The evidence in question is no longer false. What you fear really could happen. When your body convincingly plays along, this clever cliché flies out the window.

I know (and anyone that really knows me knows) that I am petrified of dental work. First, there is the uncomfortable film that you have to awkwardly bite down on and hold in your mouth for a dozen x-rays. And this is just the warm-up! I don't like pain. I don't like needles. The ones dentists use are so menacing that they purposely show off their agility training to keep them out of your sight. I hate the high-pitched sound of the drill. Before it even makes contact with my teeth, I register a threat. The sound alone is piercing. But also, the vibration of the drill against my teeth feels like a metal fork scraping across a porcelain plate—*over and over again*. Then there is the smell of something burning. I clutch the armrest of the chair, sweat, (sometimes profusely), and endure the procedure that always seems like it takes an eternity to finish!

Despite this fear, I have been to the dentist enough times to have the experience of too little novocaine and the subsequent feeling of a drill running over a nerve that is not completely deadened. It HURTS! The pain is real. I have past evidence that dental work can hurt. I memorized and rehearsed about 150 scriptures that encourage me to have no fear. None of them have made me less afraid of dental work. Don't get me wrong; it is very important that we know what God says about fear and commit these things to mind and heart. All I am saying is that confessing them aloud and being admonished by well-meaning Christians did not expel my fear.

The day before writing this chapter, I went to the dentist. This book is written especially for when declaring, "No Fear!" is not enough. The story is worth taking the time to tell because it includes all of the components of facing fear spoken about in this book. It includes love, truth, and community. It is also real, honest, and personal.

The backstory goes like this. Many months ago, I met Jerry and Linda Richman. Linda had asked me, among others, to speak at a Christian retreat weekend that she was facilitating. I agreed. Very early on, she brought a few of us together with our spouses to dine at her home. I was the only one attending without my husband. This is where I met her husband, Jerry. I did not know anyone personally. Jerry initiated a conversation with me. Jerry asked about my family. I had just started becoming comfortable with saying that I was separated. It had been 18 months. I was embarrassed. I felt defeated. I had no words and very few friends, and I struggled to make sense of it all. Therefore, I said very little, except to those that God sent in to support me and help navigate through these uncharted waters. But this night would be different. I barely knew Linda, and I didn't know Jerry at all. But in response to Jerry's inquiry about my family, I managed to utter the words, "I am separated."

Jerry was kind. While I don't remember all that he said, what I do remember is the love and compassion I experienced from this man. It was genuine and free of judgment. As the evening was wrapping up, Jerry gave me his business card and suggested if I needed anything to contact him.

I had been walking around with a cracked crown and a filling that had broken, creating a jagged edge that routinely scraped my tongue. There was also a hard bump on my gum. While I wasn't in any pain, I knew that that these things needed attention. Otherwise, and inevitably, my ability to speak to make a living would be compromised. I would have to face the fear of dental work if I intended to fulfill my purpose. If I were to continue to speak and build up God's people, I would have to get in the room with that which I feared. This time it would not be limited to a mental exercise; it would be the real thing.

Compounding my fear of dental work was the fact that I had no dental insurance. Nor did I have the ability to absorb a large bill. Several times, it occurred to me to reach out to Jerry. But my fear of dental work and inability to pay anything substantial prevented me from doing so. Finally, I got up the nerve and sent Jerry a message on Facebook. Here is what I said,

> Good morning Jerry!
>
> I love the profile picture. What an experience! Where were you and Linda?
>
> I am in need of a huge favor. As you know, I speak for a living. I have not had dental work in quite some time. This is partly due to a lack of insurance and equally because I am really afraid of dental work. It creates a tremendous amount of anxiety for me. I am certain having put off my dental needs for the past 4 plus years has resulted in several things now needing to be addressed.
>
> Actually, it's a little embarrassing to admit to such neglect. Since being separated in 2013, I have continued to slowly get back on my feet. In order to address my dental needs, I am wondering if you would be willing to work with me on a payment plan over a longer period of time than usual?
>
> I look forward to hearing back from you soon.
>
> Kim

Jerry got back to me, and I was in his office within one day. It was an experience I will not soon forget. The office was visually stunning and included art from Jerry's travels around the world. The décor and the art all seemed to complement each other. When it did not, it was on purpose, highlighting Jerry's taste in art.

Instead of individual rooms, the treatment area was an open floor plan. Three or four dental chairs, complete with set-ups, were separated by a series of eye-level walls. The set up permitted Jerry to flow back and forth from patient to patient. My first thought was that everybody would see and hear me scream!

Not only did the office express Jerry's love for art, but it also conveyed continuity. Though different, everything seemed and felt connected. Even the staff seemed like one unit. Despite differences and individual personalities, everyone was intensely interested in the patient. There was a steady flow of validation, from complementing my hazel eye color, to acknowledging my smile, and reassuring me that my teeth were not in as bad of shape as I believed. But I noticed something else. Jerry, Natalie (his dental assistant), Cindy (the dental hygienist) and Jessica (the receptionist/office administrator); all were open concerning their lives. They shared themselves—not the falsely "perfect" people that lead the rest of us to think that we must have stepped out of line when God was handing out perfect lives. These were real people with real stories that provided me impeccable service.

They shared without shame and without apology. Jerry is Jewish and Natalie is Christian. They talked of their respective faiths openly. But even more than talking about them, they practiced them with each other and in front of me. Cindy, the hygienist, told me that she had been with Jerry since he began his practice. They behave as brother and sister. The love they have for each other is obvious. The love Jerry shows for his staff is also obvious. In his office, and now in the notorious dental chair, love was running downhill to me.

I was somewhat comfortable because my understanding from the consultation was that x-rays would be taken (harmless except for the discomfort of the bitewings), an oral exam would be performed, and then we would discuss a treatment plan. No needles; no drill; no need to panic. The fact that my dental needs had not approached the epic levels that I had imagined was good news. The bump was a bone, not a tumor. The crack in the crown was porcelain and not the underlying metal. There was a filling that was partially broken, and I had one cavity. After years of no dental work, I was happy with the results. But it's what Jerry said in between the story he was telling that caught my attention. He said that he wanted to go ahead and take care of the broken filling that scraped my tongue, fill the cavity, and have Cindy clean and polish my teeth. What I heard was, "Needle, drill, and pain."

Jerry asked me to trust him. I chose to and allowed him to numb my mouth and give me several needles, the number of which I lost count. The needles did not hurt nearly to the degree I had imagined they would. As I exerted effort in clutching the chair, Jerry said, "You are in control. If there is something you would like to tell me, lift your hand. If there is a comment, you want to make, lift your hand. And if you feel any pain, lift your hand. I will stop and address it."

But what was rather amazing was that Jerry did not wait for me to raise my hand; he frequently stopped to ask how I was doing and whether or not I felt pain. I faced my fear of dental work. But I didn't do it alone. Like Moses and Esther, I experienced a tremendous amount of love beforehand as well as during the procedure. Jerry, Natalie, Cindy, and Jessica welcomed me into their community for the two hours I was present. I received loving, non-judgmental concern in exchange for my anxiety. I was able to face needles, the high-pitched drill, the smell, and the spraying of tooth enamel as the drill did its work. Finally, it was finished.

When I approached the counter to pay, I was pleasantly surprised to learn that Jerry had absorbed almost the entire cost of the procedure, leaving me with an amount I could pay right then!

I am not so naïve as to think that this small dental community of dentist and staff is impervious to the challenges. Every business has problems to be solved. And this practice is no different. Dr. Jerry Richman is in business to make money, and that requires leadership, systems, and clearly defined roles. To think that in 33 years of dentistry Jerry has been successful without a glitch in the system or conflict among the workers in his community is unrealistic. No community, whether business or social, is perfect. But in Jerry's work community, there seems to be a high regard for people above the problem—for relationships and results. I have been a beneficiary of their love and community, which gave me the courage to triumph over fear.

At one point, the question came up as to what I was working on. I relayed that I was finishing this book: *Face It with Love: The Guide to Conquering Fear*. Natalie said, "I guess it doesn't get anymore real than this!" Nope, it doesn't! The fear I experienced leading up to and during the actual appointment was real. I was anxious and sweating. I gripped the arms of the chairs so hard. My body was tense. But I remained in the chair, submitted to the shrill sound of the drill and the vibration I felt on my teeth— hoping that a pain didn't pierce through at any moment. It didn't. But even if it had, I would have prevailed in the room with fear. A cavity was filled and an old filling replaced. I left happy. Anyone that thinks that the fear I experienced was limited to my mind, has not experienced fear.

The Bible Offers No Support

The Bible just doesn't support the idea that fear is nothing more than something conjured up by the mind. It's not an illusion. Fear is neither false, nor unreal. If fear didn't exist, we wouldn't be talking about it! But we are. Concerning fear, we say things like, "Don't be afraid!" "Fear not!" "Just pray!" "Have faith." By themselves, all these words do is reinforce fear and the temptation to hide. We hide because we are afraid.

When we find out a child fears what's in the dark, we comfort him. But we dismiss the same fear in an adult by telling them to just get over it! Fear neither respects age, nor any other qualifier we assign to people. A grown man penned these words,

> Take my side, God—I'm being kicked around, stomped on every day. Not a day goes by without somebody beating me up; they make it their duty to beat me up. When I get really afraid, I come to you in trust. I'm proud to praise God; I am fearless now, I trust in God. What can mere mortals do?[46]

King David, celebrated as a man after God's heart, was afraid! David had killed a lion, a bear, and a Philistine giant. He had slewed armies. And yet, he admitted to being afraid! What David experienced was real. It might be hard to imagine a King being physically assaulted everyday. However, to be mentally and emotionally abused on a daily basis and to receive death threats, it is quite conceivable that he would feel fear. Whatever was occurring was substantial enough to evoke fear and cause David to run to God. He ran to the one that loved him. He ran to love. And that love expelled fear. And it was important enough to write about.

Fear Is Real

My friend, fear exists. It is real. It affects you and me. All the bravado in the world may hide what we fear, but it does not negate it. We may fool others and deceive ourselves by boldly boasting, "No fear!" Nonetheless, we do not fool the spirit. Stormie Omartin, in her book, *The Power of A Praying Wife*,[47] writes, "There are many things in the world to be afraid of; only a fool would say otherwise."

Ongoing bombings in Israel, recent beheadings of Christians by ISIS, Iran's insatiable appetite for nuclear weapons, the International Monetary Fund's expected inclusion of the Chinese Yuan as the newest reserve world currency, displacing that of the U.S. dollar, and the refugee crisis occurring in Europe all represent threats to the balance of world power. All contribute to the climate of fear being experienced around the world.

And what about here in America? We too live in a culture that is increasingly defined by fear. There is the upheaval among blacks and whites that has resulted in senseless deaths among citizens and police. There's the Department of Homeland Security, inaugurated shortly after 9/11, to protect us from future terrorist attacks on American soil. Recently, I glanced at the front page of their website that declares September as National Preparedness Month. A link routes to the page that begins with the following words,

This year we are asking you to take action now – make a plan with your community, your family, and for your pets. Plan how to stay safe and communicate during the disasters that can affect your community. We ask everyone to participate in America's Prepare-A-thon and the national day of action, National Prepare-A-thon Day, which culminates in National Preparedness Month on September 30.

In America, more guns have been purchased over the past few years than at any other time. USA Today reports,

> Newly released August records show that the FBI posted 1.7 million background checks required of gun purchasers at federally licensed dealers, the highest number recorded in any August since gun checks began in 1998. The numbers follow new monthly highs for June (1.5 million) and July (1.6 million), a period which spans a series of deadly gun attacks — from Charleston to Roanoke — and proposals for additional firearm legislation.[48]

Nearly all of the major news outlets, including, CNN, FOX, The Washington, Post and New York Times, are all reporting an increase in gun sales. Just recently on Facebook, a long time friend posted a picture of herself at an indoor shooting range. Her post read, "Entered the world of gun ownership today. Sig Sauer 280, rosewood handles. Hip holster. Extended magazine. Watch out!"

Fear is real. And that's just the fear experienced in response to threats against us. But also, consider our voluntary efforts to scare people into action. Marketers and advertisers have perfected fear tactics to sell products. Director Alfred Hitchcock, known for inciting terror in his movies, revealed one tactic when he said, "There is no terror in the bang, just the anticipation of it."

Marketers show us images and tell us stories about what might happen, and then they present us with a product or service that can reduce the likelihood that it will happen. Fear sells. All of us have bought it. Fear is about the anticipation of negative outcomes that are painful and must be avoided at all costs! And boy do we pay for it! We pay with money we don't have and time we didn't plan. Nearly every major industry profits from us being afraid! Consider just a few of them. Politicians use fear to gain votes. A distressing 30-second commercial dashes to mind. In 2008, during the democratic primaries, Hillary Clinton approved this message. Against a dark backdrop, with eerie music and a sobering voice, we hear, "It's 3 a.m. and your children are safe and asleep. But there is a phone in the white house and it is ringing. Something's happening in the world. Your vote will decide who answers that call. Whether it's someone who already knows the world's leaders, someone who knows the military, someone tested and ready to lead in a dangerous world."

Nearly, all politicians use fear in some form or another. Whether addressing terrorism, an impending currency crisis, the cost of healthcare, or any other reality we face, the politician becomes the "product" that can avert any negative outcomes.

The Beauty Industry exploits human beings' fear of aging to sell us a plethora of anti-aging creams and cosmetics. The Self-Help Industry plays on the fear of not being good enough, right enough, or smart enough, and then they provide an abundance of resources to re-invent yourself, re-position yourself, and ultimately, enjoy yourself. And these are just a few of the industries that use fear to entice you to buy their products.[49]

This book is not an attempt to convince you and others of something you already know and feel in your hearts. Fear has invaded our lives, perhaps more vehemently now than any other time in recent history. And it is not finished. Fear seeks total domination over the way we think and behave toward God, each other, and ourselves. Through this book, I desire to add value to the broad conversation concerning fear. More importantly, I believe in the pages that follow there lies a practical answer for those facing fear. We need faith and action to converge. We need love to replace fear-based actions. We need to know what that love looks like, what it feels like, and how to cultivate it. And we need to know now! That's because love is the opposite of fear. Therefore, we need more love and less fear.

Another Fear Tactic: Hijack the Body

British politician and writer Benjamin Disraeli said that fear makes us feel our humanity. It whispers our limitations, persuades us to feel our smallness, and reminds us of our mortality. Fear speaks to our bodies. In a vulnerable moment Job remarks, "For my sighing comes before my food, and my groaning's are poured out like water. For the thing, which I greatly fear, comes upon me, and that of which I am afraid befalls me. I was not *or* am not at ease, nor had I *or* have I rest, nor was I, *or* am I quiet, yet trouble came *and* still comes [upon me]."[50]

Adding to this in Job 4:14 and 15, Job states, "Fear and trembling seized me, which made all my bones shake. Then a spirit passed before my face; the hair on my body stood up." Fear touched Job and he felt it. Fear was a physical experience for Job. Another writer attest that fear causes physical reactions to occur in our bodies. Psalm 48:6 reads, "Fear took hold of them there, and pain as of a woman in birth pangs." And consider Psalm 55:5, "Fearfulness and trembling have come upon me, and horror has overwhelmed me."

Luke, the Physician, confirms that fear can wreak havoc mentally, emotionally, and physically, saying, "And there will be signs in the sun, in the moon, and in the stars; and on the earth distress of nations, with perplexity, the sea and the waves roaring; men's hearts failing them from fear and the expectation of those things which are coming on the earth, for the powers of the heavens will be shaken."

In his book, *Be In Excellent Health*,[51] Dr. Henry Wright traces a variety of physical ailments and diseases to their spiritual origin. Whether or not we think Wright reads too much into things, or makes giant leaps to connect the dots for us, studies support his claims.

In 1995, two physicians, along with the Centers for Disease Control and Prevention and Kaiser Permanente's Health Appraisal Clinic in San Diego, launched a study to measure Adverse Childhood Experiences (ACE).[52]

In an article in Psychology Today (2015), Donna Nakazawa writes, "[For] a child who [has] experienced adversity, the relationship between mental and physical suffering is strong: the inflammatory chemicals that flood a child's body when she's chronically stressed aren't confined to the body alone; they're shuttled from head to toe."[53]

The reality is boys and girls become afraid, and grown men and women do too! Fear affects our emotional, social, and physical well-being. It robs us of joy and peace. Face it. It is inevitable. American motivational author and speaker, Jack Canfield noted, "Everything you want is on the other side of fear."

Preparation vs. Panic

The slippery slope in writing a book about how to conquer fear is that, at some point, fear has to be addressed. But in doing so, I am at risk of stirring the very thing I seek to squish. That's why it's helpful to distinguish panic from preparation. Panic is a reaction to something anticipated to happen, or something in the wake of what has already happened. There was panic in Ferguson, MS when an unarmed Michael Brown was killed by police officer Darren Wilson. When the grand jury decided against indicting Wilson, community outrage was immediate. Businesses were burned to the ground, cars set on fire, and hundreds of shots were heard in the wake of the decision not to prosecute the white officer. Black people and sympathizers were angry. Horrified by what seemed to many as blatant injustice and fearing no other remedy, panic seized many, and a city was destroyed as a result.

If panic is an automatic reaction, then preparation is a deliberate action. It is a planned response to something anticipated. Panic is driven by emotion. Prayer, wisdom, and instruction motivate preparation. As economists suggest an impending currency crisis in America, some are listening and preparing by following advice to liquidate assets, buy gold and silver, and store water and nonperishable food items for up to three months. These actions are not done out of panic, but rather as a way to minimize the impact of a financial crisis. Whether we adopt this response or do nothing at all should arise from our personal prayers. God supplies all of our needs according to His rich, unending supply, and whatever we do should be based on our personal faith and trust in God.

Panic is inevitable. Preparation is not. But if we are to conquer fear with love, then we need to understand the spiritual nature of fear, the strength of our cause, and the quality of our community. Fear is real. It is a spirit and not simply something made up in our minds.

face it *with Love*

CHAPTER 8

You Are Worth It

The state of our soul is a vital factor when facing fear. Our will and mind either align with God or not. This is true despite how aggressive fear becomes in taunting our senses with our mortality. It is an ongoing decision to trust God, sometimes in the face of overwhelming odds. Wrestling for domination of your mind can be like trying to maintain your balance on a boat in choppy water. It takes effort and the grace of God. Our spirit knows no fear. Our spirit has been recreated in God's image. It is flawless. And it is mature. However, our soul is neither flawless nor mature. Our soul is susceptible to fear. When we call upon God, He strengthens our soul, not our spirit. Our spirit doesn't need strengthening. It is already strong and fearless. Of the soul Psalm 138:3 (NKJV) speaks,

> In the day when I cried out, You answered me, And made me bold with strength in my soul.

Fear is content to lurk deep beneath the raging emotional waters of anger, resentment, hate, and suffering. They provide clever camouflage. But even more damaging than these are the still waters of doubt. I came across a quote recently that sums up the ordeal this way: "For so many years I lived in constant terror of myself. Doubt had married my fear and moved into my mind, where it built castles and ruled kingdoms and reigned over me, bowing my will to its whispers until I was little more than an acquiescing peon, too terrified to disobey, too terrified to disagree. I had been shackled, a prisoner in my own mind."[54]

Certainly, we have all questioned God, others, and ourselves. We want to know the rightness of an event, or particular course of action. We want to know the validity of information presented to us. And at various times, we wonder whether or not we have what it takes to meet the challenges that we face. Even Jesus questioned God, both in the Garden of Gethsemane and on the cross. Agonizing in the Garden, Jesus appeals to His Father for some other course of action to be taken to remedy mankind.[55] On the cross, Jesus questions His Father, saying, "My God, My God, why have You forsaken Me?"[56]

Canadian author, Yann Martel in his book, *The Life of Pi* writes, "If Christ spent an anguished night in prayer, if He burst out from the Cross, 'My God, my God, why have you forsaken me?' then surely we are also permitted doubt. But we must move on. To choose doubt as a philosophy of life is akin to choosing immobility as a means of transportation."

It is not what we doubt that prevents us from reaching our goals, fulfilling our dreams, and in other ways venturing beyond our comfort zone. Rather, it is when doubt has become a way of life that we refuse to live. For many of us, there are at least one or more areas in which God would like us come alive and others would too! And the truth is that each of us wants to be alive.

We need to be alive—passionately alive. For when we live, others live. Howard Thurman (1899-1981), a theologian, civil rights activist, and writer, speaks of this need, saying, "Don't ask what the world needs. Ask what makes you come alive, and go do it. Because what the world needs is people who have come alive."[57]

Much more is meant by being alive than living your physical life. Christ makes us alive spiritually. Then God intends every other aspect of our being to follow suit. Each of us is passionate about someone and/or something. It's in our DNA. Life is meant to be lived. Words are meant to be thought and spoken. Feelings are meant to be felt. Experiences are meant to be processed. Life is supposed to be full of wonder and awe and moments that take our breath away. Life has a flow and an unforced rhythm to which every heart aspires. I know because we are made this way. We are hard-wired to grow, change, and improve others and ourselves. Not that we can do any of this on our own. We must respond to God's love and grace.

Doubting God

Although we breathe, so many of us miss out on life. Satan sees to it. He does so by getting us to live in a climate of doubt. Indecision, confusion, anxiety, suspicion, and uncertainty all indicate doubt. To doubt is to fear. Fear is about anticipating outcomes. To different degrees, we doubt God's love and fear

His wrath. At the end of the day, Moses wondered whether or not God would protect him. Would God rescue Moses from Pharaoh? Or like before, would God leave Moses fending for himself? Moses had reason for concern.

The last time Pharaoh sought to kill Moses, God seemed oblivious. Moses decided to run to safety. Now, being asked to return and confront Pharaoh, Moses might have experienced the painful memory of feeling alone when he needed God. If in his mind God was not present then, how could Moses trust Him to be there now? For certain, God is always present. To God, yesterday, today, and tomorrow are all the same and all are occurring now. That Moses did not perceive God did not mean that He was absent or unaware of Moses dilemma. That God chose to delay intervening on Moses and His people's behalf for forty years was both His prerogative and His plan. That Moses could not see the whole of God's plan or the value in any one of its parts must be credited to his humanity and not Divine fault. Moses' questions of God were sincere. And God took time to answer each one. God loved Moses. He understood his frailty. But also, and perhaps more importantly, God understood that the place of Moses' vulnerability was also the place of his healing. If God were to heal Moses, (that is reform his thinking, restore his faith, and reconcile him to their cause), Moses would have to return to the place of his pain and fear. Moses shuddered at the thought.

And so do we. Doubt often divulges old wounds that we would rather have left alone. But God's love is relentless to heal every part of us. And the success of our hopes and dreams, the cause for which we are created, demand nothing less. After Anthony and I separated in 2013 and he expressed his intent to divorce, I felt like one colossal failure. All my efforts had been insufficient in producing the marriage God desired for us. My schooling and self-initiated works had proven useless. Still, for years I believed that there was one more thing I could do! I believed that if I could only be quiet enough, submissive enough, sexy enough, and supportive enough, my relationship would improve, and God and Anthony would be pleased with me. It was painful to learn that my labors improved nothing. A further blow was when my husband asked me to leave the church I had helped build, and my pastors felt it in my best interest to find another church and pastor to whom I could submit and pay my tithes. While these pastors' heart went out to me, they expressed being uncomfortable supporting both Anthony and I, since we were each in full-time ministry.

It has always been extremely important to me to respond favorably to the authority of God. So, you can imagine the displeasure I felt from God. I discounted God's love for me. I mean, how could He love me. Three of the most important people in authority over me, both directly and/or indirectly, concluded I was rebellious. Scripture makes it very clear how God feels about rebellion. Saul immediately comes to mind. In I Samuel 1:23 we find God's sentiment, "For rebellion is as the sin of witchcraft, and stubbornness is as iniquity and idolatry. Because you have rejected the word of the Lord, He also has rejected you from being king."

Surely, three of the most important people could not all be wrong about me. And if they cut me off, surely I was doomed in God's eyes. I believed that. To be separated from God is to be separated from His love. But thanks to God, my doubting His love for me did not alter His love for me. That's because His love for me comes from a sovereign act of His will. What this means is that His love for us depends on no one and no thing. He loves us simply because He chooses to love us. It's His right. Paul writes in Hebrews 6:13 and 14, "For when God made a promise to Abraham, because He could swear by no one greater, He swore by Himself, saying, Surely blessing I will bless you, and multiplying I will multiply you."

"No one greater," means that there was no one in greater authority than God to decide such a matter. If no living thing has greater authority than God, then certainly nothing less has such authority. I doubted God's authority to love me as a sovereign act of His will, whether I was good or bad, right or wrong, sinful or righteous. My desire is to be in good standing with God. But this has much more to do with Him than I. I earnestly desire and choose to be kept from practicing sin. But it is the grace of God that enables me to do so. Twice in John 5 (verses 19 and 20), Jesus reiterates that He can do nothing in His own strength. Ten chapters later in John 15:5, Jesus tells the disciples, "I am the vine, you are the branches. He who abides in Me, and I in him, bears much fruit; for without Me you can do nothing." It's my connection to God and Jesus that is responsible for any success I experience personally, relationally, and in ministry to others.

During this especially painful time, I doubted God. Still, in my distress, God began teaching me that nobody had the right to define me. While others are free to draw whatever conclusions they choose about me, what really matters is who God says I am and who I chose to be. Jesus makes this clear in John 10:17 and 18. I love the Amplified Version, which says, "For this reason the Father loves Me, because I lay down My [own] life so that I may take it back. No one takes it away from Me, but I lay it down voluntarily. I am authorized and have power to lay it down and to give it up, and I am authorized and have power to take it back. This command I have received from My Father." Despite our doubts, God loves us because He chooses to love. There is simply nothing we can do to change this. Moreover, God commands that no one can take away my right and ability to choose who I will be.

So, what about this banner of rebellion to which I had been assigned? The truth is, I was rebellious. All of us are until we come to Christ. At the cross, Christ took the spirit of rebellion away from me. In exchange, He gave me the spirit of submission and humility. I choose to submit to God and those in authority over me. I no longer accept that I am rebellious. Rebellion cheapens the grace of God that is the life of Christ given to me.

God can handle our doubts about Him. He delights in making believers out of us. Ironically, Abraham (the Father of Faith) doubted God! Genesis 17:17 records Abraham's response when God tells him that Sarah would have a baby and that she would become a mother of nations; kings of peoples shall be from her. The verse says, "Then Abraham bowed down to the ground, but he laughed to himself in disbelief. 'How could I become a father at the age of 100?'" God made a believer out of Abraham. He made a believer out of Moses, Esther, Job, the disciples, and me. And God will make a believer out of you, too! And He commonly begins in the place of your distress, anxiety, and fear. David writes, "I called on the Lord in distress; The Lord answered me and set me in a broad place."

Satan is appeased when we doubt God. Fear has a way of making us question things we believe to be true, but may not have been proven to be true. Everything we believe to be true will undergo the scrutiny of testing. How else can what we believe be validated? James weighs in on the necessity of testing what we say we believe.

> Consider it nothing but joy, my brothers and sisters, whenever you fall into various trials. Be assured that the testing of your faith [through experience] produces endurance [leading to spiritual maturity and inner peace]. And let endurance have its perfect result and do a thorough work, so that you may be perfect and completely developed [in your faith], lacking in nothing.[58]

Doubting Self

If fear can't count on us doubting God, it tempts us to doubt ourselves. Although in the grand scheme of things this is good, it is immediately harmful. Once fear seized Moses, he questioned who he was and his ability to speak effectively.[59] He was undone by his failure and questioned his right and ability to speak and do business on God's behalf.

I did too. After the separation, I not only doubted God, but also myself. I feared that I was disqualified and no longer would be effective in speaking on marriage and relationships. For almost two years, I remained silent—*partly numb, partly fearful.* I doubted God's ability to use me in the manner I once dreamed and believed was possible. Doubt exposed a deep-seeded fear of not being heard. And now I had a *reason* not to be heard.

Like Moses, I had a previous record of success. I spoke and authored a few books. Pharaoh provoked Moses. Separation provoked me. He was afraid. So was I. He ran. I shut up. I felt humiliated and embarrassed for Anthony, my family and myself. Although we had helped many families, we failed to care for our own. Like the proverbial saying goes, "The carpenter took care of everyone else's house while neglecting his own. We had years of unhealthy dynamics between us. And I was supposed to be a "relationship expert." Now, I had my doubts that anyone would listen to what I had to say.

In late 2014, I remember God distinctly saying to me, "Before, you spoke and wrote because you wanted to be heard. Now, you must speak because something needs to be said. And I want you to say it."

My whole life was about improving the quality of relationships, beginning with marriage. I was born for this. It is my purpose and my passion. It's what makes me come alive. In fact, when I am speaking and spending my entire life with an audience of ten or thousands for those few minutes, I feel very, very alive. Second, to time spent with God and third to time spent with loved ones, spending time writing and speaking is my highest purpose. So, no matter how deep I hid, nor how far away I ran, the strength of desire succeeded every time. The only difference between writing and speaking then and now is the reason why I do it.

Don't get me wrong. I would like to be heard. I would even love being heard. But it is no longer the reason I write or speak. I may not be named among the best writers and speakers. But that doesn't matter now. What matters is that I write and speak.

Before, it was about me. Now, it is about God. Moses' first success in delivering the Hebrew slave was about him and what he could do. The second time he set out to deliver the children of Israel was about God and what He could do. Moses questioned God's provision and protection. God used Jethro, Zipporah, and their community to provide for Moses. God Himself would protect Moses. God has used and continues to use family, a few increasingly dear friends, and Joy Christian Center Church to provide restoration to me. He alone will protect me. In this, I must trust. And so must you.

A song that has become dear to me during this time is called, "Wings" (2006) by Alberto and Kimberly Rivera. Hopefully, you find the lyrics encouraging too.

> Nothings gonna hold me back.
> I'm gonna fly so high,
> So high away,
> Fly.
> When I saw some of you,
> You took from the Lord your NEW wings.
> You had this look on your face that said,
> "Yeah, these are new,

But I still have the memory of how it felt when
I flapped my broken wings."
And I saw this fear in your eyes.
What will it feel like to flap my new wings?
Will I have the pain? Will I still remember?
And then, I saw the Lord look into your eyes,
And they penetrated and then He said, "THE PAIN
SHALL CEASE."
He said, "Even the MEMORY shall be released.
Even the pain I shall take upon Myself.
For I will NOT give you a NEW THING that will cause
you pain.
So, DON'T BE AFRAID to fly,
For everything that I give is good.
You will Fly in My goodness,
Fly in My love,
Safely under My wings.

You will fly in My faithfulness
Fly in My comfort.
Fly in My mercy."
So, STAY CLOSE to Me,
Fly with Me,
Don't EVER go away."

This is your time. Your season is not coming; it is here. It is
happening now. Your questions are genuine, your limitations are
real, and fear is most certainly attempting to prevent you from
taking the next step. Nevertheless, it is time to move. It is time to be
and do all that is in your heart. You matter. Your desires, hopes, and
dreams matter. They are your cause. They are the cause for which
you must fight. They are the strength of your desire. And they just
won't let you to quit. Your commitment is far beyond a feeling. It is
the skill you now must apply and develop. And you can!

God has spoken to you and He is speaking to you. You have been tested by circumstances of tragedy, loss, accusation, humiliation, and shame. In the past, it was about you. Now, it's about God. As you trust God, your place of vulnerability will become your place of victory. In the same place where you were condemned, you will rise. Respond to His love, and discover the grace to do what you have been unable to do on your own. God is forever for you. Believe.

Doubting Others

Many years ago, Anthony and I sat in my then pastor's office. I remember being asked whether or not I believe Anthony loved me. My gut response was an immediate and emphatic, "No." I felt the dagger pierce his soul. But the truth is that I couldn't receive love from him, or anyone. I didn't feel lovable. I did not believe I was lovable. After years of performing for love, I remained empty. This was neither Anthony's fault, nor something he could fix. I doubted love. Therefore, I doubted Anthony's love.

In the years since, I have learned to receive love. And I am still learning. I love Paul's heartfelt prayer for us in Ephesians 3:14-19. It says,

> For this reason I bow my knees to the Father of our Lord Jesus Christ, from whom the whole family in heaven and earth is named, that He would grant you, according to the riches of His glory, to be strengthened with might through His Spirit in the inner man, that Christ may dwell in your hearts through faith; that you, being rooted and grounded in love, may be able to comprehend with all the saints what is the width and length and depth and height—to know the love of Christ which passes knowledge; that you may be filled with all the fullness of God.

Doubting others did not stop there. Now separated, I doubted others would receive anything I had to say about marriage and relationships. This presented a huge internal conflict. My passion was and is writing and speaking on love and relationships. Upon Anthony announcing our separation and his intent to divorce, I experienced a mass exodus of people from my life. Ministerial relationships that once were, were now no more. Understandably, there are many reasons people make the decisions that they do. And it's okay. Still, I suffered a loss of relationships and credibility.

Who would believe what I had to say? What if they questioned my authority? What if they concluded I was not contrite enough, broken enough, or repentant enough? Then, I think of all the prolific writers and speakers of which I am least. I think about those in authority that enjoy far greater credibility than myself. Moses experienced some of the same conflict and questions. His passion and purpose was to deliver God's people. He too questioned whether the elders would believe God sent him, as well as the words God had given him to say.[60] Esther questioned whether or not the king would receive her when she had not been summoned.[61]

Admittedly, I have suffered from "Almost Syndrome"— almost good enough, almost smart enough, almost enough, almost . . . *you fill in the blank!* I remember the spies Moses sent out to survey the land God had given them. Here's what the majority had to say upon return, "There we saw the giants (the descendants of Anak came from the giants); and we were like grasshoppers in our own sight, and so we were in their sight.[62] Only Joshua and Caleb said otherwise: "Let us go up at once and take possession, for we are well able to overcome it."[63] I have felt like a grasshopper in the eyes of others.

We doubt others because we fear what they may do to us. And what can they do? Others can expose our weaknesses, criticize us, reject our manner and way, question our authority, laugh at us, and harm us emotionally and even physically. The disciples feared that the Jews would do to them as they did to Jesus, and so they hid. The continued preaching among themselves instead of to those that needed to hear the gospel of Christ. In Matthew 10:28, Jesus addresses the disciples' fear of men saying, "And do not fear those who kill the body but cannot kill the soul. But rather fear Him who is able to destroy both soul and body in hell."

Humanity inherited fear when Adam and Eve sinned. Adam and Eve doubted God, each other, and themselves. In Deuteronomy 28:65-67, referencing the fear God's people would experience at the hands of others, we read,

> There among those nations you will find no peace or place to rest. And the Lord will cause your heart to tremble, your eyesight to fail, and your soul to despair. Your life will constantly hang in the balance. You will live night and day in fear, unsure if you will survive. In the morning you will say, 'If only it were night!' And in the evening you will say, 'If only it were morning!' For you will be terrified by the awful horrors you see around you.

We that believe in the finished work of Jesus Christ no longer have to live under the fear of others. God has given each of us someone(s) to love and something to do. We may doubt whether the intended beneficiaries will receive us. Maybe they won't. But always remember, the outcome belongs to God. We can and should believe the best in every situation. However, our success rests in preparing for and completing God's assignments. There will always be those that mistake our confidence in God for arrogance, or our gentleness for passivity. There will always be those that reject our authority and assignment. Concerning these, Jesus instructs His disciples, "But if any place refuses to welcome you or listen to you, shake its dust from your feet as you leave to show that you have abandoned those people to their fate."[64]

Satan always uses a three-pronged approach. He comes to steal, kill, and destroy. If fear can't rob us of our connection with an unconditionally loving God or kill us in despairing of ourselves, then doubting others responsiveness to us is equally effective in destroying us. The antidote to fear is love. Our strength lies in receiving the love of God and loving others as a sovereign act of our will. Like a tattoo on the arm, God has placed a seal over the heart of all those that believe in Christ. Of this kind of love, Solomon writes, "Love is invincible facing danger and death. Passion laughs at the terrors of hell. The fire of love stops at nothing—it sweeps everything before it. Floodwaters can't drown love; torrents of rain can't put it out. Love can't be bought, love can't be sold; it's not to be found in the marketplace."[65]

The condition and preparedness of our soul to face fear depends largely on how we receive and respond to love.

face it *with Love*

CHAPTER 9

A Case of Mistaken Identity

We have so feminized love and submission that many men think they neither need, nor will consciously benefit from either. In movies, we make love about the romance of women. We call them "chick flicks." We make love about women in books. We call them "Romance Novels." And we make love about women in sermons. We call it, "The Marriage Series."

But love isn't about women. Love is neither male, nor female. Love is about God. Although love has characteristics that we often define as feminine and masculine, the truth is that Love is Spirit. If we don't resolve this one truth, then we will forfeit the real power of love. Love is a weapon. Love is also a fruit of the Spirit.[66] It is one of few weapons of its kind. As a fruit, love is edible and intended to be eaten. Love must be taken in and digested before it can be activated in our lives. Consumption is the means of activation. Activated love is a life-giving, life-sustaining, reforming, restoring and reconciling force. That love transcends time, place and space and gender is impressive. Still it is often hard to distinguish love from the vessel it uses.

A friend came to me, frustrated, saying that she had helped a family pay for groceries and utility bills on a couple of occasions. And it seemed like every other month they requested her help. My friend was unable to support this family on an ongoing basis. She felt bad because the family's need was real. To this family, my friend and a provider were one and the same. The problem is that God, not my friend, says that He will supply their needs according to the vastness of His resources. While God used my friend to meet their need on a few occasions, she was neither God, nor their provider. I suggested the next time they call with a request that she refer them to some of the community organizations available to help them.

Confusing the identity of love, which is Spirit, with the person or thing through which it flows is easy to do. Love feels good. And boy is it powerful! It reminds me of one of my all time favorite movies, *The Matrix*. It's during the last scene when Neo dies. Trinity speaks to Neo. Here's what she says,

> Neo, I'm not afraid anymore. The Oracle told me that I would fall in love and that that man... the man that I loved would be The One. So you see, you can't be dead. You can't be... because I love you. You hear me? I love you.

Afterward, Trinity kisses Neo and says, "Now get up!"

Neo does get up. He fights and he wins against Agent Smith. And it happened just like Morpheus told Neo earlier, that when he was ready, he would not have to dodge bullets. Unlike the bullets he tried to dodge and ultimately surrendered to before, Neo stood still and was unaffected by the deadly rounds of fire.

When Trinity received and embraced love, she was no longer afraid. Neo was the primary beneficiary. He won in the place in which he previously lost. It's that kind of love—God's love, that guts out fear and pushes past possible that is responsible for the heroics of Moses, Esther, the three Hebrew boys, the disciples, and the apostles.

Copycats

Aside from feminizing love, there are a couple of other reasons it might be difficult for many to receive God's love. The harder of the two to explain is like a computer virus. A computer virus is a bug that infects a computer system and is capable of reproducing itself. A virus can corrupt files and in other ways disable the computer. Now bear with me a moment as I offer a basis for what I am about to say.

The truth is: God is Spirit, God is Love, and God is one. Therefore, Spirit is Love and Love is one. Practically speaking this means that, " There is one body and one Spirit, just as you were called in one hope of your calling; one Lord, one faith, one baptism; one God and Father of all, who is above all, and through all, and in you all."[67] Paul adds to this writing in Galatians 3:28, "There is neither Jew nor Greek, there is neither slave, nor free, there is neither male nor female; for you are all one in Christ Jesus."[68]

In I Corinthians 12, Paul sets out to explain how we all can be so different, yet equally valuable and necessary in marriage, family, church life, and workplaces. He does not base our value on gender, appearance, or our social or economic status. Paul compares us to the human body writing, "For as the body is one and has many members, but all the members of that one body, being many, are one body, so also is Christ."

Right before this, in verse 11, Paul says although there is a diversity of gifts it is the One Spirit working all and in all; "But the same Spirit works all these things, distributing to each one individually as He wills." In Philippians 2:2, Paul encourages God's people saying, "Therefore if *there* is any consolation in Christ, if any comfort of love, if any fellowship of the Spirit, if any affection and mercy, fulfill my joy by being like-minded, having the same love, being of one accord, of one mind."

God does not have separate love for male or female. Paul encourages us to have the same love. There is One Love received, experienced, and shared among us that believe in Jesus Christ and to the benefit of all. In our biblical, rightful, and at times forceful stance against same-sex marriage, gender fluidity, and gender-neutral themes, we are at risk of throwing the baby out with the bathwater. Satan is smart. He is also spirit. And spiritual intellect supersedes natural intellect. We could very well be making an avoidable error by throwing something good and useful away, while taking a stand against and eliminating evil.

Satan is trying to accomplish, by natural means, what God intends to accomplish by the Spirit. He draws his inspiration from God. Satan does not create things. He is a copycat that steals and distorts what has already been created. It seems Satan beats God to the punch every time because we typically recognize and respond to things we see in the physical realm before those things we see in the spirit. Paul reassures us that

Satan does not have one up on God when he compares Adam to Christ. In I Corinthians 15:45-47 he writes, "The Scriptures tell us, 'The first man, Adam, became a living person.' But the last Adam—that is, Christ—is a life-giving Spirit. What comes first is the natural body, then, the spiritual body comes later. Adam, the first man, was made from the dust of the earth, while Christ, the second man, came from heaven."

We see this same order with Abraham: first the natural, then the spiritual. Ishmael was the son of Abraham and Hagar—*man's natural ability*. But being beyond natural childbearing ability, Abraham and Sarah conceived Isaac by Divine ability. Similarly, there was Elizabeth that birthed John the Baptist, the natural forerunner of Christ. And then there was Jesus that was conceived by the Spirit. First, there is the natural resemblance of a thing, and then there is the spiritual *and real thing*.

So, now let's put all this together. Here's the bathwater, or the resemblance of unity: Make a society in which all human beings are one by erasing the gender lines. Using mankind's natural ability and free will, Satan is making one human being out of two. Sound familiar? It should. Reread Galatians 3:28, "There is neither Jew nor Greek, there is neither slave, nor free, there is neither male nor female; for you are all one in Christ Jesus."

In 2015, Dictionary.com added the term gender-fluid. It is an adjective meaning a person whose gender identity, or gender expression, is not fixed and shifts either over time or depending on the situation. Postgenderism is a movement in which its adherents advocate the removal of gender in society.

George Dvorsky and James Hughes, Bioethicist from Canada and the United States, respectively, wrote a paper entitled, "Postgenderism: Beyond Gender Binary." Here's a quote from the abstract.

> Gender is an arbitrary and unnecessary limitation on human potential . . . Postgenderists contend that dyadic gender roles and sexual dimorphisms are generally to the detriment of individuals and society. Assisted reproduction will make it possible for individuals of any sex to reproduce in any combinations they choose, with or without "mothers" and "fathers," and artificial wombs will make biological wombs unnecessary for reproduction.[69]

Big words aside, Dvorsky and Hughes state that *gender is unnecessary* and that *gender roles and differentiation of the sexes is detrimental.* If this isn't a full frontal attack on Genesis 1:27, which says "So, God created man in His *own* image; in the image of God He created them male and female. He created them," then I don't know what is.

And Genesis 2:21 and 22 state, "And the Lord God caused a deep sleep to fall on Adam, and he slept; He took one of his ribs and closed up the flesh in its place. Then the rib, which the Lord God had taken from man, He made into a woman, and He brought her to the man.

Satan is attempting to do in the natural what God has already declared He will do by the Spirit. Genesis 2:24 reads, "Therefore, a man shall leave his father and mother and be joined to his wife, and they shall become one flesh." And Paul writes in Ephesians 1:9 and 10, "Having made known to us the mystery of His will, according to His good pleasure, which He purposed in Himself, (10) that in the dispensation of the fullness of the times He might gather together in one all things in Christ, both which are in heaven and which are on earth—in Him."

What is God doing by the Spirit? He is making us one— male and female, Gentile and Jew, slave or free. We are one insomuch as we abide in His Spirit, His Love, and His truth. It is not an external sameness, but rather an internal sameness. What is consistent among us is God's love. What is similar is our conformity to Christ.

And Satan's best chance of achieving this uniformity is by merging genders. And he is strongly vying for our participation and approval. Here are a couple of young demonstrative, hugely popular disciples intent on doing away with gender. During a You Tube interview about her music video, "Wrecking Ball," (2013), Mylie Cyrus said, "I don't relate to what people would say defines a boy or girl and I think that's what I had to understand. Being a girl isn't what I hate; it's the box I get put into. I feel completely like I am not tied to either gender or to an age, I feel, you know, like an infinite cosmic thing, and that's what I want people to feel." In a June 2015 interview with Time Magazine, Mylie said, "I'm just equal. I'm just even. It has nothing to do with any parts of me or how I dress or how I look. It's literally just how I feel."[70]

Will and Jada Smith's teenage son Jaden announced that he is going to buy "girl clothes," then self-corrected and said, "I mean clothes."[71] Jaden is at the forefront of popularizing a teenage cross-dressing style trend by wearing skirts and dresses. Both Mylie and Jaden are so vocal and demonstrative about erasing gender lines that they incite Christians. Anger and fear motivate us to respond sharply, and at times rudely. History suggests that many will inevitably make it their cause to address this newest social concern. Some will even been ordained by God to do so, but not all of us. And likely, not even most of us will receive such an assignment. Confronting evil at this level requires a tremendous amount of love and intentionality instead of fear or anger.

It is dangerous to become so pre-occupied in taking a stand against a thing. In doing so, sometimes what we do stand for can easily get lost. I believe this has contributed to us losing the battle against redefining marriage (as if we can even change what God ordains). As Christians, we have been so entrenched in opposing same-sex marriage that we have neglected marriage, which we believe is biblically right and desirable. Hence, divorce continues at unacceptable rates in the church. And marriage is not as desirable as it once was among young people. Sometimes standing for something is the most effective method of standing against something else. James drives the point home when he says, "Therefore, submit to God. Resist the devil and he will flee from you."[72] It is in submitting to God that we establish and promote what is right. But also, in submitting to God, we are standing against and resisting the devil. If, as with same-sex marriage, we spend more time standing against gender fluidity than focusing on becoming one by conforming to Christ, we will again lose both footing and influence.

We are throwing the baby out with the bathwater. Moreover, we make it increasingly difficult for brothers and sisters in Christ to see that unity among us is what God is after. God's love is genderless. Love is also ageless and timeless. These are facts. And despite Satan's miscarriage of these truths, they remain true and worthy of our pursuit. Remember when Jesus said, "A new commandment I give to you, that you love one another; as I have loved you, that you also love one another. By this, all will know that you are My disciples, if you have love for one another."[73] Feminizing love, merging the sexes, and Hollywood erode the real value and strength of God's love.

Hollywood

Hollywood has also duped many into thinking of love as a three-letter word: sex. Hollywood depicts foreplay as hot and steamy looks and super romantic poses fit for a movie screen. This leaves most people disappointed when the lines and looks don't work at home. Still, many of us enjoy keeping up to date with celebrity marriages, divorces, and extra-marital affairs. As a whole, Hollywood has more to do with form and fashion, rather than substance and function. Love is cheapened when viewed through a Hollywood lens.

While feminizing and romanticizing love make it less desirable for men, confusing gender lines reinforces the need for specificity. I believe it is Satan's hope that we passionately take a stand against same-sex marriage and gender unification. For while we are vehemently taking a stand against these things, we forgo taking a stand to become one in Christ. We dismiss the necessity of receiving love from God and each other. And what we have not received, we cannot impart on others.

Romanticizing and feminizing love, as well as rejecting the physical differences and merits of gender, obscures the real attributes of love and the ones critically needed to overcome doubt and fear. Love's identity is not in our maleness or femaleness. Although God's love can reveal itself through almost anyone, anything, and at anytime, we ought not reduce love solely to a person, place, thing, or time. God's love transcends all of these. Paul affirms that it was not Jesus, but rather God (and His love) at work in Jesus. II Corinthians 5:19 reads, "For God was in Christ, reconciling the world to Himself, no longer counting people's sins against them. And He gave us this wonderful message of reconciliation."

I remember teaching this scripture to a group in Peru using a glove and my hand. I held up a lifeless glove and said, "This is you and me before Christ." We are dead in sin. Then, I lifted my hand and said, "This is Christ. He has been knocking at our door for a long time. When we open the door, He comes in and begins to share fellowship with us." I slipped my hand into the glove and began to move my fingers. In this same manner, when He interacts with us, we come alive. The glove is only alive and moves insomuch as it is filled and infused with life. But in and of itself, the glove can do nothing. Jesus sums it up this way in John 15:5, "I am the vine, you *are* the branches. He who abides in Me, and I in him, bears much fruit; for without Me you can do nothing."

Love is neither male, nor female. It is not a feeling, nor is it physical. Yet, love can use all of these things to make itself known and experienced. By identifying love in gender terms, we limit our experience of love. The identity of love is Spirit. Spirit Love is the most powerful force in the universe. Love cannot be controlled, contained, or coerced. When we experience this love, it can take our breath away, in ecstasy. But also, love can inspire us to take action that may result in pain. To get in the ring with fear, we need both ecstasy and passion. And get in the ring we must, because in the words of American writer Judy Blume, "Each of us must confront our own fears, must come face to face with them. How we handle our fears will determine where we go with the rest of our lives: to experience adventure, or to be limited by the fear of it."

Knowing the kind of love that results in the willingness to get in the room with that which we fear depends on letting go of myths. In addition to falsely believing love is feminine, or that we can best experience and express love by all becoming the same on the outside, there are at least two other myths about love. Holding onto these lies inevitably undermines our experience of God's love.

Love Isn't Supposed To Hurt

We have all heard some version of "love hurts." And many believe it to be true. There are quotes and songs that tell us so. We have our own experiences that say it's so. But is it? When I think of how vast God's love is for us, when I think of the joys and pleasures of love that He intended for us, it is difficult to accept that love and pain can flow from the same spigot. Even more difficult to experience at the same time are two opposing ideas. First, that God's love is everything good and beautiful. God's love is pleasant to taste, touch, feel, hear, and behold. The opposite of this love is unpleasant, hurts, and is in other ways painful. The idea that we are to associate love with pain makes love highly undesirable. While the choices we sometimes make for the sake of love may result in pain, love does not cause pain. Love isn't supposed to hurt.

Likely, you have heard the paradox another way. There is a conflict between the idea of a loving God, and a God who would allow terrible things to happen. Consider the child who is sexually molested by an uncle, and questions how such a good God can allow such bad things to happen. Or, the teenager that blames God for the death of a parent, wanting to know why, if God loved him so much, He would cause such pain. It is easier to blame someone or something else then suffer through our own ignorance as to the ways and means of God. It's easier to conclude love hurts than to look for a deeper, more rational cause for our pain.

For instance, God gave man the earth as a gift to rule in the same way He ruled the heavens. In the Garden of Eden, man (not God), chose to heed to Satan. This was the result of human reasoning. Ever since, mankind has been deciding for himself what is best. The fact that we have free will is God's choice. That we choose what is hurtful to others and ourselves is our choice. When Adam and Eve exercised their free will in the Garden, God did not interfere. It wasn't because He couldn't intervene. Instead, it was because in doing so, God would have violated His decision to gift the earth to man to have dominion. Adam, like many of us today, did not ask for help when his decisions brought unfavorable consequences. God's hands were tied, so to speak.

Moreover, if God curtailed one man's free will, then He would have to curtail every man's free will. All of us have done things that have resulted in loss, harm, and pain to ourselves and others. In fact, if you and I really think about it, the greatest and most prolific lessons we've learned have come as a result of another's suffering from our choices. It is not love that hurts others. Instead, it is separation from or absence of love that causes pain. We all have felt it.

I remember the grievous tears I cried after admitting to having committed adultery. While I was not caught, I could not live with myself. I violated my conscience and everything I held dear. Realizing suicide was not an option for me and that running away might bring more attention and harm to others, I chose to confess what I had done to my husband. I will never forget the look of betrayal and hurt in his eyes. It reminded me of the scene in the movie, Braveheart when William Wallace (Mel Gibson) discovers it is Robert the Bruce that betrayed him. Gibson appeared like a balloon full of air pierced by a pin. There were no words as all strength and life had left his body.

David adds words to what Wallace and Anthony might have felt in Psalm 55:12-14 (NLT).

It is not an enemy who taunts me—I could bear that.
It is not my foes who so arrogantly insult me—I could

have hidden from them. Instead, it is you—my equal, my companion, and close friend. What good fellowship we once enjoyed as we walked together to the house of God.

Love did not cause this hurt anymore than God sanctions sin. Men and women, who were their equals, inflicted King David, William Wallace, and Anthony's pain. Men and women that lack love often hurt those closest to them. In nearly every case, the betrayer chooses self-interest over God's and others' interest. By choosing myself, I hurt my husband, my children, and all those that have taken or are familiar with "Radical Love," the 12-week marriage skill-building course I co-created. I hurt another family. Still we cannot fault love. Love is not selfish, nor does it insist on having its own way.[74] It is the absence of God's love that gives rise to selfishness and demands its own way.

Love is not painful. It is always good and always feels good. However, what we sometimes choose to do for love hurts like hell. It is understandable and easy to extol love when we are in the midst of doing what may hurt for the sake of love. We tell ourselves things like, "I'm doing this because I love you." Whether it is sacrificing a much anticipated event to stay home with a sick family member, a single mom working three jobs to provide for her children, or parents refusing to bail a son out of jail: all are motivated by love. In these examples, one person suffered from disappointment, another suffered from fatigue, and the last suffered from grief. None of these people suffered from love.

Some people reading this may believe I am splitting hairs. But it's important to distinguish love from that which causes pain. If love hurts, then human instinct would cause us to avoid it. And if we spent our time avoiding love, we could not benefit from its power to overcome fear. An anonymous writer sums up the lengths we go to in order to avoid discomfort.

> All we do is avoid pain. We have bodily pain. We drink because thirst hurts, we eat because hunger hurts, and we build houses and wear clothes because the cold and rain hurt. All of this requires money, so we must work. We avoid the walls and the obstacles in our way because it hurts to knock into them. We have sex and masturbate because it causes us to suffer if we don't satisfy our sexual instinct. And so once we are fed, watered, sheltered, and sexed, all we achieve is a state of painlessness, not pleasure. And this soon turns into boredom; the terrible feeling that life has no value, which we try to avoid at all costs.[75]

Jesus Distinguishes Love From Pain.

It is clear that Jesus loved His Father. He loved His Father's life more than His own life. The father also loves Jesus and says so in Matthew 3:17; "And a voice from heaven said, 'This is my dearly loved Son, who brings me great joy.'" The Father shows love for Jesus by placing everything that was taken from Adam's hands back in His hands. That means that Jesus was in control. He had both the right and the authority to make whatever decisions he chose. Fast forward to the Garden of Gethsemane. Jesus inquires as to whether or not there was some way to restore mankind, other than death and separation from His Father. Luke 22:42 records Jesus' appeal; "Father, if you are willing, please take this cup of suffering away from me. Yet I want your will to be done, not mine." For Jesus, being separated from His Father was unthinkable. To be separated from love was unbearable. The very thought of either was excruciating. If becoming our sin was the suffering in the cup, then separation from love was the last swig.

Imagine being out in space and suddenly realizing that your oxygen supply was interrupted. Life would cease. But before it did, our body might react violently. Jesus felt all of this and for all of us. Luke the Physician writes, "He prayed more fervently, and he was in such agony of spirit that his sweat fell to the ground like great drops of blood."[76]

Not once do we read Jesus confusing His pain with love. Love was love, and it remained good to Jesus. Pain was pain and it remained all things separate from love. Neither God, nor love caused Jesus pain. No doubt, Jesus experienced pain physically, emotionally, mentally, and spiritually. David elaborates on what Jesus' experience might have been like in Psalm 22. He begins with words we later hear Jesus say, "My God, my God, why have you abandoned me? Why are you so far away when I groan for help? Every day I call to you, my God, but you do not answer. Every night I lift my voice, but I find no relief."

And then we find an even more in depth depiction of what separation from love may have felt like in verses 14-21.

> My life is poured out like water, and all my bones are out of joint. My heart is like wax, melting within me. My strength has dried up like sun-baked clay. My tongue sticks to the roof of my mouth. You have laid me in the dust and left me for dead. My enemies surround me like a pack of dogs; an evil gang closes in on me. They have pierced my hands and feet. I can count all my bones. My enemies stare at me

and gloat. They divide my garments among themselves and throw dice for my clothing. O LORD, do not stay far away! You are my strength; come quickly to my aid! Save me from the sword; spare my precious life from these dogs. Snatch me from the lion's jaws and from the horns of these wild oxen.

Jesus chose to suffer. It was an intentional decision on His part. He chose to become sin and suffer death and separation from God and Love as a result. Jesus loved His Father so much that He trusted Him to death. Jesus loved us so much that He died a painful death to pay a debt He did not owe, so that we could experience a love that we could never afford.

What you and I may choose to do for love can and sometimes will hurt. But let us not think love is hurting us. What we do for love can be costly. And at various times, we willingly pay the price. For Jesus, that cost included the cross. We know that judgment for sin had been carried out when Jesus acknowledges being separated from God, saying "My God, My God, why have You forsaken Me?"[77]

And then John writes,

Jesus knew that his mission was now finished, and to fulfill Scripture he said, "I am thirsty." A jar of sour wine was sitting there, so they soaked a sponge in it, put it on a hyssop branch, and held it up to his lips. When Jesus had tasted it, he said, "It is finished!" Then he bowed his head and released his spirit.[78]

Distinguishing love from pain is necessary if we are to fully embrace either. That's because they are contrary to one another. To lump love and pain together deprives us of the fullness of God's love and the fullness, albeit temporary nature, of pain. Love lasts forever. Pain does not. Love inspires us to do some wonderfully amazing and incredible things. And pain is not without its own ability to steer us, clear us, and move us into God's perfect will for our lives.

Love: A Sovereign Act of Will

The experience of mutual love is by far the most desirable kind of love between people. When honesty, humility, kindness, validation, trust, patience, honor, devotion, self-control, unconditional acceptance, and affection are reciprocated, it is powerfully energizing. And when these things are shared between husband and wife and accompanied by sexual love, nothing rivals this human experience. It's an overwhelming feeling of being deeply connected from the inside out. It would be nice if mutual love were exhibited all the time and with all people. War, crime, and unbridled self-indulgence would be things of the past. Unfortunately, this is not the case. And it is good for us that God neither waits, nor depends on reciprocity to love. If He did, we all would be doomed.

God's love is different. In addition to being Spirit, God's Love is sovereign. He loves us as a sovereign act of His will and choosing. The dictionary defines the word "sovereign" as self-governing. God's love is self-regulated. That means it begins and ends with Him. Jesus speaks of His Deity and Divine Love in Revelations 22:13, saying, "I am the Alpha and the Omega, the First and the Last, the Beginning and the End."

God's love depends on no one and no thing. It stands alone. It requires neither approval, nor reciprocity. I remember doing a short stint hosting a radio program. My friend and co-host always ended the program by saying, "I love you, and there is nothing you can do about it!" Reggie told listeners that loving them was his right; whether or not they liked it, agreed with it, or reciprocated.

Israel loved God, left God, and returned to God often throughout its history. One time God cites their evil conduct as misrepresenting Him among the nations to which they had been scattered. In Ezekiel 36:21-23, the Prophet records God's disposition on the matter. God makes it clear that He is bringing them back to their own land not because they deserved it. Rather,

> I am doing it to protect My holy name, on which you
> brought shame while you were scattered among the nations.
> I will show how holy My great name is—the name on which
> you brought shame among the nations. And when I reveal
> My holiness through you before their very eyes, says the
> Sovereign LORD, and then the nations will know that I am
> the LORD. For I will gather you up from all the nations and
> bring you home again to your land.

God was not responding to a cooperative people. He acted on behalf of an uncooperative people. That's what Sovereign Love does. It does not require participation of the one to whom it is bestowed. Paul attests to this in Romans 5:8 (AMP):"But God clearly shows and proves His own love for us, by the fact that while we were still sinners, Christ died for us." God loves us and forgives us because of who He is, not because of who we are or what we have or have not done. God is love. Therefore, He loves us. We are spared eternal separation from God because of what Jesus did, not what we do. Paul again makes the sovereignty of God's love clear to the Ephesian Church saying,

For it is by grace [God's remarkable compassion and favor drawing you to Christ] that you have been saved [actually delivered from judgment and given eternal life] through faith. And this [salvation] is not of yourselves [not through your own effort], but it is the [undeserved, gracious] gift of God; not as a result of [your] works [nor your attempts to keep the Law], so that no one will [be able to] boast or take credit in any way [for his salvation].

God's love is an independent act of His will. Only a love that is contingent on no one, or no thing has the authority and power to overcome fear. This is the kind of love we need operating in us to strengthen our cause and empower us to face that which we fear. And we are able to love in this manner because we are first loved in this way. John writes,

There is no fear in love [dread does not exist]. But perfect (complete, full-grown) love drives out fear, because fear involves [the expectation of divine] punishment, so the one who is afraid [of God's judgment] is not perfected in love [has not grown into a sufficient understanding of God's love]. We love, because He first loved us.[79]

Until we receive God's love for ourselves, exercising it is mere imitation. Imitating is best suited for children, as it lacks the substance necessary to tackle the big jobs like those things we fear. In Sudan (2014), at eight months pregnant, Miriam Ibrahim was sentenced to lashes and then death by hanging for marrying a Christian man and refusing to renounce her Christian faith. Forced to give birth while shackled to the floor, the 27-year-old maintained her love and devotion to Christ as a sovereign act of her will. Ibrahim was willing to die for the cause of Christ. Her soul was healthy as she identified with Christ. The strength of her cause none can dispute. And the quality of hope she found in a worldwide community supporting her decision enabled her to face the fear of death and come out of it with her life. But it was sovereign love that inspired her decision to stand for that which she believed. In her words, she said, "Faith is life. I always remember the image of Jesus and He died on the cross for us. We should love and defend Him." She also thanked her faith for protecting and teaching her not to be afraid of "any evil." "I'm happy, despite the difficult circumstances, what happened, what I faced was a test of my faith. I succeeded because I am convinced of what I do."[80]

Miriam went on to say that she hopes other Christians were empowered by her experience that they might not feel intimidated. To this cause, she devotes her life. Love from and for God emboldened Ibrahim to take a stand at the risk of her life. Only a love that requires no one and nothing can accomplish such a feat. Only a soul that identifies with Christ, receives the richness of God's love, and possesses the strength of a dream turned cause and the backing of a quality community can do what Ibrahim did.

Perhaps not nearly as compelling as Ibrahim's story is the more recent experience of Kim Davis. Davis is an elected clerk of court in Rowan County, Kentucky. In September 2015, Davis entered the national spotlight when she refused to issue marriage licenses to gay and lesbian couples, following the Supreme Court decision sanctioning the right for same-sex couples to marry. Davis was held in contempt of court and consequently jailed for defying the court order. Kim's rationale for refusing to issue marriage licenses following Court order follows.

> Over four years ago, I heard a message of grace and forgiveness and surrendered my life to Jesus Christ. I am not perfect. No one is. But I am forgiven and I love my Lord and must be obedient to Him and to the Word of God. I never imagined a day like this would come, where I would be asked to violate a central teaching of Scripture and of Jesus Himself regarding marriage. To issue a marriage license which conflicts with God's definition of marriage, with my name affixed to the certificate, would violate my conscience.81

Like Ibrahim, Davis identified with Christ, received God's love, displayed resolve in her devotion to scripture, benefitted from community, and was willing to incur whatever the cost of her refusal to issue marriage licenses. While Christians disagree on whether or not Davis should have acted in the manner that she did, none can argue her courage in taking a stand. Like Ibrahim, Kim Davis loved God as a sovereign act of her will, and that love proved to be independent of any intimidating consequence dangled in her face.

It is this kind of love alone that inspires us to face that which we fear. It's this kind of love that best conditions our soul, strengthens our cause, and facilitates real community.

CHAPTER 10

The Power of Love

The God kind of love of which I speak fulfills dreams and funds causes. It does so by inspiring us to get in the room with that which we fear. You know nearly every book on success speaks about the power of a clear vision. However, few address the necessity of overcoming fear to achieve success. And even fewer discuss *how* to overcome fear. The role God's love plays in enabling us to get in the room with that which we fear is indispensable. Without love, we cannot prevail against fear. It is perfect love, that is, God's love that drives out fear.[82] God has provided no other means to accomplish such a formidable task. We all need this kind of love operating in our lives personally and relationally. That God would allow what we want and desire most, the reason for our existence, to be blocked by fear almost seems cruel. But even greater than what we dream, and even greater than the purpose for which we were created, is God's desire for us to know His love.

Few words adequately convey the power of God's love. Solomon,[83] a accepted as the wisest man of his time, explains the power of God's love this way in Song of Solomon 8:7, "Many waters cannot quench love, nor can the floods drown it. If a man would give for love all the wealth of his house, it would be utterly despised."

I offer that if water can't quench God's love, then fire can't extinguish it. Ask the three Hebrew Boys thrown in a fiery furnace, heated seven times hotter than normal. The love shared between them and God was indestructible! Upon realizing this kind of love did not yield to the fire, an interesting exchange occurred between the King and his servants in Daniel 3:24-26,

> But suddenly, Nebuchadnezzar jumped up in amazement and exclaimed to his advisers, "Didn't we tie up three men and throw them into the furnace?"
>
> "Yes, Your Majesty, we certainly did," they replied.
>
> "Look!" Nebuchadnezzar shouted. "I see four men, unbound, walking around in the fire unharmed! And the fourth looks like a god!"
>
> Then Nebuchadnezzar came as close as he could to the door of the flaming furnace and shouted, "Shadrach, Meshach, and Abednego, servants of the Most High God, come out! Come here!"
>
> So, Shadrach, Meshach, and Abednego stepped out of the fire.

God is love. And this love is virtually indestructible. It lasts for always. And we are the intended recipients of God's sovereign, unending, unbreakable love. Here's what Paul says in Romans 8:38 and 39 (NLT),

> And I am convinced that nothing can ever separate us from God's love. Neither death nor life, neither angels nor demons, neither our fears for today nor our worries about tomorrow—not even the powers of hell can separate us from God's love. No power in the sky above or in the earth below—indeed, nothing in all creation will ever be able to separate us from the love of God that is revealed in Christ Jesus our Lord.

Love Overpowers Money

When this kind of love is operating, not even money or the promise of wealth can come between people. Laddawan Tong-Keaw, called "Pink," is a 13-year-old who lives in one of Thailand's orphanages. She travels approximately 100 miles round trip by bus to attend the top government school, after having passed a stiff entrance exam.

The infamous Reality TV Star Kim Kardashian visited the orphanage in 2014. Both Kardashian and Pink agree that their connection was immediate. Kardashian was so struck by Pink that she offered her a life of wealth and glamour through adoption. Pink declined the opportunity, saying that she wanted to study in Thailand and help her homeland by helping the orphans with whom she was raised. In Pink's words, "But the other children here are like brothers and sisters to me and I couldn't leave them behind. They are my family and I couldn't just go away and leave them."[84]

In the same article, Kardashian told DailyMail.com of her experience with Pink saying, "When you meet someone that you really connect to like this, you can't help but think like how you could change their life. And I think that looking into adoption would be amazing."

Any number of things might have contributed to the connection experienced between Kardashian and Pink. However, what is certain is that Pink had a fierce love and resolve for her people. While Pink was excited about being on TV and the thought of an overnight lifestyle upgrade was a real possibility, it was love that empowered a little girl to choose to suffer with her people instead of finding happiness only for herself.

Like Moses and Esther, Pink chose to identify with her people. Though separated by time and life paths, the same love enabled them to act courageously and defy the fear of loss. Love is just that powerful, and it knows no age. Love is timeless. It transcends gender, circumstance, countries, origins, and all things created by man. Love is impervious to death.

Love Out-Muscles Death and Opposition

Kate Ogg, an Australian mother, asked to hold her newborn son after he was pronounced dead in March 2010. He was born at 27-weeks and weighed only 2 lbs. Skin to skin Ogg laid her son on her chest and spoke to him of her love. After about two hours of caressing him, the newborn began showing signs of life. Doctors dismissed a gasp of air as reflexive. The mother put some of her breast milk on her finger and her son and offered it to her son who accepted it and began breathing normally. Ogg had this to say,

I thought, 'Oh my God, what's going on? A short time later, he opened his eyes. It was a miracle. Then he held out his hand and grabbed my finger. He opened his eyes and moved his head from side to side. The doctor kept shaking his head saying, 'I don't believe it, I don't believe it.'[85]

Believe it! Love out-muscles death. The Oggs provide proof. Today, Jamie Ogg is 5 years old! He and his twin sister live with their parents in Sydney, Australia. Love defies all. According to the Apostle Paul, this kind of love never fails.[86] With a one hundred percent success rate and a zero percent fail rate, we not only need, but also require God's love to achieve our dreams and fulfill our respective missions in life and relationships. To think otherwise is foolish.

That's because love melts opposition. Dreams, relationships, and our missions in life present us with challenges. Sometimes that opposition comes in the form of circumstances. At other times, it comes in the form of people. And sometimes the very people we love are opposed to the person God has made us to be and the tasks He has given us to do. Matthew 5:44 explains how we are to love our enemies. Proverbs 25:21 and 22 reads, "If your enemy is hungry, give him bread to eat; if he is thirsty, give him water to drink; for in doing so, you will heap coals of fire upon his head. And the LORD will reward you."

A friend told me of her materialistic husband. She had longed for a simpler life: a smaller home, less extravagant cars, and deeper relationships that are more meaningful. It created rivalry and resentment within their marriage. They lived large. They worked hard and played hard. They made a lot and spent a lot. Despite disdain, her husband made sure to upgrade her to the newest car or gadget on the market. She disliked materialism's lure to focus exclusively on external things. Instead, my friend regarded the wellness of people's hearts. When her objections went unheeded year after year, she turned to God. She came to the understanding that her husband belonged to God, and if there were to be real and lasting change, then God would have to orchestrate it. She decided to love and accept him exactly as he was and trust God to change his heart if it was His will.

I spoke to her a few months ago and learned that they downsized their cars and have decided to sell their house. When her husband's posts show up in my Facebook news feed, they clearly reflect a man that had begun to value people over things. My friend can't pinpoint the day, time, or particular incident that prompted his change. But she did say that making the choice to love him and let him off her hook both made him available to God and resulted in her peace. It is tough when opposition comes from within our own homes. The fear of rejection and abandonment can keep us dancing in hurtful circles, or futilely trying to fix loved ones.

Love Summons Us Into Rest

For years, I believed I was rebellious, more disgracefully known as "unsubmitted." I loved God and still do love God. Ever since I received Christ in 1982, all I desired to do was make His name famous. I told everybody I knew how gentle and kind I had experienced the God of the universe to be. I am certain I was labeled fanatical; I felt that way. No one had ever captured and held my attention as Jesus Christ did, and after all these years, still does. I became a greedy reader and consumer of His Word. I desired, above all, to please Him. Since God hates pride and all things rebellious, I grew to be overly concerned with submission to those in authority over me. I thought that if those in authority over me did not find me submissive, then surely God wouldn't either. Fearing rejection from God to the best of my human ability, I conformed to corrections issued by my husband and others in authority. It got to the point that anytime I disagreed, or exercised my own will, I was slapped with the label "uncommitted," or one of its variant forms such as disrespectful, unsupportive, or strong.

Each time it was even hinted that I was rebellious it felt like the dagger in my soul was twisted. It happened so often and for so long that I believed I was rebellious. Despite turning to God accepting Christ's submission for my rebellion, I continued to condemn myself, harmonizing with my husband and those in authority over me. Encouraged to leave the church I helped start, it was recommended that I find another pastor. Here's what I was told.

> You should be covered by the pastor of a church to which
> you are submitted and pay your tithes. Because you are a part
> of a church ministry, you should join a church and submit to
> that pastor. That pastor should rightfully cover you. I trust
> you understand.

What I didn't understand then and what I understand now is that all are declared rebellious in Adam; Also, all are declared righteous in Christ. This means that I was rebellious. But after having accepted Christ, I am no longer rebellious. I have a new nature—a Divine Nature that is "submitted," and pleasing to God. And although I may act in a rebellious manner, I am submitted. I am no more rebellious because of a rebellious action than I am a duck because I choose to quack. I am submitted. I practice submission. And on occasion, I may rebel.

Fear has a way of bullying us to accept things about ourselves that simply are not true. When powerful people tell lies, their power does not make the words true. Shortly after I arrived at the church I now attend, the pastors prayed with me. With no prior knowledge concerning my situation or my past, they spoke words very closely to these:

> You have been falsely accused. God sees and knows your heart and loves you. He is pleased with you. You are submitted. You are approved by God and have no need of the approval of men. Be healed restored and do what God has called you to do.

From that time on, they have affirmed me. They confirm who I am in Christ. As with all I am assured, it is not by our own works or efforts that we are right in God's eyes. Rather, it is that we are in Him that was, is, and will always be submitted to God. I no longer have to work to be submitted. I am submitted. Paul writes, "For all who have entered into God's rest have rested from their labors, just as God did after creating the world."

Finally, I could rest in the knowledge of who Christ made me to be. The struggle to decide whether or not I was 'really' submitted was over! I was submitted. Not even Jesus always experienced submitting as easy. Struggling with the temptation not to submit is not rebellion. Temptation and the ensuing struggle is not a sin, as some believe. Inevitably, like Jesus and every other Christian, I will be tempted not to submit. And my hope is to win all of those battles. But in the case that I lose them, it is just a battle loss, not a change of team.

God's love brings rest to our troubled souls. Rest is powerful and essential to becoming who God desires us to be. It is necessary to fulfilling the purpose for which we are created. When we are anxious, it is because we are afraid. And we become afraid because we do not have control over the outcomes we desire. Paul writes to the Philippians about this very thing.

> Don't worry about anything; instead, pray about everything.
> Tell God what you need, and thank him for all he has
> done. Then you will experience God's peace, which exceeds
> anything we can understand. His peace will guard your
> hearts and minds as you live in Christ Jesus.[87]

The Christian life is based on rest. Jesus said, "Come to me, all of you who are weary and carry heavy burdens, and I will give you rest." Fear works our nerves, affects our bodies, and in other ways creates unrest inside of us. Striving against fear, whether by attacking it or avoiding it, wears us out. And if we are honest, much of the fight has been conducted according to our own understanding and strength. That was the case with me. I worked hard to be submissive. The harder I worked, the more I felt condemned. There were days I felt hopeless. The day I heard, "You are submitted," The fight was over. A burden was lifted. I could rest in the truth that I was submitted.

Fear keeps us on edge, thinking, wondering, and weighing potential outcomes. We become restless and annoyed with people, places, and things that expose our fears. Love summons us to rest that we might renew our strength and act responsibly toward all.

Love Causes Us To Act Fearlessly

Whether it is to experience deeper intimate connections with those you love, experience better health, speak publicly, get a college degree, win a triathlon, or excel in your chosen work, it matters not. Your desire and dream must become the cause for which you fight. It has to be strong enough to cause you to do what you would not otherwise do. So, the strength of your cause matters greatly. Here's a real example. I was eyeing the new Apple Watch. It debuted just before my birthday. A friend inquired as to what I wanted for my birthday. Naturally, I thought it would make a great birthday present. I wouldn't use the word 'love' here, but let's just say Apple products fascinate me. One morning during my quiet time with God, I remember distinctly hearing these words, "You can have whatsoever you desire. But for every material thing taken, spiritual insight is risked at best and forfeited at worse. Therefore, choose wisely."

What I understood was that natural things are often at odds with spiritual things. That which we see with our eyes is physical and temporary, but that which we can't see is spiritual and eternal. Paul speaks about this in II Corinthians 4:18. (NLT)

> So, we don't look at the troubles we can see now; rather, we fix our gaze on things that cannot be seen. For the things we see now will soon be gone, but the things we cannot see will last forever.

I desired spiritual insight. Despite my infatuation, I told a friend that I did not want an Apple Watch for my birthday. It would just become another digital distraction stealing time and attention from my pursuit to know God. The strength of my cause to know God 'caused' me to choose spiritual insight over the natural enjoyment of a brand new Apple Watch. While choices vary in degree of difficulty, the strength of our cause is an important factor in determining what we choose. Love empowers us to make such choices.

George and Kimmi founded and operate the 5th Street Mission. It is a Christian organization that provides food, clothing, and character development to a Latino Community in Buford, GA. George and Kimmi love this community. Sometimes upwards of fifty children converge on their apartment. Their kitchen has become a food pantry. Every day, they prepare meals for the children. Their spare bedroom has enough clothes to outfit a small army. For the past four years, George and Kimmi's time and resources have been devoted to improving the lives of the families in this community. They love the children and their families as their own flesh and blood. This love has caused them to sacrifice their house and possessions.

Love Helps Us Take Risks

Love causes us to do things that some may not understand. Others may find it grievous. And still others may vehemently disagree with our actions. Love improves our willingness to take risks. In a 2013 article in the Huffington Post, "Nine Ways Falling

In Love Makes Us Do Strange Things,"[88] Jacqueline Howard writes that love can turn us into 'daredevils'. The article sites a study performed by The Journal of Risk Management that states, "Risk-taking behavior in men and women shows that men are more willing to take unnecessary risks for a romantic partner."

New York Times Op-Ed writer, Arthur Brooks writes,

> She was 25. I was 24. We spent only a couple of days together and shared no language in common. But when I returned to the United States from that European music festival, I announced to my parents that I had met my future wife. Of course, I had to convince Ester first. So, I tackled the project as if it were a start-up. I began by studying Spanish. Before long, I'd quit my job and moved to her native Barcelona — where I knew no one except her — in hot pursuit. The market pressure was intense: Men would shout wedding proposals to her from moving cars. But I pressed on, undeterred. It took two years to close the deal, but she finally said yes, and we married.[89]

Love actually motivates us to take risks, some more calculated than others. But whenever we face fear, we are taking a risk. Love provides the help we need to take risks. The more hazardous the potential outcome, the more love we require.

Love Lessens Pain

Whether in our minds or in reality, fear amplifies the experience of pain. My oldest daughter, Taylor, is pregnant. She and her husband, Phillip, decided to enlist the support of a birthing coach. Rebecca Munlyn (their Birthing Coach and a family friend), explains it this way:

> Fear causes the body to engage in a "fight" or "flight" mode. This prevents the body's natural ability to produce

endorphins (the body's natural pain killers) by restricting the flow of oxygenated blood. Both endorphins and oxygenated blood are required for a more comfortable and safe birthing experience. Relaxation provides the optimal condition for the body to produce the endorphins that reduce pain.

Love helps us relax and feel safe despite what might be going on around us. When we are relaxed, our bodies have the benefit of oxygen rich blood and endorphins. Dr. Arthur Aron, Researcher and Psychology Professor at State New York University, finds, "That some of the areas of the brain activated by feelings of intense love are the same areas that drugs use to reduce pain."[90]

Sean Mackey, MD., PhD., and Chief of the Division of Pain Management at Stanford writes, "When people are in this passionate, all-consuming phase of love, there are significant alterations in their mood that are affecting their experience of pain."[91]

Drs. Aron and Mackey agree that love lessens our experience of pain. I doubt the medical industry is ready to throw in the towel or revenues generated from prescribing painkillers. However, the fact that there is emerging agreement that loving relationships reduce pain and/or increase our ability to endure it is noteworthy. Consider the Civil Rights Movement in the 1950's and 60's. Men and women (both black and white) fought a long, hard, brutal, and deadly battle for racial equality in America. One of the main leaders of the movement, Dr. Martin Luther King Jr., consistently preached that, "Nonviolence demands that the means we use must be as pure as the ends we seek." For King, love was the purest means by which freedom fighters could accomplish their goal. One of the six principles contained in King's non-violent ideology reads, "Non-violence is a way of life for courageous people. It is active, non-violent resistance to evil. Non-violence is aggressive spiritually, mentally, and emotionally."

We might easily substitute God's love for non-violence. Sit-ins, boycotts, and marches were all non-violent ways to object to discrimination. As a consequence, freedom fighters endured brutality and imprisonment. That love enabled these men and women to endure such hostility and not retaliate is phenomenal. Love is the only force strong enough to maintain self-control when everything else wants to lash out in revenge! Love is so powerful that it accepts temporary pain and loss in exchange for long-term victory. In pursuing our cause, there will be setbacks, detours, and unanticipated terrain; there's just no way around it. But when love constrains us, our ability to manage adversity, distress, and pain increases exponentially.

Love Is Ferocious

According to Galatians 5:6, love powers faith. The more love we experience, the more dangerous we become. That's because love makes us bold and fierce. Love makes us act even at risk to our own welfare. In Hebrews 11, we read about some pretty amazing and dangerous things that happened by faith working through love.

> It was by faith that the people of Israel marched around Jericho for seven days, and the walls came crashing down. It was by faith that Rahab the prostitute was not destroyed with the people in her city who refused to obey God. For she had given a friendly welcome to the spies. How much

more do I need to say? It would take too long to recount
the stories of the faith of Gideon, Barak, Samson, Jephthah,
David, Samuel, and all the prophets. By faith, these people
overthrew kingdoms, ruled with justice, and received what
God had promised them. They shut the mouths of lions,
quenched the flames of fire, and escaped death by the edge
of the sword. Their weakness was turned to strength. They
became strong in battle and put whole armies to flight.
Women received their loved ones back again from death.

We may enter the room with fear having just the meow of
a kitty cat. But we invariably come out with the roar of a lion.
We roar not because we always get that which is desirable, but
because we faced the threat and did not surrender. Consider the
roar of these in Hebrews 11.

> But others were tortured, refusing to turn from God in order
> to be set free. They placed their hope in a better life after the
> resurrection. Some were jeered at, and their backs were cut
> open with whips. Others were chained in prisons. Some died by
> stoning, some were sawed in half, and others were killed with
> the sword. Some went about wearing skins of sheep and goats,
> destitute, oppressed, and mistreated. They were too good for
> this world, wandering over deserts and mountains, hiding in
> caves and holes in the ground.
>
> All these people earned a good reputation because of their
> faith, yet none of them received all that God had promised.
> For God had something better in mind for us, so that they
> would not reach perfection without us.

God's love worked through those devoted to Him to act
in the presence of fear. God delivered some in life and others
through death. But all earned respectable status. Their virtue

had nothing to do with the outcome. They were counted worthy because they got in the room with that which they feared. And it was their faith being fueled by God's love that empowered them to walk into the room.

Hebrews 11 gives me a new appreciation for those that believe God and may not experience the outcome they desire here on earth. I think of cancer patients who believed God healed and He did only through death, instead of life. We can't conclude the merits of one's faith solely by the outcome that occurs. Nor can we assume that those triumphing over incredible adversities are any less faithful than those that succumb to the same adversities. All we can do is love and support the uniqueness of each individual. In the end, God will separate the wheat from the tares. All we can do is love. In fact, this is all God asks of us. Jesus speaks in Mark 12:29-31 (NLT),

> The most important commandment is this: 'Listen, O Israel! The Lord our God is the one and only Lord. And you must love the Lord your God with all your heart, all your soul, all your mind, and all your strength.' The second is equally important: 'Love your neighbor as yourself.' No other commandment is greater than these.

This isn't the kind of love that is watered down, shallow, and erotically displayed across Hollywood movie screens for our sensual consumption. Nor is it the kind of love that relies on emotion to sway a crowd, calling concerts worship services. And it is not the kind of love that lends itself to philosophical debate.

Paul adds that this kind of love, "Is not jealous *or* envious; love does not brag and is not proud *or* arrogant. It is not rude; it is not self-seeking, it is not provoked [nor overly sensitive and easily angered]; it does not take into account a wrong endured. It does not rejoice at injustice, but rejoices with the truth [when right and truth prevail]."[92]

I wonder what our marriages, families, and church communities would be like if God's love was working through our lives? We can't continue to say we know God, while His love eludes us. Many of us have been deceived. Some of us think that our accomplishments excuse us from humility and politeness. Others believe their office or gifting justifies their arrogance. And others equate opulence with love. But perhaps greater than all these deceptions is the assumption that God's love is at work in us when we display no change in manner or way year after year. John sums it up this way: "We know that we have passed out of death into Life, because we love the brothers and sisters. He who does not love remains in [spiritual] death."

All of us can do kind things. But all of us are not kind. We can all do loving things, but all of us are not loving. We are called to be love, then do love. In order to be something, we must receive something. It is true that upon receiving Christ, we received the love of God. The love of God is within us. However, just because something is in us does not mean it is working for us.

Several years ago, I found a wonderful fiber powder supplement. I added it to my daily regime to regulate my bowels. The bottle clearly says to drink water afterwards. On one particular occasion, I was in a hurry and did not follow the instructions. The fiber was in my body, but wasn't doing what it was designed to do. That's because it requires water to dissolve and influence the digestive system. I drank water. Several hours later, and to my relief, I was once again regulated. Albeit a graphic illustration, it makes the point. We can have the substance of love in us, yet it may not be affecting our soul and body the way God intends it to. A love that has not changed us will not change others no matter how well we teach, preach, or evangelize. Our sideshows may draw people to the big tent, but only the love of God can transform a heart.

Ferocious love trumps fear. John gives the reason why in Revelations 12:11, saying, "And they have defeated him by the blood of the Lamb and by their testimony. And they did not love their lives so much that they were afraid to die." The love of God was evident in the shedding of Jesus' blood. Our acceptance of this blood does more than cover us as in the Old Testament. It thoroughly cleanses us and makes us right with God in Christ. We were reborn in Christ's image to be full of God's love and to live unique and exceptional lives. When we truly receive God's love, we become devoted, loyal, fierce, and honorable. We become warriors with a weapon no one can steal because it is a fruit that has been digested. And one we find sweet to our soul.

Each of us has someone to love and something to do. All of it is on the other side of fear. How well our soul is nourished by God's love, the strength of our cause, and the quality of our community determines the degree to which we experience success. Without love, we can do nothing of eternal value.

CHAPTER 11

Receive Love

If we are going to defeat fear, we need love. It's just that plain and simple. That the Church, collectively and individually, is not experiencing God's love is obvious to us and to everyone. It is obvious in the rate at which we are divorcing. It is obvious in the way that we speak to one another. It is obvious in the way we behave toward one another. We have allowed the world to dictate how we hug—*shoulder level, one or two slight taps on the back, lower body at least one foot apart*. Really? And the world influences a whole lot more than that. It dictates what we watch, what we eat, what we wear, what we buy, and generally how we live our lives and act in our relationships.

It amazes me how many pseudo-Christian resources are available on leadership and marriage. Many extol God in their writings, shellacking on a few scriptures like a smooth coat of lacquer on a unfinished piece of furniture. However, these same books offer human prescriptions for the spiritual ills we face. We have flocked to leadership conferences, but the leadership in many homes continues to suffer. Many of us have been to marriage seminars, workshops, and even counseling, but our relationships lack the kind of love that distinguishes us as true disciples of Christ.

It could easily be said that the teaching and advice offered are not the problem. Understandably, it could be that readers and listeners fail to apply the information to their lives. This is likely true in some cases, but certainly not in all. There are many people who identify themselves as 'Type A' personalities. These doers, overachievers, perfectionists, and workaholics thrive on implementing "to do" lists. Give them the manual, and they will get it done. But some things cannot be feigned. Love is one of them.

Sadly, we say and even insist that we possess the love of God. But we do not, nor should we. The love of God is not for us to own, package, or market. God's love is supposed to be lived and shared among us in our homes and communities. But we are afraid of love because love renders us vulnerable. We cannot control God's love. We can't regulate love like we can regulate church services, church business, and how or to whom resources are distributed. We have the unique privilege of participating with God's love. We do so by first receiving it, and then responding to it.

I know many will say that upon receiving Christ, we received the love of God. And this is true. Paul, however, points out the need to access that which we have received through Christ: "Therefore, having been justified by faith, we have peace with God through our Lord Jesus Christ, through whom also we have access by faith into this grace in which we stand, and rejoice in hope of the glory of God."[93]

Access Granted

What grabs my attention are the words, "we have access by faith into this grace which we stand." In other words, we are standing in something and yet we still need access. The love of God is in us, but we still we need to access it. Have you ever downloaded a file from the Internet to your computer and when you tried to open it, you received the message, "Access Denied"? Whatever is in the file is not available for your use and benefit. Such is the case with many that have received Christ. We are not benefitting from the awesome and terrible power of love. We're not moving mountains, healing the sick, casting out demons, or performing miracles. These are the results of faith working through love. Having the love of God and accessing this love are two different things.

On our computers, there may be a few of reasons why access has been denied. It could be that the file folders are intended only for an administrators' use. If you are not an administrator then you cannot access the files and will instead receive an error message denying access. Another reason why access might be denied is that your computer detects a virus in the file and, in order to prevent it from corrupting your entire computer, it denies it access. Generally, you can manually override this action through your security settings. One other reason access may be denied is that the hardware on the computer is incompatible with the new software.

Fortunately, when we received Jesus Christ we received the necessary hardware. God, the Holy Spirit lives in us. The Holy Spirit has taken up residence in us. Moreover, our spirit was recreated and now is compatible with God's Holy Spirit. As it was with Christ, so it now it is with us. John 1:12 tells us that the word became flesh. That means the entire Bible is inside of us! Think about that. Every verse in every chapter, of every book of the Bible is already in us! Hard to believe, but nonetheless true! God's Word is the hardware. It is intact and capable of handling uploads from our spirit to our soul, that is, to our mind and awareness. We are equipped to run God's Love software program.

Moreover, God's love files are not corrupt. We have received an incorruptible seed that abides forever.[94] Finally, we have administrative approval to access God's love files. Fear tries to prevent God's love from penetrating our hearts and dismantling our well-oiled defense machinery. Fear constantly throws glitches into the system, freezing the page called, "our past," spooling accusations, and inundating us with targeted ads that have some proven appeal to us. Despite this opposition, we can still choose to receive God's love and override fear.

Rooted and Grounded

All who believe in Christ stand in the love of God, albeit all do not enjoy full access to it. And those that have gained access may not be rooted and grounded in God's love. Paul speaks about this very thing to the Ephesian Church:

> Then Christ will make his home in your hearts as you trust in him. Your roots will grow down into God's love and keep

you strong. And may you have the power to understand, as all God's people should, how wide, how long, how high, and how deep his love is. May you experience the love of Christ, though it is too great to understand fully. Then you will be made complete with all the fullness of life and power that comes from God.[95]

The greater works spoken about in John 14:12 require deeply imbedded love. Only when we are rooted and grounded in love can we produce fruit year after year until Christ returns. I am not a gardening enthusiast, although I love flowers (especially Peruvian Lilies). Once they are planted and take root, the beauty of their colors and foliage can be enjoyed every year without effort on my part. The soil fertilizes the planting. The rain waters them and the sun summons their beauty beyond the surface. Unlike annuals that must be dug up and new seedlings planted each year, perennials reproduce on their own. God's love produces on its own. God's love is sovereign and behaves as a sovereign act of His will.

God has planted His Love in the soil of our hearts. The fertilizer of faith is there too.[96] The Holy Spirit rains upon us, and people and circumstances sometimes beckon our love and sometimes subpoena our love. When we intentionally receive and respond to God's love, we grow immeasurably. We advance from manually exercising love, to being exercised by love. It becomes involuntary, like a beating heart. This is what Paul means in Galatians 2:20 (NLT),

My old self has been crucified with Christ. It is no longer I who live, but Christ lives in me. So, I live in this earthly body by trusting in the Son of God, who loved me and gave himself for me.

Around 2008, I began practicing sitting still before God and thanking Him for pouring His love out in my heart. I would inhale deeply and deliberately envision myself taking in God's love. At first, I could only sit briefly. But then, I was able to be still for longer and longer periods, sometimes with the aid of worship music.

When all kinds of hurtful untrue rumors began swirling around me leading up to separation, I remained quiet. This was partly due to being numb. However, I felt no hostility toward those that spoke unkindly of me, and I felt no need to respond. The silence of friends screamed louder and hurt more deeply than the harshest words of my enemies. I did not realize just how many would vacate my life at a time I felt I needed them the most. I often thought how little we all knew then and how much we loved. And how much we all know now and how little we love. It wasn't supposed to be this way and yet it was.

With fabulous precision, God's love had prepared me for these moments. Sitting still week after week years' earlier, intentionally receiving God's love now held me together and bridled my tongue. The people I loved and do love most summoned this love. What emerged from my heart and to my own wonder was kindness, gentleness, self-control, longsuffering, and compassion. I firmly believe, have experienced, and now know beyond doubt that hurt people do not have to hurt people. Jesus didn't. And this time neither did I.

When we are still in repose, we are open and can receive God's love. God can accomplish amazing things in us and through us. God's love does to us what He wants love to do through us. Love happens to us, so that love can happen through us. Let love not only happen to us, but also let us pursue love. Oh, that we become God's love personified on earth. May we aspire to be love to them that are without such love.

But first, we must become rooted and firmly grounded in God's love. For this to happen, we must experience the kind of love that liberates us, celebrates our uniqueness, and encourages the best in us. It's the kind of love that speaks life and hope to our hearts. God's love affirms who He made us to be, rather than condemning who we pretend to be. God's love relaxes our muscles and releases tension in our souls.

The beautiful fact that we can relax and be ourselves with God and others is to the remarkable credit of love. And think about it; in the presence of the God that knows everything there is to know, about anything there is to know, what is there to figure out when we can just ask? Or, where is there to go in the presence of Him that is everywhere all the time? What is there to do in the awareness that God is omnipotent and said that it is finished? There is but one thing to do. Rest and believe. In Matthew 11:28, Jesus says, "Come to me, all of you who are weary and carry heavy burdens, and I will give you rest."

In Psalm 23:1-3 David writes, "The Lord is my shepherd; I have all that I need. He lets me rest in green meadows; He leads me beside peaceful streams. He renews my strength. He guides me along right paths bringing honor to His name." Since the Lord is God and God is love, we might aptly say that Love is our shepherd; therefore, we have all that we need. Pause and think about this. In this very moment, the moment your eyes and brain reach these words, you have everything you need. In this moment, you fully attend to these words. The ringing of your cell phone, or an interruption of another kind may cause you to leave this moment and enter the next. But while there in this moment, you have everything you need. God promised. Sometimes our inability to see that God's love has met our needs could be that we misunderstand our real need. God does not. And He is the one that promised to supply all our needs according to His resources.[97] And still there are times when love chooses to suffer. Writing of his own experience with love, Paul writes the Philippian Church, "Not that I was ever in need, for I have learned how to be content with whatever I have. I know how to live on almost nothing or with everything. I have learned the secret of living in every situation, whether it is with a full stomach or empty, with plenty or little."[98]

The secret of which Paul speaks is learning how to be content with what we have and doing everything through Christ's love. We need so much of this love too. Paul again speaking in Philippians 1:9 and 10 writes, "I pray that your love will overflow increasingly, and that you will keep on growing in knowledge and understanding. For I want you to understand what really matters, so that you may live pure and blameless lives until the day of Christ's return."

What really matters is love. Love is responsible for producing the pure, blameless life of Christ. Love allowed David to rest by peaceful streams where his roots could go bury deep in the earth to be watered and strengthened. Tina Turner recorded the song, "What's Love Got To Do With It" (1984). The chorus reads,

> What's love got to do, got to do with it?
> What's love but a second hand emotion?
> What's love got to do, got to do with it?
> Who needs a heart when a heart can be broken?

Love has everything to do with it! Though love is not an emotion, it can use our emotion. And we most certainly need a heart, although it can and may be broken. Without love, we have little hope of overcoming fear to fulfill our dreams and achieve the cause for which we live. Roots produce fruit and love produces dreams.

Love Produces and Reproduces

The abundance of life and power in God's love is supposed to produce something. God's love is teeming with life, creativity, authority, and power. And it is good for us that it is. We need all of these things to achieve our dreams and finish the race to which we have been assigned.

Receiving love sweetens the experience of our worth to God, others, and us. To hear and believe that we matter is one thing, to feel it is another. We must believe, experience, and know that we matter. Feelings do for our souls what color did for black and white television. Feelings amplify our experiences whether for good or bad. Add high definition and we see sharper and clearer images

before us. Seeing and hearing the sights and sounds of God love, as well as having the added benefit of feeling His love, enables our roots to go down deep and with ease. Having our roots in love, deep beneath the surface soil, is beneficial. Aside from the soil of our own hearts, there is topsoil—*the people and circumstances in which the highest amount of our daily activity occurs*. People and circumstances are constantly changing, since they are affected by that which is above and below. When we are firmly fixed in God's love, not only can we successfully weather surface tension, but also, we can produce and influence the topsoil.

And like God, love needs a body to produce in the earth (in our relationships and in our work). As we receive love and become increasingly more rooted and grounded in love, something amazing happens; we become love personified. John 1:1 helps us see this. In it, we are told that God is Word. Earlier, we learned that God is Love. Now in John 1:14, we find these words: "So, the Word became human and made his home among us. He was full of unfailing love and faithfulness."

God's Word, that is, Love became flesh and blood. John, of course is speaking of Jesus. Love became (a) man. But also, this man was full of this unfailing love and devotion. Jesus was in God's love and the love of God was in Him. They were one.

> Christ is the **visible** image of the **invisible** God. He existed before anything was created and is supreme over all creation, for through him God created everything in the heavenly realms and on earth.⁹⁹

Jesus is the love of God revealed. If we are in Christ, then all things that are true of Jesus are true of us. We are both in God's love and we are full of God's love. Today, we are the love of God revealed. Imagine millions of us conscious of and in God's love, and imagine that love filling us with faithfulness, devotion, power, and might! What an invincible force we become against personal and relational threats, not to mention threats to the Church at large.

When God's love becomes us, we involuntarily speak with love, touch with love, and honor and obey with love. God's love becomes as natural to us as breathing. We won't know how to do anything else but love. I don't know about you, but if God's love is all things good, all things pure, and all things beautiful, then I want this love constraining me. And I desire that everything bad, impure, and ugly cycle through this love. That God's love becomes our flesh is our best hope for bringing the reign of Jesus Christ to our own lives and the lives we are given to influence. Our finest and only option in conquering fear is choosing to become increasingly full of this remarkable, undefeated love. We can do this because, according to Paul, there is no law against it![100] There is no limit as to how much love we can experience. We can't max out God's love! It's just not possible. But we can only receive God's love now. We can't receive for yesterday, nor can we receive it for tomorrow. It is only available now.

Here and Now

That's not intended to be a clever sales pitch to get you to impulsively buy. God's not selling. Love is not for sale. That's part of its huge appeal and genuine beauty. It transcends all of the categories that we like to slice and dice and place people. God's love will have none of that.

God's love is available to all every single moment of every single day and in whatever moment we find ourselves. It is always here and now. It is a present tense experience. In Matthew 6:31-33 Jesus speaks of food and clothing needs, telling His disciples,

> So don't worry about these things, saying, 'What will we eat? What will we drink? What will we wear?' These things dominate the thoughts of unbelievers, but your heavenly Father already knows all your needs. Seek the Kingdom of God above all else, and live righteously, and he will give you everything you need.

The take away is this. God has us! We need not be consumed with fear and striving to get our needs met. But we are because we neither trust love, nor do we live here and now.

Jesus instructs them, "Now when they bring you to the synagogues, magistrates, and authorities, do not worry about how or what you should answer, or what you should say. For the Holy Spirit will teach you in that very hour what you ought to say."[101]

Jesus told the disciples that when it was time for them to speak, the Holy Spirit would give them words to say. When God's love is our milk and meat and is well digested, there is a high probability that we will utter that which God desires, and scarce concern that we will not. And in the remote chance we do, God is well able to work it together for the good of His will. Love is that tenacious. When we are present, we are of the utmost usefulness to God. When we abandon the past and let go of trying to control the future, we can be here and now. Our thoughts, feelings, and all of our bodily parts are available to respond to the moment we are in. Some Christians will suggest that the whole idea of 'being present' in this way constitutes 'new age' thinking and is neither biblical, nor practical.

But God is love. Love is not obligated to time, place, or space. Love is omnipresent. Of faith that functions through love, Paul has this to say in Hebrews 11:1, "Now faith is the substance of things hoped for, the evidence of things not seen."

In most bible translations, the word "now" appears at the beginning of Paul's statement. Now is present tense. In fact, faith only works in present tense. We do not have faith for the past. It is over and we do not need it. We do not have faith for the future. It has not come. All we have is faith for here and 'now'. And that faith depends on the fuel of God's love. One of the things I am not proud of is learning as a child how to cope with straightforward people that I love (and especially those to whom I am accountable) by emotionally detaching and retreating inside. Having experienced the pain of detachment, a friend confronted me. She asked when I withdrew where did I go. No one ever asked. I didn't have an answer. So she asked to go the next time I withdrew, to which I forcefully said, "No!" My friend then said that if I had been with Jesus, I would reappear all the better. But I did not. She described me as depressed, downtrodden, self-piteous, and victim-like. So, she suggested that I consider inviting Jesus to come with me the next time I felt the need to detach. Honestly, I never thought about asking Jesus. It all seemed so normal to me. But this was the first time someone I cared about voiced the pain I caused so clearly. I could not ignore the impact or her feedback.

Sure enough the next time came. It was how I learned to respond when I felt unheard and insignificant. I withdrew from those painful feelings and the people that contributed to them. *Now* and once again, I felt ignored and unimportant. With machinelike precision, I withdrew. Past practice had perfected this response. I was on autopilot. But this time, I would take my friend up on her idea and invite Jesus along. He accepted immediately, taking my hand. We walked hand in hand, into what seemed like it was back in time. I thought so because I experienced a little girl looking up to Jesus every few steps. We finally reached a door. With that same clockwork regularity, I reached out to open the door. It was really dark inside. As we walked into the room, Jesus completely illuminated the room. I could now see what I could not see in all those years before. The devil's imps all around! They sat u-shaped, with the opening of the "u" facing the door. And there were two rows of them, the second row slightly elevated like the bleachers in a stadium. Typically, I would have walked into the "u" and sat down. The imps would then close the "u" forming a circle around me. In the past I sat there, harassed by their insults. I am not sure how long I stayed each time. However, I eventually emerged.

But 'NOW' was different. Jesus asked whether or not I still wanted to go and sit in the midst of the devil's imps. The choice was an easy one; I didn't. We turned around and left the room. I shut the door never to be entered again. Yes, I have been tempted to return in response to feeling disregarded and meaningless. But knowing what is in that dark room, it will never be the same place of deceived comfort to me. That room is no place for me. Another's love enabled me to enter the room. Another's love gave me the choice to stay or go. Another's love made seeing my true condition easier. It made accepting an inviting, yet hostile reality easier. It made choosing easier. Temptation still sometimes entices me. But NOW, I refuse.

We can experience our past resolved when we are "here and now," allowing love and faith to replace past responses to present problems. Like me, each of us has developed well conditioned responses to things that have hurt us and caused us to be afraid. Only faith working through love transcends time, and this is required to heal our past and seize our future. The power and beauty of love only can be experienced here and now.

Kelly Gissendaner, reportedly, had such a moment. After being convicted of murder and sentenced to death for masterminding the murder of her husband, Doug, in 1997, Gissendaner experienced remorse, graduated from a prison Theology program, and became a source of inspiration to fellow prisoners. At least three appeals were made for clemency, Kelly desired and for her sentence to be lessened to life in prison. It wasn't. Kelly Gissendaner was the first female executed by the State of Georgia in 70 years. After two execution dates came and went and then a five-hour delay, there was good reason for hope.

Disappointment in hand, Kelly continued to trust God's ability to deliver her from death, as she was strapped to the gurney. Reports say that sobbingly, Gissendaner apologized to the victim and his family. Then began singing the hymn, "Amazing Grace." Needless to say, Kelly was present. All of her faculties engaged in the moment. Any fear of death was overcome by her simply being in the room. Though the outcome proved to be unfavorable to human sensibilities, God delivered her from death through death's door. She is free. Indeed, for Kelly fear is banished forever. Love trumped fear. Faith worked through love in the execution room, even while she lay helplessly strapped to a gurney. I think her daughter's words to the swollen crowd believing with Kelly provide the exclamation point.

> To see all of you here is incredible. There are tons of you. We want to thank you so much for being here. We chose not to see our mother today and instead present ourselves to the Parole Board and plead for our mother's life. We are still fighting. Do not lose your faith. Thank you.[102]

Notice the word 'here' in the first and third sentence. Kelly was present here and now. Her children were present here and now. And what became a community in this moment was also here and now. Faith, working through love, enabled all to endure what none of these desired. The power of love can be seen, experienced, and sometimes felt only in the present. How many times have we failed to notice God's love, moreover experience it for ourselves because we were preoccupied with our past or consumed by the future? How many times have we missed some of the best loving God offers through people because we refuse to be here now? Facing that which we fear is not so much about getting the outcomes we desire every time. It is about experiencing the love of God in such a manner that yields deep, resounding peace in our often-troubled souls. The power of love does all this and so much more. The secret to experiencing this love is being present.

Right Focus

We hear much about the importance of having a vision. Vision enables us to plan our way and trust God to direct our steps. Routinely, I coach individuals that desire to grow spiritually, personally, and in their relationship with others. When asked what each desires, all too often I hear what a person does not want to have happen. Or like so many, we focus on the wrong outcome. I am guilty. For years, I battled with my body about losing weight. When friends asked my goals, one of them was inevitably to lose weight. After many unsuccessful attempts, I felt like a failure. I couldn't lose weight.

On an unrelated trip to the doctor, I expressed my frustration about not being able to lose weight. Reflexively, she flat out said, "That's the wrong focus." Without explaining she said, "Here's what I want you to do. Go home and continue to eat as you have been doing. Over the next month, I want you to drink a lot of water. Don't sip it throughout the day, but drink a bottle of water 4 or 5 times a day. I did. When you return we will talk further." Her instructions provided immediate relief to me. She wasn't asking me to remove items from my diet as I had been instructed so many times before. Instead, she encouraged me to continue eating as I had been and change nothing.

I returned in a month and discovered I had lost weight— *5 pounds to be exact!* She still did not explain why wanting to lose weight was the wrong focus. Rather, she asked that I purchase a Vita-Mix, one of these commercial high-powered blenders that can turn things into soup and ice cream, as well as crush nuts and knead dough. Once purchased, she recommended that I shop for kale, spinach, broccoli and other green leafy vegetables, carrots, apples, and other fruit. The Vita-Mix came with all kinds of green juice recipes and she encouraged me to use them. In addition to the water, the doctor wanted me to drink 20-24 ounces of green juice made up largely of fresh vegetables everyday. I was eating all kinds of vegetables. Some I simply disliked. Others I would not eat even when cooked. A few weeks in, I distinctly remember going out to dinner with my family and ordering a vegetable plate. Never before had I done that. My youngest daughter, Jordie, who was about eight at the time said, "Mom, nobody goes out to dinner and orders just vegetables!" Well, since eating 'clean' is trendier today, more people do order just vegetables, but back then most didn't!

Shortly after this, I went back to the doctor. Again, to my surprise I had lost another 12 pounds. My doctor told me, "Your body will crave what you give it, whether good nutrition or bad. Give your body the good stuff, and your appetite for the bad stuff will diminish." I had not changed the other things I was eating. I just ate increasingly less of them. My pastor recently said almost the exact same thing!

Put the good stuff in and the bad stuff has to go out! Scripture attests to this truth. Light causes darkness to flee. The more light we have, the less darkness there can be. Darkness disappears when confronted with light.[103] Ephesians 5:8 says that we were at one time full of darkness, but now that Christ has entered our hearts, they are (full of) light. As light increases, darkness decreases.

God has an affinity for adding and multiplying. We should too. In the Garden of Eden, God's instructions to mankind were:

> Be fruitful, multiply, and fill the earth, and subjugate it [putting it under your power]; and rule over (dominate) the fish of the sea, the birds of the air, and every living thing that moves upon the earth.[104]

The best way we can stimulate change is by adding that which is desirable to that which is not. When I began consistently adding water to my diet, my taste for soda and juice waned. Most are too sweet. Except for an occasional half bottle of ginger ale and maybe a swig of sweet tea, I drink water. It doesn't require any effort. My body just prefers it.

In most cases, the traditional way we diet doesn't work. And when it does, the improvements are short-lived. That's because many weight-loss diets focus on the removal of foods from our dietary regime: a little at a time of course. However, once food is removed, we neither have sufficient good stuff in our system to regulate us on its own, nor do we have the mental energy and willpower to manually maintain our choices. In 2012, ABC News reported that weight loss is a 20 billion dollar industry. How many of us contribute to this industry over the years? How many times have we lost weight, only to be disappointed by the weight returning? Focusing on the weight gets more weight.

Having relapsed often, I can tell you the struggle is real. But the real struggle is not to lose weight, but rather to live healthfully in an unhealthy world. I desire to continue to add healthy choices to my routines, like more water, more green juice, and taking the dogs on longer walks. Jesus understands the power of healthy habits overcoming unhealthy habits, love prevailing against fear, and good triumphing over evil. Paul writes about it in Hebrews 2:11 (NKJV)

> For both He who sanctifies and those who are being sanctified are all of one, for which reason He is not ashamed to call them brethren,

When we focus on fear, we become more afraid. In fact, whatever we focus on we bring to life. Whether it is real or perceived matters not. Whatever we give attention to will loom larger and larger in our lives. Not only so, but that which we attend to in our mind and practice in behavior will eventually control our lives. Paul says it this way in Romans 6:16, "Don't you realize that you become the slave of whatever you choose to obey? You can be a slave to sin, which leads to death, or you can choose to obey God, which leads to righteous living."

If we are to get in the room with that which we fear to fulfill our dreams and achieve God's purpose for our lives, then it will be love that ushers us in. This means we will have to focus more on love. We will have to eat more of the good stuff. The goodness of God is what brings us under the influence of love. And if we are to be intoxicated, then I can think of no better substance than love to intoxicate us!

CHAPTER 12

The Thirst Quencher

Admitting that we need love is hard for most. Many of us have learned to live without the genuine love of God for so long that we are convinced we're fine without it. We spend our time and energy working, spending time with our kids, volunteering, and helping others so that we don't have to be alone and feel the pain of our love deprived souls. We hide our neediness behind ministry and busyness, unable to be still. We appear devout, but only to those that also have not experienced God's love. We act religious, but reject love. And yet, we suffer for that which we perceive to be love. Like the parents who love their kids and try to give them everything they didn't have, and experience unnecessary hardship in doing so. Or like pastors that refuse the help of the flock so as not to burden any, but suffers need by depriving God's people of sharing good things with those that contend for their souls.105 Most often, when we cannot admit need, pride is the culprit.

But sometimes we don't realize we are in need of something until we receive it. For several weeks, a dear friend suffered with chronic fatigue. She believed that in addition to routinely adding too many things to her plate, her exhaustion was due to all the extra hours of working to complete a time-sensitive project. Once the project was completed, she took off for several days and unloaded her plate in hopes of regaining her strength. Still, she was tired. I suggested she see a doctor. She did. A blood test revealed that she had an iron deficiency. She began taking iron supplements and within a few days, she felt remarkably better. A blood test alerted my friend to her need for iron. However, it wasn't until her body received the iron that it reflected improvement.

Knowing something is not the same as receiving it. We can know in our head that God loves us, but have not received His love inside. Let the discrepancy between knowing God's love and failure to reflect His love in our relationships convince us that indeed we have not received the love of God. God loves us intensely. He wants us to experience His love so thoroughly that we neither have to be supervised, nor forced to yield to His requests. If this were in fact the case, our marriages, families, churches, and communities would be favorably different.

We thirst for God's love and don't realize it. Jesus wept upon entering Jerusalem because in His own words, "If you had known, even you, especially in this your day, the things that make for your peace! But now they are hidden from your eyes."[106]

Our thirst is apparent in a landscape littered with casualties. And some of those sufferers include us that profess to know God's love. We behave as though we are unloved. And I don't mean we occasionally "dabble" in this. Many of us are repeat offenders.

We lack the graces of a kind, gentle spirit, showing preference for the health and well being of others. To the impairment of all, we hold onto people and things far longer than necessary. And we let go sooner than appropriate. We live hidden in the tall grasses of suspicion, cautiously peering through their sway to protect our self-interest. Certainly, this neither reflects love, nor does it bode well for the Church.

We can't continue to claim to know Him whom we have not personally experienced. The world just isn't buying the charade anymore! Disheartened Christians are finished with the sideshow. But also, recent affinity for whole foods, clean eating, and clean living appeals to similar desire in many for unprocessed, unrefined Christianity and holy living. For this to happen, we must receive and experience the unadulterated love of God. Concerning the same, John writes,

> That which was from the beginning, which we have heard, which we have seen with our eyes, which we have looked upon, and our hands have handled, concerning the Word of life, the life was manifested, and we have seen, and bear witness, and declare to you that eternal life which was with the Father and was manifested to us— that which we have seen and heard we declare to you, that you also may have fellowship with us; and truly our fellowship is with the Father and with His Son Jesus Christ.[107]

John was not speaking *about* Christ; rather he was speaking *of* Christ. John was speaking from having had personal encounters with Christ. It was not only his encounters of which he spoke. He uses the word, "we" to include the Apostles and other disciples that also had personal experiences with Christ.

Knowing About God Is Not A Thirst-Quencher

If knowing that God loves us were sufficient to conquer fear and fulfill our dreams, then why does this knowledge fail our faith in the hour we seemingly need it most? As we receive and experience God's love, we can overcome every fear that has ever beset us from birth to now. We can conquer every fear that will inevitably confront us, as well as every fear our mind constructs. It is only the fulfillment of our hopes and dreams that waits for us to cross the hot, unforgiving desert sands of fear. The degree to which we defeat fear equals the degree to which we accept God's love. We take love from Him that we can't see by faith. And we take love from those we can see by acknowledging love, accepting love, and showing gratitude for love.

When my friend began taking the iron supplement, her body rewarded her with energy to continue the pursuit of her dreams. When we continuously receive God's love, we are also rewarded with the wherewithal to overcome whatever fear stands in our way of our dreams. Genuine love necessarily results in changes in the way we think, behave, and experience life and relationships. I John 3:14 reads, "We know that we have passed from death to life, because we love the brethren. He who does not love *his* brother abides in death."

When we accept love, then we can give love to others both in word and deed. This kind of love is not reliant on reciprocity, good response, or the negative things others say and do. The strength of our love can be measured in what we do for others of our own choosing. Paul writes, "We then who are strong ought to bear with the scruples of the weak, and not to please ourselves. Let each of us please *his* neighbor for his good, leading to edification."[108]

John adds, "Love has been perfected among us in this: that we may have boldness in the Day of Judgment; because as He is, so are we in this world."[109] Love searches for the best in us and builds upon it continuously. Love focuses on the good. And when we mess up, as we sometimes will, love reminds us of whom we are *to* God, who we are *in* God, and what we can accomplish *through* God. Love quenches our thirst and spoils our appetite for the profane. Love feeds us and nourishes all that God places in us to be and to do.

One Agenda Two Outcomes

God has one agenda. He is making a family for Himself, to become a nation of people that will rule a future earth. Revelations 21:1-3 assures us that one day there will be a new heaven and a new earth.

> Now I saw a new heaven and a new earth, for the first heaven and the first earth had passed away. Also, there was no more sea. Then I, John, saw the holy city, New Jerusalem, coming down out of heaven from God, prepared as a bride adorned for her husband. And I heard a loud voice from heaven saying, 'Behold, the tabernacle of God *is* with men, and He will dwell with them, and they shall be His people. God Himself will be with them *and be* their God.

The various desires, dreams, and causes, to which each finds their God-given affinity, have at least two certain outcomes. First is that our thinking, attitudes, and behavior are transformed to reflect Christ. As we pursue our hopes and dreams, they change us. They change our relationships. They change our priorities. They refine what we value. They make us more Christ-like! That's why answering our prayers and fulfilling our dreams is so vitally important to God! Through them, He loves us into the likeness of Christ. When we accept the pursuit of our dreams, and before it's all over, like Christ we will have given our all. Songwriter, William McDowell writes,

> Fill us up and send us out. I don't want to go to heaven with my life on full—full of visions, full of unrealized dreams, full of strategies, full of songs, full of businesses that could change the world, but I held onto them because I got comfortable and complacent. When I get to heaven I want to hear Him say, 'Well done good and faithful servant'. That's what I want to hear because I know that I have done everything I supposed to do. So, I want to live a life poured out.

Oh that the love of God would ignite the dreams and visions that lay dormant in some. That God's explosive love would reignite the dreams and visions that people and circumstances have tried to extinguish in others. The flames of His love consume our hopes and dreams and set us ablaze. The intensity of this fire makes for an iron clad will that stops at nothing to bring God's plans and purposes to pass. And hereby we devour fear! With nothing to lose and everything to gain, we are joyfully poured out.

Paul testifies to the Philippians, "But even if I am being poured out as a drink offering on the sacrifice and service of your faith [for preaching the message of salvation], still I rejoice and share my joy with you all."[110] And then he tells Timothy, "For I am already being poured out as a drink offering, and the time of my departure [from this world] is at hand and I will soon go free."[111]

When our desires and dreams take on the strength of the cause for which we live and breathe, then we will pursue them with reckless abandon. Those that do so find out eventually that it will cost them everything that means anything to them. One cost we all incur is the purging of every ounce of fear to which we have given refuge. Sometimes knowingly and at other times unknowingly, we have allowed fear to subvert our thinking with false beliefs. Love seeks to overthrow these lies by challenging and replacing each with truth and alternate outcomes.

I was acquainted with Jeff and Amanda for several years before they approached me for counseling. Jeff was a faithful blue-collar worker, contributing steady income to the family. He was kind-hearted and helpful. He seemed unsure of himself, frequently glancing at his wife as if seeking a nod of approval.

Amanda was a tenured professor at a local university. She was accomplished and highly motivated. Amanda loved Jeff. It was obvious in the way she spoke to him, as well as the way she spoke about him when in and out of his presence. Amanda was a natural nurturer, showing affection with ease and fluidity. But she was frustrated and complained that no matter how much she told and showed Jeff that she loved him, he didn't receive her love. Their conversations rarely reached the depth necessary to facilitate a favorable change.

Jeff admitted to not feeling adequate. Although he joked about "marrying up," the implications had a far more reaching effect than was obvious to those that chuckled with him. Upon exploring what he meant by "marrying up," Jeff divulged that he did not feel worthy of Amanda. I ask him whether it was Amanda of whom he did not feel worthy, or whether in general he did not feel worthy. He admitted generally not feeling worthy of Amanda, of God, of love, and virtually of any good that came to him. Well-meaning parents that desired the best for Jeff, but obviously did not know how to cultivate the best, constantly criticized him. Jeff's take away was that he was neither good-enough, right enough, or lovable enough for anyone. Until Jeff accepted the truth, that in Christ he already was good enough, right enough, and lovable enough, no amount of love, whether in word or deed, could penetrate his heart and cause healing.

Jeff needed to agree with God, if at first all he could offer was willingness to agree. Then he could learn to mentally agree with God that he is lovable. Only then could love begin to penetrate and mend his heart. That happened for Jeff. Instead of criticism, he experienced celebration from others. Oh, the joy of love! That we too would be willing to mentally agree with God that we are lovable. And like Jeff may the outcome be refreshingly different and quench our thirst for love!

The second outcome God achieves through our hopes and dreams benefits others. Whatever God gives us to be and do, He has the benefit of others in mind. God considers the good of all—*even when things don't seem to go well for all.* Jesus teaches us this by commandment in Mark 12:30 and 31,

> And you shall love the LORD your God with all your heart, with all your soul, with all your mind, and with all your strength. This is the first commandment. And the second,

like it, is this: You shall love your neighbor as yourself. There
is no other commandment greater than these.

We love God with all of our hearts as we live out His intended
purpose for our lives. And this necessarily means fulfilling our
God-given dreams. When we love God first, we love others best.
Sometimes, saying yes to God means saying no to others. Such is
the case when safety requires establishing boundaries with those
that continuously harm us. A child that routinely steals from his
parents to support a drug habit may revoke his freedom to come
and go from their home. The locks may be changed to prevent
entry when they are not home. And short visits for a meal, or
some other activity are welcomed over longer stays. Or, they may
choose to visit with their son in a public place like a restaurant.
Whatever the newly introduced boundaries, they won't be
pleasant to the child accustomed to having his way. Yet, they are
a very real and necessary response to managing the property and
possessions God has given them. By establishing boundaries,
the parents demonstrate love for God and best love their son
by refusing to willingly contribute to unhealthy behavior. Such
boundaries work together with everything else God is using to
win the heart of their son and his freedom from drugs.

As we pursue our dreams and become the people God
planned for us to be, then others reap the benefits. As Moses
became the man God designed, a nation of people gained their
freedom. As Esther became the woman God imagined, a nation
of people was spared destruction.

Hopes and dreams make us thirsty. Perhaps like me, you
didn't know that was for what you truly thirsted. Maybe, like

me, you tried all sorts of things like drugs, sex, playing victim to gain support, feigning illness to get sympathy, over-achieving, performing, intellectual pursuits, or whatever else fills your blanks. Quite possibly, you have found, or will find that it is a drink from the deep well of unconditional love for which we all thirst. For this love, we must turn to Christ, as did the woman at the well.

The woman at the well in John 4 thirsted. Like many of us, she had yet to become the woman God had envisioned. Her desire for love was exploited, perverted, and reduced to seeking sexual satisfaction by going from man to man. Perhaps her dreams of a beautiful, intimate marriage was squashed. Maybe her hope turned to despair. Whatever the case may be, she did not know her thirst, nor had it been quenched. That Jesus discerned the woman had five husbands is the searching of a thirsty soul.[112]

Never Thirst Again

Oftentimes, our thirst for something must be aroused. Advertisers are keen to this. Before asking us to buy, they play show and tell with us. It's a spin off of the "show and tell days," when many of us were in elementary school. Those of us that recall selecting a toy or other item from home and bringing it to class. Each student would take a turn to show the item and tell the class about it. In school days, there was no sale's pitch at the end. But with advertisers, there is a pitch and we buy.

In Genesis 2:18-23, God raised Adam's desire for another like himself by bringing the animals to him in pairs to name. Imagine seeing animals in pairs, pair after pair, and being assigned the responsibility of naming each pair. What desire might arise? Likely,

Adam began experiencing the desire for another. But before he could ask, God answered by making Adam another like him.

Now, we find a Jesus tired, sitting by a well in the Sychar (soo-khar') a city in Samaria. Sychar comes from the Hebrew word, "shekar" (shay-kawr). The word means "drink," especially the kind of drink that is strong and intoxicating. Though in other places in scripture the word, "shekar" has a negative connotation, we are remiss in thinking Jesus would offer anything damaging. And to do so here would be contrary to the purpose for which He engaged a Samaritan woman. She was already damaged.

Sitting by the well, the thirsty Jesus asked an approaching woman for a drink of water. The woman recognized that Jesus was Jewish. But like Adam, who didn't recognize his need for a partner until God showed him pairs of animals, this woman was clueless to her real need. How many of us can recall searching for something and not being quite sure what that something was? The discourse between Trinity and Neo in The Matrix (1999) sums up the search.

> Trinity: I know why you're here, Neo. I know what you've been doing . . . why you hardly sleep, why you live alone, and why night after night; you sit by your computer. You're looking for him. I know because I was once looking for the same thing. And when he found me, he told me I wasn't really looking for him. I was looking for an answer. It's the question that drives us, Neo. It's the question that brought you here. You know the question, just as I did.
>
> Neo: What is the Matrix?
>
> Trinity: The answer is out there, Neo, and it's looking for you, and it will find you if you want it to.

Like Neo, the woman at the well was also looking for an answer. Five husbands[113] later, she had not found one. So, here she is engaged with the answer and doesn't realize it. She says, "I know the Messiah is coming—the one who is called Christ. When he comes, he will explain everything to us."[114]

In the beginning she thought Jesus was nothing more than a common man that happened to be Jewish. In fact, three times she objected to his request. The first time, the woman pointed out that Jews refused to have anything to do with Samaritans. So, why would he be asking her anything? And while neither she, nor Jesus raised gender as a reason not to engage, John notes the disciples' concern in Verse 27.

> Just then, his disciples came back. They were shocked to find him talking to a woman, but none of them had the nerve to ask, "What do you want with her?" or "Why are you talking to her?"

I love how Jesus always seeks to elevate the conversation. He did not respond directly to their cultural differences. Instead, In John 4:10 Jesus says, "If you only knew the gift God has for you and to whom you are speaking, you would ask me, and I would give you living water." His focus was on answering her real need. But her focus was on finding ways to avoid what was deeply intimate and personal. So, she remotely admitted to needing and desiring this water Jesus had no way of delivering it to her. Verse 11 reads, "But sir, you don't have a rope or a bucket and this well is very deep. Where would you get this living water?"

Ah, in these words we get our first glimpse of her spiritual awakening. With interest in what Jesus was saying, the woman asks, "Where would you get this living water?" That they were already by a well of water means the woman was now considering the possibility of another well. Perhaps the woman was either still more asleep than (spiritually) awake, or more fearful than trusting of this stranger. Before Jesus could answer, she questions His authority saying, "And besides, do you think you're greater than our ancestor Jacob, who gave us this well? How can you offer better water than he, his sons, and his animals enjoyed?"[115] In other words, she asked Jesus, "Who do you think you are?" Again, Jesus elevates the conversation to answer her real need. In John 4:13 and 14, He responds by telling the woman, "Anyone who drinks this water will soon become thirsty again. But those who drink the water I give will never be thirsty again. It becomes a fresh, bubbling spring within them, giving them eternal life."

In other words, the woman never again would have to look outside of herself for love. Love would not only be in her, but it would become a fountain springing up and out of her capable of satisfying her and others. The source of love would be inside of her and she would be able to draw from it at any time and have as much as she desires. Jesus knew she needed a permanent answer to her routine frustration. He gave her one.

Needless to say, the woman now wanted this water! Oh that we too might elevate the conversation with those that object to Christ's love. How many today are looking for the devoted, unconditional, and empowering love of Jesus Christ and don't know it? Moreover, how many of us that profess Christ reject the love of God because it doesn't come through the race or culture of people we find desirable, or because it comes from people that don't seem to have the wherewithal to help themselves let alone us, or because we simply feel superior in some way.

Now that Jesus had captured the woman's attention and desire for the water that would end her thirst, He lays His proposal of water side by side with the manner in which the woman had proposed to obtain this water. Jesus knew that she desired love and devotion. And she sought to get that through men. So, Jesus asks for her husband. The woman admits to having no husband. And when Jesus discloses that she had five husbands and the one she was currently living with also wasn't her husband, the woman perceives Jesus to be a prophet.

All of us have looked and continue to look for the unconditional love and devotion that empowers us and makes us come alive! We all desperately need and want to feel alive—*very, very alive!* This is the only thing that can change our marriages, families, churches, and communities. We must wake up and be alive! This won't happen unless we become love on steroids. Our ability to influence the people and systems to which God assigns us is limited without this kind of love. Jesus influenced this woman and propelled her forward from knowing about God to experiencing Him on the spot. Can our love do that? Jesus did it by elevating the conversation. And this will require that we first be elevated. Experiencing God's love elevates us.

Pursuant to newfound love and devotion, the woman asks Jesus why the Jews insist on worshipping in one place, while the

Samaritan's worship in another place?[116] For us, it would be like asking why this denomination versus that, or mega-churches versus smaller ones, or any number of doctrines and preferences that treat Jesus' body as a chop shop, dividing and monetizing God's people for personal gain. Jesus' answer in John 4:21-24 still applies to us today.

> Believe me, dear woman; the time is coming when it will no longer matter whether you worship the Father on this mountain or in Jerusalem. You Samaritans know very little about the one you worship, while we Jews know all about him, for salvation comes through the Jews. But the time is coming—indeed; it's here now—when true worshipers will worship the Father in spirit and in truth. The Father is looking for those who will worship him that way. For God is Spirit, so those who worship him must worship in spirit and in truth.

Notice Jesus says that both know about the One they worship—*the Samaritans know little, perhaps nothing at al, while the Jews know a lot.* This is a credit to neither the Jews, nor Samaritans. Knowing *about* God, quoting scriptures, preaching from a pulpit, and tithing and volunteering in church outreach programs is not only insufficient, but ineffective in bringing about the epic kinds of changes we pray and desire to see. Only the genuine love of God working through true disciples is capable of facilitating wholesale change, whether we are speaking of change in one heart or many. It's not the church you attend, the pastor under whom you serve, or the resources available to you. The proof that we are receiving God's love in this hour is worshipping the Father in spirit and truth. When we do, we prove that we *know*

Him, we don't simply *know about* Him. This is what Jesus told the Samaritan woman in John 4:23 and 24: "But the hour is coming, and now is here, when the true worshipers will worship the Father in spirit and truth, for the Father is seeking such to worship Him. God *is* Spirit, and those who worship Him must worship in spirit and truth."

Love inspires devotion. It just does. We worship whom and/or what we are most devoted to. It's the natural unforced rhythm of love. Still, after all of this, the woman did not know that Jesus was the one she sought. Read what she tells Him and His response.

> Woman: I know that Messiah is coming (who is called Christ). When He comes, He will tell us all things.
>
> Jesus: I who speak to you am He.
>
> The woman was stunned. Verse 28-30 (AMP) reads,
>
> Then the woman left her water jar, and went into the city and began telling the people, "Come, see a man who told me all the things that I have done! Can this be the Christ (the Messiah, the Anointed)?" So, the people left the city and were coming to Him.

Surely, up until this point the woman was relying upon her own understanding and ability to meet her needs, albeit unsuccessfully having had five husbands.

I wonder how many times we have been in a discourse with the answer to our problem and didn't realize it. May God open our eyes that we too may see! For when we receive and experience God's love, like the woman, we will also leave our own water pots—*that is, our own brands of self-reliance* and go and speak to people we do not know, in places we might not ordinarily choose, to rescue God's people and bring them to Christ. That's what love does. That's how love behaves. God's love transcends race, culture, gender, denominations, economics, geography, and any other circumstance known to mankind. It's just that powerful!

But like the woman at the well, we too will require those who press beyond our objections and push past what we deem possible and love us intentionally and aggressively. We need people in our lives that love us by constantly elevating the conversation and thereby speaking to the deeper needs in our lives. And it is doubtful that God can call upon us to love others in this "won't take no for an answer" way, unless we have been loved and surrender to love.

Truth Be Told

If we are brutally honest with ourselves, like the woman at the well many of us have and still seek this kind of love through people, places, and things. We live in a sexually saturated and perverse society. To think we have been unharmed is naïve. I am not just talking about before becoming Christians, but also after professing allegiance to Christ. Some of our unhealthy patterns and ways of relating to others continue up to this very minute. It saddens me that many earnestly desire to be free from all kinds of bondage—sex, drugs, gluttony, materialism, and otherwise. Many pray, fast, move their geographical location, let go of bad alliances, and follow the twelve, six, or three steps to freedom. Still they do not attain the freedom they seek. Certainly, all do not lack faith.

Perhaps it is not faith that is needed, but rather a genuine encounter with God's love. Hopefully, up until now, this book has revealed the basis and power of love to accomplish God's will in people's lives. We saw that Moses was thrust into his destiny by the love of Jethro, and Zipporah. Moses overcame his fears of death, authority, being alone, rejection, public speaking, and a general sense of inadequacy. His willingness to face his fear won the freedom of a nation of people. Moses observed the Jewish rituals like praying, fasting, and celebrating the feast days. He also changed geographical locations and gave up the company of the elite. But none of these things alone were sufficient to fulfill his dream to deliver God's people from Egypt. Only after having received God's genuine love does a heroic Moses emerge.

Then there is Esther. We watched Mordecai's love hurl her toward her destiny. Esther was reluctant to approach the King uninvited for fear of death. She accepted the possibility of death, and approached him anyway. By doing so, she spared a nation of people from certain destruction. Mordecai was a Jewish elder and raised Esther to pray, fast, and observe the Jewish feasts. Esther also moved geographical locations, from the city to the palace. Though she lived among the gentile elite, her heart remained with her people. But none of these things alone was responsible for fulfilling her dream to save her people. Only after having received God's genuine love do we discover a courageous Esther.

Space does not permit to tell of the bravery of Job, Ruth, David, Joseph, the disciples, and many others who did many amazing feats in God's name. All received the love of God. All gave love. All were inspired to a devotion that led them to fulfill their dreams and complete their purpose to the benefit of others.

Each owned his life. Each was full of hopes and dreams. And each had a community to receive and give love.

Truth be told, my Christian friend, you also need to experience the water of love if you are to accept responsibility for your life, pen the story, or achieve your dreams to your personal fulfillment (and to the betterment of all). And while this water may already be inside you, it will need to bubble up and become a fountain flowing out of you as living water to God and others. A major hindrance to receiving this love is fear.

Fear of Love

Fear leaves us languishing from thirst for love. Largely, fear of love is the greatest fear common to all. Adam and Eve determined this when they proclaimed to hide from God because they were afraid that God would punish them. But God is love. And love doesn't punish us. We are punished by disobedience and sin. It was the sin that God judged and condemned, not mankind. Man's refusal to part company with sin by covering it up was responsible for his destruction.

That's exactly what happened to Achan and his clan. God told the Israelites that when they plundered Jericho they were not to take any of the spoils for themselves. God had reserved that first military maneuver and the spoils of war for Himself by cursing them. Achan and his family decided to keep some of the spoils for themselves and carried them out of Jericho. Here's what followed according to Joshua 7:19-25,

> Now Joshua said to Achan, "My son, I beg you, give glory to the Lord God of Israel, and make confession to Him, and tell me now what you have done; do not hide it from me." And Achan answered Joshua and said, "Indeed I have sinned against the Lord God of Israel, and this is what I have done: When I saw among the spoils a beautiful Babylonian garment, two hundred shekels of silver, and a wedge of gold weighing fifty shekels, I coveted them and took them. And there they are, hidden in the earth in the midst of my tent, with the silver under it." So, Joshua sent messengers, and they ran to the tent; and there it was, hidden in his tent, with the silver under it. And they took them from the midst of the tent, brought them to Joshua and to all the children of Israel, and laid them out before the Lord. Then Joshua, and all Israel with him, took Achan the son of Zerah, the silver, the garment, the wedge of gold, his sons, his daughters, his oxen, his donkeys, his sheep, his tent, and all that he had, and they brought them to the Valley of Achor. And Joshua said, "Why have you troubled us? The Lord will trouble you this day." So all Israel stoned him with stones; and they burned them with fire after they had stoned them with stones.

Love did not punish Achan. His insistence on taking and holding onto what God cursed did him in. Still many of us fear love, supposing it can harm us. This is particularly problematic for those of us that profess to know Christ. If we fear love, then we can neither receive, nor give love. And if only love can conquer fear then where does this leave us? It leaves us on this side of our hopes and dreams. It leaves an emotional void in the relationships that matter most. We become a vault without a key. Our hopes and dreams are locked up. We are left with an abyss between knowing God's will for our lives and being able to fulfill it. It leaves the lives we are given to influence deprived. Paul opens I Corinthians 13:1-3 by sharing our condition without love.

If I could speak all the languages of earth and of angels, but didn't love others, I would only be a noisy gong or a clanging cymbal. If I had the gift of prophecy, if I understood all of God's secret plans and possessed all knowledge, and if I had such faith that I could move mountains, but didn't love others, I would be nothing. If I gave everything I have to the poor and even sacrificed my body, I could boast about it; but if I didn't love others, I would have gained nothing.

I especially appeal to those that minister each week from pulpits around the world. For wherever the Church is, we have led her there. In whatever state we find her, it is also where we find ourselves. If the people of God are afraid of love, it is because we are afraid. We may shout the, "No Fear" mantra from the pulpit and strut with the words, "No Fear" on our t-shirts. We may fool some of God's people with our bravado, but we won't fool all of them. And we definitely do not fool God, or the spirit of fear. That we have drawn nearer to God with our words, and yet our hearts remain far off, is a lie and mockery. Isaiah prophesied about this very thing by saying, "Because this nation approaches [Me only] with their words And honors Me [only] with their lip service, But they remove their hearts far from Me, and their reverence for Me is a tradition that is learned *by rote* [without any regard for its meaning]."[117]

Speaking of the Pharisees, Jesus repeated Isaiah's words in Matthew 15:7-9. In Verse 19, Jesus continues by saying that we are ruined by what comes from our hearts, "For out of the heart proceed evil thoughts, murders, adulteries, fornications, thefts, false witness, and blasphemies." Luke chimes in and adds, "A good man out of the good treasure of his heart brings forth good;

and an evil man out of the evil treasure of his heart brings forth evil. For out of the abundance of the heart his mouth speaks."[118]

Finally, in his very first letter written to the Galatians, Paul writes, "Do not be deceived, God is not mocked; for whatever a man sows, that he will also reap."[119] There are the words we speak and the lives we live. When they are different, we invite destruction upon ourselves and contribute to the stumbling of others. For as with our children, so it is with those we lead. They may hear and even applaud our great and swelling words, but they learn and repeat what they witness in our actions.

Pastor, Minister, Chosen by God. I implore you to allow these words to sink into your heart and continue the good work God has begun in you by cultivating the fruit of a meek and quiet spirit. Let our only aim be the peaceable fruit of a life aligned with God. I write you as one soaking in the warm waters of God's love as He resolves my own discrepancies. It hurts me to think of all the times Paul's words to Titus regarding God's chosen were true of me. "Such people claim they know God, but they deny him by the way they live. They are detestable and disobedient, worthless for doing anything good."[120]

It is the experience of God's love that improves our responsiveness to truth and willingness to change in cooperation with healing and restoration. In the absence of these, we are as whitewashed tombs that look beautiful on the outside, but inside are full of all uncleanness.[121] Paul warns of this sort of thing in II Timothy 3:1-5,

But know this, that in the last days perilous times will come:
For men will be lovers of themselves, lovers of money, boasters,
proud, blasphemers, disobedient to parents, unthankful, unholy,
unloving, unforgiving, slanderers, without self-control, brutal,
despisers of good, traitors, headstrong, haughty, lovers of
pleasure rather than lovers of God, having a form of godliness
but denying its power. And from such people, turn away!

Let us see to it that none of the above be named among us. For if we have preached the love of God to others, but fail to receive its life transforming power for ourselves, then what hope do we have? In Psalm 32:4-6, David expresses what it feels like when there is disagreement between what is on the inside of us and what we portray outwardly. Our body wears and tears; we cry and moan and we become increasingly weary as we try to hide guilt and shame. That's because we weren't meant to live two lives, but rather one cohesive life. Love resolves the discrepancy. To know this brings me great joy. To experience this is powerful.

Today, the grace of God is upon us in a unique way. Where sin increases, grace increases even more.[122] With personal, marital, church, and world turmoil increasing more and more, grace is abounding and summoning us to the epicenter of God's love that is in Jesus Christ. Jesus came to release us from fear, but first we will need to receive from the epicenter of love and soak in the waters of revival. There is no other way. John reminds us that perfect love is the only thing that forces fear to leave us. "Such love has no fear, because perfect love expels all fear. If we are afraid, it is for fear of punishment, and this shows that we have not fully experienced his perfect love."[123] Love is our only hope in conquering fear.

We Fear Exposure

We must have love if we desire to be successful in our relationships, work, and ministry, and to fulfill our dreams. Still, there are many reasons we fear the absolute and very thing we need. One reason we fear love is that it exposes our raw, unlovely insides. If love would guarantee confining its disclosure to the good and uniquely wonderful things about us, then we would have no fear of love. Bring it on! But love also reveals the unlovely parts of us—*our weaknesses, limitations, faults, temptations, and pretenses.* The same "perfect love" that topples fear also discloses and dismantles all that is incompatible with Christ. God's intent is not to destroy us by such revelations, although it can certainly feel that way. When we truly see some of the things we have done for what they really are, it is both disturbing and humbling. To learn the lengths we sometimes go to in order to preserve *our lives, our way, our position, our things, our rights, etc.* can be humiliating.

Love shows us who and what we are, as well as who and what we could be. But we fear such exposure because we believe we have much to lose. However, it's not really that we have so much to lose. We are overly concerned and play to the fiddle of what others think of us. And often we are more attached to who we erroneously consider ourselves to be than becoming who we really are. My youngest daughter recently encouraged me by texting the following quote:

Be fearlessly authentic.

Being fearlessly real means accepting God's love in every area of our lives: in the good, in the bad and in the ugly. Perhaps this is why the masses could so easily relate to Jesus. With Jesus, they could be completely themselves. They also were given options and invitations to become something else. That's the power of love. It's about developing a thirst for what is good, pure, and holy. It's about sending out repeated invitations to love's reception. And ultimately, it is about leaving the choice of whether or not to attend to each invitee. Love is always about choice

When we choose to be real, it means that we are present in the moment. We choose to reveal whatever God may prompt us to reveal in that moment, even when it reflects poorly upon us. We trust God with how it all works out for us, whether or not it is in our favor. We thirst for unconditional love because we thirst for guilt-free living. We experience freedom from guilt when we are open and honest with those who love us. David sums up the way I felt after having confessed committing adultery eighteen years into marriage and betraying those I loved, as well as everything for which I stood, wrote about, and counseled. David writes,

> Oh, what joy for those whose disobedience is forgiven,
> whose sin is put out of sight! Yes, what joy for those whose
> record the Lord has cleared of guilt, whose lives are lived in
> complete honesty![124]

At that moment, and even now, if no one else forgave me, I still experienced and know the forgiving love of God. Today, there is no charge or accusation that can come against me in this because I have been cleared. Though a very painful self-disclosure, it changed the course of my life from pursuing significance to pursuing love in all, with all, and through all.

We Fear That Love Equals Pain

Love doesn't cause pain. A quote by an anonymous author resonates with the notion that love doesn't hurt. He wrote, "Everyone says that love hurts, but that's not true. Loneliness hurts. Rejection hurts. Losing someone hurts. Everyone confuses these with love. But in reality love is the only thing in this world that covers pain and makes us feel whole again."

Love covers pain and makes us feel complete again, but not before addressing our pain. That's why whenever we enter new and loving relationships, old, painful, and unhealed wounds rush to the surface. Instinctively, our desire to be healed recognizes this new relationship as an opportunity for healing. And though we may sometimes choose the wrong people and wrong relationships, the underlying desire is the same: to be healed and made whole. If we meet, greet, and interact with others as they are and not how we want or need them to be, we can see their wounds and hear and feel them as well.

Since God designed all healing to take place in relationships, each new relationship offers this possibility. Try as we might, we won't be able to indefinitely press and hold our hurts down or keep them at bay. Imagine trying to hold a balloon filled with air underwater. As soon as we slacken our grip, the balloon pops back to the surface. Love causes us to loosen our grip and alleviates fear, making us available us to receive comfort and support. When we relax all that is wounded and distorted in our thinking is able to rise to the surface. At the surface, there is light, hope, and truth. Here is where real and lasting healing occurs. It's supposed to work this way.

Healing only occurs in relationships. Only that which is brought to the light and acknowledged has the possibility of being healed.

It saddens me when well-meaning Christians tell those bound by undesirable behavior to pray more, "confess" scripture, and generally just "try harder." If Jesus used this logic with Lazarus, I wonder to what extent he would have become frustrated, depressed, and eventually given up hope? Lazarus was raised from the dead and alive unto God, but he was still bound by his grave's clothes. Jesus loved Lazarus. Love recognized that although Lazarus was conscious and present, he still was tightly bound and could not see for the cloth covering his face. Instead of encouraging Lazarus to have faith, pray more, recite scripture, and work harder to get free, Jesus solicited the help of Lazarus' family and community to loosen him from the cloth.

> Out came the man who had been dead, his hands and feet *tightly* wrapped in burial cloths (linen strips), and with a [burial] cloth wrapped around his face. Jesus said to them, 'Unwrap him and release him.'

Contrary to belief, we cannot free ourselves, nor can we maintain our freedom by self-effort. Love signals our hurts to come forth in the same manner as Jesus beckoned the lifeless Lazarus. Love then offers time, place, and space for the process of healing to occur. Lazarus' sisters were love personified. They became his community of unconditional love. No doubt, Lazarus' burial clothes carried the stench of death. It was messy, dirty, and perhaps even unsanitary. But love doesn't mind.

When fear causes us to refuse love's gentle pleadings for what ails us, we forfeit the opportunity to be healed. However, when we are desperate for healing, we give up the need to appear a certain way, smell a certain way, and behave a certain way. People succeed when what is in them is greater than what lies ahead of them—whether good or bad, helpful, or harmful. Our love and passion for a thing must compel us at the risk of failing. Concerning the light bulb, Thomas Edison that said, "I haven't failed. I just found ten thousand ways it didn't work."[125]

And it was Baseball Hall of Famer (1982), Hank Aaron that hit 715 homeruns surpassing Babe Ruth's 39-year old Major League record. Aaron went on to finish his career with 755 home runs (1976), a record that would stand until Barry Bonds 756th homerun in 2007. Aaron's motto: "Keep swinging. Whether I was in a slump or feeling badly or having trouble off the field, the only thing to do was keep swinging."[126] Failure is inevitable, however success is not. Fear is inevitable, however receiving the kind of love that inspires and activates us to do great things is not. Our desire for healing and wholeness must grow beyond our fear of loss of friendships, position, reputation, money, and possessions. We will lose people and things we value. There is no amount of insulation that can protect us. But this is a book about overcoming fear to fulfill our dreams and God-given purpose. And the health of our soul and body is relevant to this very thing. John agrees, saying "Beloved, I pray that you may prosper in all things and be in health, just as your soul prospers."[127] John wrote those words to Gaius, a man whom he loved and highly respected for obeying God's truth. John desired that Gaius physical condition reflect his spiritual condition. Whether Gaius was experiencing physical health or challenges at the time of this writing we really don't know. What we do know is that like us, Gaius was on a journey to realize his dreams and fulfill the assignment given him by God. John urged him to continue. I urge you to continue.

God desires the total restoration and reconciliation of our soul. By spinning a web of fear around our dreams, Satan attempts to deny and delay this from happening. God knows just how sticky these webs can be. He also knows that once trapped, more sticky threads are spun, further immobilizing prey. Yet, under careful watch, God allows it all to happen. That's because God knows dreams inspire, compel, and push us to wrestle and fight from the inside out, like a caterpillar emerging from its cocoon. And He also knows the quality and strength of the community He has placed around you to bring you into your destiny. To overcome fear, we must fight from the inside, as well as from the outside. Love accomplishes both. Fear of love forfeits both. Love heals, restores, and reconciles our souls to God, others, and ourselves. Love also fulfills dreams. And somehow, love manages to accomplish both at the same time!

face it *with Love*

CHAPTER 13

Love Trumps Fear

Love always wins. Love always trumps fear. Love is tenacious in that way. Love fueled the faith of Moses, Esther, the Prophets of old, Joseph, Jesus, the Disciples of Christ, and virtually all others that refused to let go of their Divine purpose. And it will fuel you and I too, as we hold onto the dreams and visions God has given us.

Although I don't find football particularly enjoyable, it serves as a great example of the tightness of the grip Moses, Esther, and all the others had on their destiny. The idea is fascinating that the wide receiver catches the ball and devotes his heart, mind, arms, legs, and entire body to advancing the ball to the end zone. A community of ten other players, also committed to helping him advance the ball, surrounds him. Still, the receiver catches the ball knowing that there are eleven other players equally devoted to stopping him. Expecting this, the receiver tucks the ball under his arm, tight to the body, and holds on to it at all cost. He knows that he can be hit, pushed, shoved, and knocked down. Often he is. When tackled, his refusal to let go of the ball can be attributed to love and devotion to his team, the game, and winning. Love answers every objection, including fear.

It staggered me to learn firsthand how furiously God loves us. He not only fights for us, but he also rescues us repeatedly. In 1967, Marvin Gaye and Tammi Terrell released a song called, "Ain't No Mountain High Enough." The song later went on to win a Grammy award. It goes like this,

> Listen baby, ain't no mountain high enough,
> Ain't no valley low enough, ain't no river wide enough baby.
> If you need me, call me, no matter where you are,
> No matter how far; don't worry baby.
> Just call my name; I'll be there in a hurry.
> You don't have to worry.

The song sums up how God feels about each one of us. He is relentlessly committed to making sure we know how much He loves us. And He goes to great lengths to prove it. I used to think it wrong that God should have to prove His love to me. How dare me even think so highly of myself that God should have to prove anything to me? He doesn't. But He wants me to know how much He loves me because when I do, facing my fear becomes inevitable. Love inspires us to do it. And He knows that overcoming fear is the key to fulfilling our dreams and destinies. So He shows me His love over and over again, in whatever circumstance I might find myself. There is no fear big enough, wide enough, deep enough, or high enough to prevent love from having its way. Contrary to what some believe, God doesn't always wait for us to come to Him. He comes after us as a man pursues the woman that captured his eye. And He allures us to Himself. I was astounded when He drew me to love. Each time I remember how God won me to love, I become overwhelmed. The magnetism of God's love can be irresistible. I have been indelibly marked by love in real and tangible ways. For this, I am indebted to love. I will never forget one time in particular. Even now, as I recall what happened two years ago, I am filled with the serene afterglow of God's love.

It was extravagant. Some thought it wasteful. But I didn't mind because I experienced concrete love that spared no expense and presented me no bill. I had what some call a "red-letter day," only I had nine of those days in a row. Imagine that. It was significant because love reached way down, deep inside of me, where fingers cannot go. Love went beyond the muscles, tendons. and tissues to the soft, pulpy core of my soul. And He did it with such precision it was painless. I tell you God's love doesn't hurt!

The Backstory Began With Sitting With Love

In July of 2013, I spent nine of the most amazing, life-altering days of my life in Peru spending most of my time with people I had never met. My experience with God's love changed the entire trajectory of my life.

It didn't begin in Peru. A few years after having committed adultery, spending three months in counseling and deliverance, and then studying, writing, and teaching a 6-week curriculum called, "Sex In the City,"[128] I asked God for something I had never asked of Him before. I asked God to fill my soul with the love that was in Jesus Christ. I wanted to know the love that caused Jesus to become who God intended. I wanted to know the love that enabled Him to dismiss the cruel things others said of Him. I desired to know the love that didn't mind being hurt to facilitate another coming to know His Father in a deeper way. I wanted to know joy and kindness, gentleness, and how to suffer well for the sake of the gospel. I desired to know the love that heals, restores, and activates God's people. Equally important to me was to hear, see, smell, taste, touch, and feel the affection of God's love.

And so I asked to know this love that was in Christ, the love responsible for reconciling us to God. He answered, telling me to, "Be still and know love." I understood that to mean sit down, be quiet, and receive love by faith. And that's what I did. I began praying the following,

> Father, you already poured out your love into my spirit by the Holy Spirit. I am invoking my right as your daughter (or son) and heir to receive this love into my soul. I willfully open my soul that includes my mind, emotions as well as all the details of my life to the love that only comes from You. Now fill my soul with Your love. Flood my soul with the love that was in the soul of Jesus Christ. Like Jesus cause this love to overflow from me into the lives of those You have given me. You said that there is no limit to how much of Your love my soul can receive, so I keep on intentionally asking and receiving. I thank you for hearing me and answering me. And, now, I pause and wait quietly to demonstrate my availability, faith, and receipt of Your love. In Jesus' Name!

To help me focus, I used (and sometimes still use) music that spoke of God's love and desire for me and mine for Him. I did this weekly for several months. And then, periodically throughout the day, I would stop and thank God for pouring His love into my heart by the Holy Spirit. Honestly, after many weeks of this, I noticed nothing different. Weary and hope waning, I asked a few women in the church I belonged to at the time to join me. I didn't have anything to show for the time I had already invested. I could offer no testimony, which made me think some of the women only came because I was the Pastor's wife. Still, they came. We sat quietly spread out in the same room. Songs played in the background directing our attention to God's love. We usually remained an hour and closed out with a short prayer, hugs, and encouraging one another. We did this weekly and it was rather uneventful.

But then one day, my husband pushed my buttons. We had grown accustomed to taking turns. Today, it was my buttons that got pushed. Normally, I would have reacted harshly, condemning not only his behavior, but also his person. However, this time I experienced quietness, accompanied by a gentleness I had not known when agitated. Instead of lashing out, I identified with him and calmly asked how I could help. Inside I heard these words: "A gentle answer deflects anger, but harsh words make tempers flare."[129]

And then Jesus followed saying, "Take My yoke upon you and learn from Me, for I am gentle and lowly in heart, and you will find rest for your souls."[130] I had just experienced the yoke of Christ! I experienced gentleness and peace. All those weeks we had sat with one aim: to receive God's love. We asked for nothing else. We sat week after week demonstrating earnestness. And others had similar stories of saying and doing things that were so unlike them. Love had begun breathing, speaking, and in other ways living through us.

We exercised faith by making a conscious decision to receive and declare our receipt of God's love. We demonstrated trust that God would gratify us by setting aside time to be available exclusively for each download and installment of love. We were deliberate. We decided, spoke, sat, and made ourselves available for love. As was my own testimony and that of others, we knew and now know God's love.

Walking With Love

We continued to sit and invited others to join us. We were becoming love. We began behaving as love. We not only noticed the changes taking place in us, but also the changes taking place in each other. We talked about these changes, celebrated these changes, and continued thanking God for filling us and showering us with His love.

But I still yearned to know the touch of God's love. I don't know about you, but when a song resonates with me, I play it until it stops moving me on the inside. In late June 2013, I pressed the repeat button upon listening to Kirk Franklin's song, "Let Me Touch You." Here are the lyrics that captured my heart for several weeks.

> Let me touch you and see if You are real.
> Even though, I know my heart Your hands can heal.

But sometimes I get discouraged,
And I need Your strength and shield, Jesus.
Let me touch You and see if You are real.
Sometimes to me You seem so far away,
And I wonder how to make it through the day.
But if I can touch the hem of Your garment,
Your power, I know, You can heal, Jesus.
Let me touch You and see if You are real.
When I'm down let me touch You.
When I'm lonely, let me touch You.
When I'm discouraged, let me touch You.
Like I never have before,
Lord, I need You more and more, Jesus.
Let me touch You and see if You are real.
Oh, see if You are real

Around the same time, our church was finalizing plans for a Mission's Trip to Peru. It was to take place the following month. I remember the thought of going flashed across my mind and thought about it no more. The first Friday in July (2013), I received a call from the Missions Coordinator at our church. Amy started by recounting a conversation she had with the Host Pastor. A typical part of planning a mission trip is to ask the host pastor what we can bring from the States. Amy said that Pastor Ernesto and his wife, Gennina, had one request: that "Pastor Kim" accompany the team. Other than praying for me as a member of our church Pastor Ernesto did not know me, nor I him. That Friday afternoon, Amy asked if I would join the team, explaining that the Peru host church had never asked for specific people to travel and that she found it unusual that they were so insistent. I told Amy that although I felt honored by such a request, I did not have the money to accompany them to Peru. And if I did there were more pressing financial concerns that I'd need to address first. Furthermore, that at this time I did not have the emotional energy to raise the funds to go. I thanked her again and we hung up.

That was Friday. Monday morning I received a second call from Amy informing me that the exact amount needed for one more person to go had been provided for the team and furthermore, that Peru had called once again to say, "Please bring Pastor Kim, we have been praying and believe it is important she come." Before committing, I would need to speak with my husband and ensure provision for Jordan, my then 16 year old. I was satisfied that all the bases had been covered and agreed to join the team.

The song, "Let Me Touch You" remained on repeat right up through our departure on July 19th. The song resonated with my deep-seated and long-standing desire to know the pure love and affection of God. Aside from "playing doctor" with one of the neighborhood boys, my exposure to touch came through molestation, though we were fairly close in age. My most vivid recollections of touch were sexual and the pain following a fall, cut, or spanking. Shameful pleasure and pain were etched into my memory. I had no other file folders for my physical experience with touch. All touch was either categorized as sexual or leading to sex, or painful. Touch felt shameful or painful. And since I am what Dr. Elaine Aron calls a highly sensitive person, my experiences were intensified all the more.[131] I do not enjoy sharing such vulnerable information with you. But my heart and my life, past, present and future, belong to God. It is His love, the love that was in Christ, of which I boast. This is what it means to FACEIT, to be in the room with vulnerability, often in the presence of one or more, and trust God with the outcome. This is what it means to be fearless. Today, I am fearless and each time another comes to this place, I prove fearless once again.

I am fearless because my desire for you to know the love of God that I had the privilege of experiencing in Peru and ever since outweighs the fear. The fear of those that would look down upon me, rescind ministry opportunities, distance themselves from me, and otherwise exclude me from their lives is a small price to pay for you to experience God's love.

Now keep in mind that as long as I can remember, I have longed to know the pure, affectionate hand of God's touch. By now, my soul was prayerfully singing, "Let Me Touch You" on its own—albeit not nearly as well as the song itself. But that didn't seem to matter to God. He summoned me to Peru, a country in South America.

South America has a culture of touch. The culture is less formal and more personal than American or European cultures. South Americans stand and sit in closer proximity when speaking to one another and use touch frequently when expressing themselves. THEY HUG—men to women, men to men, women to men, women to women, as well as adults to children and vice versa. Men and women also may greet with a kiss. These kisses are pure, affectionate, and friendly. They have no romantic meaning. That's the culture in which I was submerged for nine days. Incidentally, the number "9" symbolizes "gift." There are nine gifts of the Holy

Spirit and nine fruits of the Spirit.[132] Nine is also the number of months of a "full-term" baby before being delivered.

One other thing that would be helpful to know as the story unfolds is that Amy, the church's Mission's Coordinator at that time, spent her formative years completing high school in Bogota, Colombia. Amy is fluent in Spanish and has served as an Interpreter for me in the past. Colombia shares the culture of touch with Peru. Amy is also a Licensed Physical Therapist in private practice. Touch was natural and part of her everyday life. I learned that she prefers "manual" or "hands on" physical therapy, which involves touch and not just a list of exercises. I sure hope you are beginning to see that the song I had been listening to and now singing on had begun materializing before my eyes! It gets better. We arrived in our summer, but Peru's winter season. It was cold. Kathy, a friend of Amy's met us at the airport. She hugged me as if we knew each other our entire lives! She was so happy to see us. And, unbeknownst to me, this was the beginning of my complete submersion into healing touch. In the past, if a friend hugged me I was on guard and could not freely receive or give a hug comfortably. Touching was common the entire trip, but I felt none of the usual shame or pain. That first night we stayed in a hotel in the city. I remember it being cold with no heater in the room. We slept 2-3 to a bed for warmth.

That next day, Kathy escorted us to Pastor Ernesto. He and his team were extremely hospitable. Pastor Ernesto is a very well respected man that exudes love and humility. I was told that he and his family have been offered housing in a well-to-do section of town, but preferred to live and relate among the people to whom He was given. His team prayed and spoke words of encouragement to several of the ladies that were with us. That night, Pastor Ernesto asked that I minister in the church he pastors. He had never heard me minister, nor did he ask for my credentials or references. And he encouraged me to share that which God had put in my heart—*he did this not knowing what was in my heart.* There wasn't the bureaucracy I was familiar with from many American churches. They were just people—men, women and children hungry for God.

I recalled wanting to minister one thing and sensing God would have me minister on love. It didn't make sense to me because these people were full of sincere love and kindness. The genuine warmth of their love was more apparent than my own. I could feel it. What could I possibly share with them? Nevertheless, I spoke on love. I do not recall what I said and Amy translated.

What I do know is that before I could finish making the alter call, people were leaving their seats and advancing forward for prayer. There was no more room. Pastor Ernesto came up to me and asks what I would have him do. I told him and the team with us just pray these words, "Be filled with the love of God." Pastor Ernesto instructed his ministers to do the same. The back doors of the church were open and it seemed like people just kept coming in. People were healed of physical illnesses. Pastor Ernesto instructed those that received healing to go back to their doctors' and confirm the work of the Lord. Many did. Once all that desired prayer received it, I turned to Pastor Ernesto and asked that he and his wife pray for me.

Pastor Ernesto led Amy and I to his office where his wife was waiting. We sat down, and Pastor Ernesto prayed, while Amy interpreted. He asked that I place my hand over my heart and he prayed again. Then he proceeded to tell me that they had been praying for me for some time. And that something was preventing me from going forward in fullness. He said that it was like I would go so far and then a bungee cord would snap me back. He told me that they wanted to help me, if I would allow them, but that they would understand if not.

I wanted help. I needed help. I was there to be helped. So, I said, "Yes." Again, he asked me to place my hand on my heart while he prayed. Then he asked me a question, "What is the struggle?" Immediately, I thought here we go again. I am going to have to recount every sin of which I repented. And I was going to have to do this in front of AMY—my interpreter, my spiritual daughter, my assistant, *neither my peer, nor my elder.* And she didn't know the half of it! But I wanted to receive whatever God had summoned me to Peru to receive. And if that meant divulging deeply personal things in front of Amy, then so be it.

But as I started to speak of those things, Pastor Ernesto interrupted me to clarify his request.

I want to know what is the struggle. I have no need for you to tell me from all that God has delivered you. I know that you have and still do repent. And you are sincere. I am concerned that you are trying to maintain your freedom of your own will and not by the grace of God. It is not the sin that concerns me. Sin has been addressed. The struggle has not. Struggles lead to sinful behavior or righteous behavior. You know both. I want to relieve you of the struggle. What is the earliest struggle you remember? Close your eyes and place your hand on your heart.

He prayed again. This time the struggle to emotionally connect with my mom rushed to my awareness. The earliest I remembered being aware of the struggle had to be around four or five years old. Pastor Ernesto said,

> I want to tell you something. I intend no hurt or disrespect. But I perceive that when your mom was pregnant with you a lot might have been going on in her life that required her attention, her action, and responsiveness. Regardless of how legitimate the details and noteworthy her response, it lessened her attention and responsiveness to you. No one can be in two places at one time. This is not a judgment against the quality of your mother's love for you. She loves you deeply. But how you have interpreted that love has much to do with the struggle. You say you struggled to feel connected. You also told me that the first few times you felt connected was related to sexual molestation. For you, meaningful connection was established through touch, affection, and pleasure that was sexual in nature. Though shameful to you, it was connection. You needed connection.

Then Pastor Ernesto said that he would like to do something for me that I couldn't do for myself. I have struggled to cut the cord of guilt and shame mostly by trying to maintain my own innocence. He asked me the following:

> "What baby, reaches up takes the scalpel and cuts its own umbilical cord?"

I said, "None."

"Then how can you presume to do this for yourself?" he pressed.

"I can't."

"Then allow me," he replied.

Pastor Ernesto went on to explain that severing the cord is legal action that ends the right, reign, and opportunity for Satan to prevent you from developing right attachments that are pure and holy. You will be able to experience deep, loving, vulnerable connections with loved ones without fear of sin and perversion. You will be free to love and be loved. And you will grow in your ability to love, as you have always desired. After this, Pastor Ernesto prayed and severed the cord by the sword of the spirit. His wife, who prayed throughout, looked at me with tears in her eyes and said, "Do you realize how long God has waited for you to come to this moment? He has been longing for you to experience His love as much as you have longed to experience it and more. And now you are here. Experience love."

We went to eat afterwards with a group that had been waiting for Pastor Ernesto. And to observe the ease these people had with their pastors and their pastors with them was unlike what I have known in the States. The pastor and his wife smelled like his sheep and preferred it that way. It was beautiful to see!

Base Camp

It was late when we made it to our next destination and where we would stay for the remainder of our trip. The place was called Kawai. It was on the beach, but it was still winter. It was beautiful, but always cold and damp. Nothing completely dried. There were 5 of us on the trip and we shared a cabin. I shared a room with Amy, and the three others with us shared a room together. There was no heating system in the room, except for the hot water heater for the shower and sink. The cold was chilling to the bone and we all decided to share beds to keep warm. We laughed at how funny it was to need to wear so many layers and snuggle up to not freeze! I immediately appreciated the heating system in the states. Little did I realize, that this too contributed to my healing. God sure is creative and now I see his beautiful hand even in the lack of heat! A sheet and blanket as thick as a pancake rested on each bed. We slept with our jackets over our pajamas and with socks and shoes on our feet. Body heat made up the remainder of our warmth.

While in Peru. I was hugged and kissed more than I had been in my entire life! Much delight was taken in me without effort on my part. The love and affection I received in Peru was abundant above all I could have ever asked. That God would arrange all of this for me in my time of deep distress is overwhelming. I can tell the experience I had with God's love in Peru is worth more than any material possession I have ever owned. No amount of money can be compared to what love did for me. And if this kind of love meant the loss of all things I had held dear, then it would have to be worth it.

In Peru, I drank long and deep from the well of God's love. But also, I was bathed in loving touches and pure affection—*without a hint of sexual innuendo!* Although I had never known such love, I had always believed it to be possible. And now I knew its reality. As if this were not enough, when we road in the van to the airport to return home, a song came on the radio. You guessed right! It was, "Let Me Touch You—*and see that you are real*" In that moment, I realized my prayer and deep longing to know pure touch, had been answered!

Scary Moments

Facing whatever our "IT" is both risky and exciting. To see, experience, and witness the lengths to which God goes to make known the love that conquers fear is breathtaking. That the taking of our breath comes when we feel most vulnerable is scary. It is frightening because when we are vulnerable we are at risk of being hurt, or hurting ourselves again. And let's face it, who wants to hurt again? It's painful. But also, we can experience the pleasure of healing when we are vulnerable. Until Peru, I had two folders for which to interpret and file physical touch—*sexual and painful.* So any time I opened myself up to physical affection, it had a good chance of being filed in one of these folders, even though I did not want it to. In Peru I gained another folder that I will call "non-sexual affection." It housed affection exchanged by siblings and friends. It also contained affection from one human being to another. For instance, comforting someone that comes to the altar, or who is experiencing the loss of a loved one, or congratulating another's success.

Our willingness to be vulnerable, accompanied by the threat of being hurt again, is the key to experiencing the extraordinary power of God's love in overcoming fear. Vulnerability is also the location of our deepest needs for His healing love and the seat of our dreams. Every fracture of soul occurs in contact, or absence of contact with people. Soft, innocent bones of the soul are broken and defiled by others, like in the case of early childhood molestation and other forms of abuse. Anger, refusal to forgive, resentment, and bitterness cause us to become dry and brittle. Such thoughts and the emotions that accompany them lead to isolation and loss of intimacy in relationship. These kinds of bones tend to break with the slightest exertion, or outside interference. Whether hard or soft such bones lack the integrity necessary to withstand threat. The result is insecure grown men and women, many of whom profess Christ. I was such a one.

However, it is the skillful love of God that exposes our vulnerability repeatedly and on purpose. Each time God hopes we oblige, and allow love to cleanse, heal, and embolden us to stand in spite of fear. Writing so candidly invites censure and the potential for misinterpretation. Still, I write because that's what love did for me. And apparently, that's what love did for Job.

> God rescued me from the grave, and now my life is filled
> with light.' Yes, God does these things repeatedly for people.
> He rescues them from the grave so they may enjoy the light
> of life.[133]

The love of God makes us come alive. But it also uncovers the hurts and pains that make us vulnerable. It exposes the false beliefs that have come to govern our behavior. Elihu (meaning "My God Is He") did this for Job. Consider the care with which he speaks to Job's heart and soul. "Look, you and I both belong to God. I, too, was formed from clay. So, you don't need to be afraid of me. I won't come down hard on you."[134]

Elihu spoke sincerely and truthfully with Job. He challenged Job's thinking. At one point, Elihu even told Job his thinking was flat out wrong. God had not caused his calamity. Nor did God punish Job. Rather, Job was punished by his own doing, with the aid of an all too eager to help Satan. Whenever our thinking is out of alignment with the One in whose image we were created, harm and unhappiness are the result. God's love working through Elihu exposed Job to truth and compassionate love. This love, mixed together with truth, overcame Job's fear of disaster, but not before it had taken all that he had. And such is the case for many of us.

God Works All Things Together

After returning from Peru and ready to enjoy the healing I experienced there, my life took a drastic turn. After 28 years of marriage, my husband left our home. I did not see it coming, not at all! Unbeknownst to me at the time, it was the same month I went to Peru, that he had made a decision to leave me. Subsequently, he asked me to leave the church I had helped start. After experiencing much internal conflict, I also relinquished my rights to Radical Love, the very successful marriage course I wrote and developed with Anthony. I lost income. I lost my home to a short sale. I had no vehicle. My youngest daughter preferred to live with her father. Many friends were silent. My mother-in-law, whom I loved dearly, passed away quickly and unexpectedly. These are the facts of my life. I had been harmed; I felt unhappy and very alone.

Pastor Ernesto and Gennina, and in front of Amy my soul lay bare. I was vulnerable. I was afraid. But I believed God brought me to this place to help me. Imagine a love so determined to

take me away from my family and out of my country to a place
I did not know, to a people whom I had never met, to heal me
in order that I may fulfill God's will and my dreams for my life.
For nine straight days, the Alarcon's, Kathy, and her mother,
Amy, and the others I traveled with (Grandma V, Michelle,
and Sonnet) became my community—my **F**ACE **I**T **G**roup
(FIG).[135] For nine days, with the help of these loving individuals,
love triumphed over fear!

It was like in the *Wizard of Oz* (1939) when Dorothy, Toto
(her dog), the Lion, Scarecrow, and Tin Man all traveled to the
Emerald City to see the Wizard. All desired something from
the Wizard. The Tin Man wanted a heart that could feel. The
Scarecrow wanted a brain to think. The Lion wanted courage
to roar. And Dorothy just wanted to go home. Each person on
our team desired something from God's Love. Unlike the five
characters in the movie, the five of us did not travel to Emerald
City. Instead, we traveled from North America to South America.
Like the Lion, I came home with courage. God's love gave me the
confidence to be who I am—the gentle, sensitive, understanding,
kind-hearted, deeply caring, emotionally affectionate person He
made me to be. I came home with the courage to receive and
give affection that is pure and untainted with sexual suggestion.
I came home with the courage to stand my ground against those
that would insinuate otherwise and in other ways cheapen and
try to steal that which God did for me in Peru.

"Love works all things together for the good of them that
love God."[136] The pain of losing and the joy of connecting shape

us into the people God would have us become. Love did all that for me. And love can do that and more for you. Love overcame the fear that my badness would overtake my goodness. Love freed me from having to maintain my goodness and condemn my badness. Love hadn't punished me all these many years. Nor is it punishing you. We punish ourselves by believing what others say and think of us instead of that which God declares true of us. Everything Jesus is, we are. In John 15:5, Jesus assures us of this,

> Yes, I am the vine; you are the branches. Those who remain in me, and I in them, will produce much fruit. For apart from me you can do nothing.

In essence Jesus says, "I am, therefore, you are." God's undeterred love for us tirelessly and grittily works to make this our living reality. We are in Him and He is in us. It is through identifying and adopting the mind of Christ, and in relationship with Him, that we fulfill our dreams and God's purposes for our lives. Toward this end, as Paul's words urged the Philippians, may they persuade us. "Let this mind be in you, which was also in Christ Jesus."[137]

Face Your Fear Fulfill Your Destiny

For some reason, God permits the spirit of fear to fasten itself to our hopes and dreams. But He does so holding the trump card. Love is the deciding factor as to whether or not we will achieve our dreams. If God's love is not operating within us, we may have marginal success at best and utter defeat at worst. I believe God is more interested in the people we are becoming than, anything we will ever do. If we are becoming the person God intends, we will be doing what He desires us to do and at the same time experience the fulfillment of our dreams.

Picture a field. In that field is a hidden treasure. Groping around the field, you stumble upon a piece of treasure. Excited by what you find, you put it back and tell no one. Invigorated, you go home, gather and sell everything you have, and purchase the entire field, believing that there must be more treasure. You set up base camp, and then you begin to inspect your purchase. Only, there is no treasure apparent. There are only weeds, rocks, dirt, dust, insects, and other kinds of animals like snakes and rodents. All represent potential threats. Still there is treasure in the field. You saw it firsthand. You bought it. But also, you bought the threat of these other things. No doubt, there is treasure and likely much more. To get it will require plowing the weeds, moving rocks, shoveling dirt, and fending off snakes, wild meat-eating animals, and bugs. In short, it will require neutralizing the threats. Paul writes,

> For it is the God who commanded light to shine out of
> darkness, who has shone in our hearts to give the light
> of the knowledge of the glory of God in the face of Jesus
> Christ. But we have this treasure in earthen vessels that
> the excellence of the power may be of God and not of us.
> We are hard-pressed on every side, yet not crushed; we are
> perplexed, but not in despair; persecuted, but not forsaken;
> struck down, but not destroyed—[138]

We are God's treasure. Our real value is hidden deep within us. There are weeds and pests made of wrong thinking, fears that rival bolder sized rocks, snakes, and wild animals seeking to attack us. Their tools of destruction are pride, shame, lust, and jealousy, resentment, and bitterness. But there is treasure in us and love intends to claim it. We are God's treasure. We are His dream. We are His joy. And His love will do whatever it takes to win our voluntary affection.

But also, you and I have a treasure—*a God-given dream*. It is hidden in the field of fear. Moses found this out early on. He treasured the victory of freeing his enslaved brother from the torture of his slave master. But upon learning of Pharaoh's anger and intent to kill him, Moses recognized he was standing in the field of fear and ran. It would be forty years later before Moses gained the courage to return to his field of fear to claim his treasure.

Esther also discovered her treasure and value that was hidden in the field of fear. It took three days of prayer and fasting, along with her entire community. She did all this before she gained the courage to return to the field of fear and lay hold of her dream to ensure the safety of her people.

How long might it take each of us to return to the field of fear to lay claim to our respective dreams? What might it take? Inevitably, it will take different things for each of us. But one thing is needful for all. That is God's love. It is the kind of love that moves boulders, cuts through stone and iron and slashes through bushes. Love does all of these things while preserving the treasure in us and empowering us to fulfill our dreams.

These two things are happening simultaneously; God is

mining His treasure in us, while we are unearthing our own. God's love is both working with us to fulfill our dreams and working on us to fulfill God's dream for a people like Himself that will one day rule the earth just as He rules the heavens. Again I refer to Paul, this time in I Corinthians 3:9 (NLT), which says, "For we are both God's workers. And you are God's field. You are God's building."

Our treasure is not in the field of dreams. Rather, it is shrewdly kept in the field of fear—the field of our frailty. To Paul, God said that His power works best and is most evident in our weakness.[139] Jesus was hidden in Mary, a woman representing frail humanity. To the foolish, such treasure went easily unnoticed. To the unbelieving, such treasure goes mistreated.

Facing that which we fear is the only way to find out what really matters to us and ultimately demand our dreams. Love's double-edged sword, which is spoken about in Hebrews 4:12, cuts through and demolishes fear, leaving us with the treasure we coveted and a dream fulfilled.

Incorporated into our dreams is God's plan to transform us into the people He would like us to be. The sword spoken of in Hebrews 4:12 is doubled-edged for this reason. It is intended to cut us, separating what belongs to God first and then what belongs to others and us second. A big part of that is cutting and separating us from fear. And, believe it or not, He prefers to accomplish this by overwhelming us with love over and over again!

Though many do not experience God's dependence on love and kindness as the primary method of wooing us to Himself, it is nonetheless true. Romans 2:4 asks, "Don't you see how wonderfully kind, tolerant, and patient God is with you? Does this mean nothing to you? Can't you see that his kindness is intended to turn you from your sin?"

My hope and prayer is that we soak in this love often and drink from love continuously. May we become so pliable and intoxicated with love that we conquer fear by mounting every obstacle that stands in the way of us answering our dream.

CHAPTER 14

What Are You Waiting For?

In the classic fictional tale "Hinds' Feet In High Places," British author Hannah Hurnard takes readers on a journey of overcoming fear through a symbolic character named Much Afraid. It is a rich and moving story about how a little girl conquers fear by receiving love from the Shepherd. I read the book many years ago. While not the inspiration for this book, I share the premise of the book. Receiving love provides the courage to face fear and fulfill dreams.

Much Afraid's dream was that the Shepherd would transform her crooked feet into hind's feet so she might leap across the mountains of life. She is transformed by the love of a Shepherd and finally advances to the high places. She is given feet like hind's feet, making it easy to scale mountains. There, Grace and Glory replaced her former companions, Sorrow and Suffering. One famous and recurring line in the book is Much Afraid's learned response to the daily challenges she faced: "Behold me, here I am; thy little handmaiden Acceptance-with-Joy and all that is in my heart is thine."[140]

Accepting challenges permitted by her loving Shepherd characterized Much Afraid's journey in conquering fear. Much Afraid learned to experience joy—*the belief that nothing could befall her that she and the Shepherd couldn't handle together.* In all things, whether or not were caused by the Shepherd, she gave thanks. Paul offered the same advice to the Thessalonians saying, "In everything give thanks; for this is the will of God in Christ Jesus for you."[141]

By receiving all as from her Shepherd, Much Afraid learned to deliver His response instead of relying on her own. Much Afraid had been laboring among the flocks of the Shepherd for some time before she was extended an invitation to fulfill her dream. Still, she was afraid. How many of us that have given our lives to Christ and been in God's service for years are afraid to pursue our dreams? It was neither money nor time or leadership skills for that matter that prevented Much Afraid. Rather, it was fear. And it is fear that prevents so many of us from taking the next step toward fulfilling our dreams.

Many of us have deserted that which is truest of us in character, manner, skill, or way because we fear what others have said or might say in the future. And sometimes we think too highly or lowly of ourselves to engage in the task at hand. Consider the teenager that thinks working at a fast food restaurant is beneath him. Or the adult that doesn't pursue a promotional opportunity for which she is well qualified because she believes it is above her. Both suffer from pride. Whether your self-esteem is too high or too low matters not. What matters is that which God says concerning us. Much Afraid dreamed of hind's feet. Although she believed the Shepherd could grant her such feet, it wasn't until she learned to trust His love by facing each thing that befell her that she was granted hind's feet.

Much Afraid learned how to rest in the Shepherd's love, trusting that if He allowed a circumstance, He also had an answer for it. In Romans 11:36, Paul suggests that whatever befalls us God has allowed it to be. He says,

> For of Him and through Him and to Him are all things, to whom be glory forever. Amen.

Therefore, there is no fear that we can't address together with God. For Much Afraid, it began by receiving the Shepherd's love. That love first came in the form of a seed. Here is the discourse that occurred between the Shepherd and Much Afraid.

> Shepherd: Then will you let me plant the seed of true Love [in your heart] now? It will take you some time to develop hinds' feet and to climb to the High Places, and if I put the seed in your heart now, it will be ready to bloom by the time you get there.
>
> Much Afraid (shrank back): I am afraid. I have been told that if you really love someone you give that loved one the power to hurt and pain you in a way nothing else can.
>
> Shepherd: That is true. To love does mean to put yourself into the power of the loved one and to become very vulnerable to pain, and you are much afraid of pain, are you not?
>
> Much Afraid (nodded miserably and then said shamefacedly): Yes, very much afraid of it.

Shepherd: But it is so happy to love. It is happy to love even if you are not loved in return. There is pain, too, certainly, but Love does not think that very significant.

Much Afraid received the Shepherd's seed of love in her heart. Afterwards the Shepherd says to Much Afraid, "I planted the seed of love in your heart, and already it has begun to make you hear and see things that you had not noticed before (bubbling water sounds, the color of flowers, birds songs, the people you see each day (your two guides))."

Love makes us come alive. Before we come alive, and thereby give life to our dreams and love others, we too must receive love. John 1:12 says that to as many as received Him, that is to receive God's love to them He has given authority to be who God intends and fulfill the dreams He places in their hearts.

John also writes, "This is real love—not that we loved God, but that he loved us and sent his Son as a sacrifice to take away our sins."[142] He makes our need to receive God's love first even clearer in I John 4:19 (NKJV). "We love Him because He first loved us." The New Living Translation writes the verse this way, "We love each other because he loved us first."

Whether we are speaking of loving God, loving ourselves, or loving others our ability to do so always depends on having received God's love first. We must receive before we are able to give. That's why clever, well-intended clichés like, "Act like you have it and you will get it," or "Do right and eventually you will feel right," or "Fake it until you make it," are misguided. All of these motivational mantras start with giving something instead of receiving something. Each statement encourages the false belief that doing something without being something first is okay with God. Worse still, that doing something for God is more important than being something to God. The order is this: receive, be, and then do. Unfortunately, even well-meaning ministers propose the reverse: do, be, and then receive. No wonder so many of us collapse. We are stressed out, worn out, and eventually sell out. This is the difference between working through God's strength and our own. Paul declares,

> Now the Spirit expressly says that in latter times some will depart from the faith, giving heed to deceiving spirits and doctrines of demons, speaking lies in hypocrisy, having their own conscience seared with a hot iron, forbidding to marry, and commanding to abstain from foods which God created to be received with thanksgiving by those who believe and know the truth.[143]

Most do not depart the faith because we arrive at an intersection and one option reads, "Lies, Doctrine of Demons, or Hypocrisy." After a long discourse on deception and the lawless one (Satan), Paul explains that the refusal to receive the love that belongs to truth results in departure from the faith. He says, "because they did not receive the love of the truth, that they might be saved."[144]

Furious love is strong, viable, and effective because it is based on truth. Receiving this love makes us bold, practical, and effective in meeting the harsh realities we sometimes face and must overcome. Quite often, those realities are cloaked in fear. God's love is furious. It provides relentless aid in addressing the circumstances standing in the way of our dreams. God's love cannot be tricked, imitated, or in any other way diminished or defeated. That's because God loves us as a sovereign act of His will, dependent on no one and no thing. Like the allegorical Much Afraid, we must continuously receive the love that is based on truth in our hearts. Furthermore, when we allow His love to grow down deep within us by accepting those things that happen to us as permitted by God, as well as draw from and give support to the communities of which we are a part, we ultimately prevail.

I love God's love. It is genderless, ageless, and "religion less." God's love is always present, always knowing, always powerful, and always ready to aid. It is not forceful. Like the love of Much Afraid's Shepherd, God's love is extremely respectful of our will and our traditions, leaving us sometimes feeling forgotten, abandoned, and even punished. Still, God's love is gentle, patient, and kind. His love is easy to receive. It is as easy as stepping in a sauna or hot tub and taking a seat.

The Way of Love

A few years ago, I was introduced to JeJu Saunas[145] located in Duluth, Georgia. It is a traditional Korean public bathhouse. Under a 35,000 square foot roof are hot tubs, showers, and saunas. In Korea, the word used is "Jjimjil," which means "heating." The Saunas' various rooms are maintained at different temperatures, from mild to extremely hot, to suit guests' needs and preferences. The walls are decorated with different woods, minerals, crystals, stones, and metals. The mood is tranquil with ambient lighting, natural colors, earthy textures, and natural aromas.

The floors are heated for lounging and sleeping. Wide-screen TVs, exercise rooms, ice rooms, heated mineral rooms, a swimming pool, sleeping quarters, and a food court also occupy the space. There is a menu of spa services from which guests can choose. There are unisex and gender specific areas for the enjoyment of all.

I absolutely enjoy this place! For a period of time, I went weekly. I especially enjoyed the Rock Salt Sauna and the hottest water spa tub. The Rock Salt Sauna is the hottest dry sauna made of pure crystal rock salt. Both of these amenities relax muscles, relieving stress and tension. The Rock Salt Sauna also strengthens the cardio-vascular system, increases blood flow, and allows you to sweat out impurities and loosen dead skin cells.

What I found most amazing about each is that I only had to pay the small JeJu admittance fee to gain access to the sauna or the hot tub. That was it! Seriously. The heat did the remainder of the work! The longer I lay and sat in each, the more relaxed my muscles became. Tension and stress surrendered to the intensity of the heat. And I didn't ask, command, or even pray that the tension and stress leave my body. I just lay in the sauna and sat in the hot tub, occasionally changing positions for comfort's sake.

This is exactly how it works when we sit and soak in God's love. We enter into the room of God's love by faith. That we are already in Him means we only need to recognize and focus on this truth. That's what it means to lay, sit, and even walk and stand in God's love. We choose to be still and aware of our location in Him, that is also in His love. This is not a matter of convincing oneself, or positive thinking. Rather, it is acknowledging and adhering our minds to the truth. Twenty-five times in the New Testament, the phrase "in Christ" is used to establish our location and to inform us what is available for us to in Christ. Ephesians 1:3 sums up all that is available to us in Christ—every spiritual blessing. Love is Spirit and as such, it falls within the category of a spiritual blessing. It says, "Blessed *be* the God and Father of our Lord Jesus Christ, who has blessed us with every spiritual blessing in the heavenly *places* in Christ."

The truth is we who believe are in Christ. And Christ is in God. Colossians 3:3 reads, "For you died, and your life is hidden with Christ in God." Everything that is available to Christ in God is now available to us that are in Christ. Paul tells us exactly how to receive it. Paul writes in Ephesians 1:5 and 6, "Having predestined us to adoption as sons by Jesus Christ to Himself, according to the good pleasure of His will, to the praise of the glory of His grace, by which He made us accepted in the Beloved."

Paul says we are accepted in Christ, the Beloved. If we are accepted in Him, then knowing his whereabouts and posture might be important to receiving God's love. Ephesians 1:19-21 (NLT) provides the answer.

> I also pray that you will understand the incredible greatness of God's power for us who believe Him. This is the same mighty power that raised Christ from the dead and seated Him in the place of honor at God's right hand in the heavenly realms. Now He is far above any ruler or authority or power or leader or anything else—not only in this world but also in the world to come.

Jesus Christ is now sitting at the right hand of God in the heavens, far above all authorities both in heaven and earth, now and forever. What this means is that love is far above the spirit of fear. Love dominates and rules over fear. When we take our rightful place, that is, seated in God's love, fear has no control over us. God speaks through King Solomon and instructs all that desire to receive love to, "Be still, and know that I am God!"[146]

The words "be still" come from the Hebrew word, "rapha." It is a verb that means to be weak, let go, release. It has been explained as causing oneself to let go, or allowing oneself to become weak. The idea is that we stop exerting our will, our way, and our own agendas. We cease from striving. What that looks like is giving up trying to control the outcomes of circumstances. Furthermore, we quit trying to fix people and control their behavior for our comfort and pleasure. Instead, we allow ourselves to just be. Hebrews 4:10 captures the idea.

For he who has entered His rest has himself also ceased from his works as God *did* from His. Sometimes we can receive God's love by simply stopping and withdrawing our minds from the external noise, and retreat within, taking our seat with Christ. For me, this is like walking in and laying down in the Rock Salt Sauna, or descending the stairs and taking a seat in the hot tub. It requires little effort. Once reclined and seated, the heat relaxes my muscles and willfulness. The longer I am in either the dry heat or heated water, the more my body surrenders and the easier it becomes to accept another idea or a different way of handling something. When I am relaxed, I am receptive. And this is when God's love makes its best advances in me—filling me, massaging my will, adjusting my thinking, and influences my behavior. Maybe that's why God speaks to us when we are asleep. These are some of the times we are most relaxed and most receptive. Elihu tells Job,

> For God may speak in one way, or in another, Yet man does not perceive it. In a dream, in a vision of the night, when deep sleep falls upon men, while slumbering on their beds, then He opens the ears of men and seals their instruction. In order to turn man from his deed, and conceal pride from man, He keeps back his soul from the Pit, and his life from perishing by the sword.[147]

To maximize our receptivity to love we need to relax. As long as we are trying to defend, protect, and preserve ourselves, love can make little headway in improving our relationships or circumstances or advancing our dreams. We need to relax.

When Relaxing Is Not So Easy

Though seemingly passive, being still can be quite an active affair. Some have great difficulty letting go and giving up control for all kinds of reasons that may all be reduced to fear. Sometimes we become anxious. More commonly, I hear of people having severe, immobilizing panic attacks. None of us are immune, albeit some seem more prone than others. It is easy to become overwhelmed by the emotional intensity of a situation to the point of inaction. And though we may "be still," we are hardly relaxed or open. Though we may be outwardly quiet, dissatisfaction screams loudly on the inside. There is so much information coming at us all the time. We hardly have time to thoroughly process one set of information and make wise decisions before the next wave of information crashes upon us. In these times, being still and letting go is not so easy. How can we receive God's love during these times?

As for the rapid fire of information, we can unplug and even plan times of unplugging. As I write, Amy is in a remote area of Columbia vacationing with her sister, brother-in-law, niece, and nephews. There is no phone access, Wi-Fi, or TV. They have each other, a farm, livestock, ample food, and plenty of time. For four days, they will remain "unplugged." I am certain all are better for it. Life will be richer, deeper, and more meaningful, and they will be refreshed all the way around.

There are also places where we can go to retreat from technology and the noise of everyday life. Several years ago, I participated in a retreat called Tres Dias. It is 3-day weekend in which Christians are immersed in the love of God. We had no watches, no smartphones, and no TV. This particular weekend was structured. But other retreats are not. They simply offer you a shelter, shower, and meals. The rest is up to you. But these are planned times away and don't necessarily help in the routines of our lives.

Recently, I quit my affair with Facebook for a week. Wow! What a difference it made. It was welcomingly quiet. I could hear almost immediately. There was no more ambient background noise with which I had to contend. There was no one else's voice with which I had to discern. I experienced peace. I could focus. There was no more competition for my attention. I could relax. I didn't realize how the amount of information and the violent, "crisis" nature of much of the information kept me on high alert— *all thanks to Homeland Security.* I couldn't relax. Sometimes we can improve our receptiveness to love simply by turning off the TV, disengaging from social media, unplugging the electronics, staying out of the stores, and relinquishing a meal or two.

Another Way To Receive Love

Unlike passively laying in a sauna, sitting in a hot tub, or unplugging from technology and other amenities we may enjoy, a third way we can increase our intake of God's love is by drinking it. Receiving God's love can be as easy as drinking a bottle of water. Let me explain. Aside from saunas and hot tubs, this is perhaps my favorite.

Perhaps I like this method so much because I absolutely love water. I am a water enthusiast. I am passionate about boating, jet skiing, swimming, and just being around water. I love sitting on the balcony in my apartment because I have a bird's eye view of Lake Lanier. Just seeing the lake is relaxing. Swimming and playing in it is near divine. That's because water reminds me so much of God's love. And I love God's love. It is everything good and pure.

Thinking love was good and bad, helpful and hurtful, rewarding and punishing was confusing. The gift of wisdom has enabled me to even see through some paradoxes. But I could not reconcile God being good and bad, pleasurable and painful. In the Bible, James says, "And so, blessing and cursing come pouring out of the same mouth. Surely, my brothers and sisters, this is not right! Does a spring of water bubble out with both fresh water and bitter water? Does a fig tree produce olives, or a grapevine produce figs? No, and you can't draw fresh water from a salty spring."[148]

I John 1:5 adds, "This is the message we heard from Jesus and now declare to you: God is light, and there is no darkness in him at all." God is not the author of confusion, nor does He play tricks with our emotions. Love is not the guessing game many of us played as young girls. We'd fetch a dandelion and pick it apart petal-by-petal saying: "He loves me. He loves me not," hoping the game ended on "He loves me." God loves us, period. End of story.

I decided that God's love was good all the time and in every way. And when I did, love was all I wanted. Don't get me wrong. I have always desired love, but now I no longer engage the weary pursuit whether or not love is trying to hurt me. It's not. That His love has no ill will toward me and causes me no harm frees me to pursue it vigorously. God's love always feels good, while the things I choose to do for love do not always yield such a result. And the same is true for you. Neither you nor I need to walk around suspicious, distrustful, and in self-protective mode. We can devote our attention and time to receiving and responding to God's love individually and within the communities God assigns. This is how we become the people He intends, overcome the fears that have often beset us and fulfill the dreams God placed inside of us. With such clarity and single mindedness, receiving God's love is as easy as drinking a bottle or glass of water.

Water A Symbol and Type of Love

Before taking a drink, appreciate love's ability to get things done in your life that up until now you couldn't do. Consider that the Bible is full of symbolism. Symbols are naturally occurring phenomena, concrete things, or people that represent a spiritual reality or truth. Here are a few. The wind is symbolic of the Holy Spirit. A signet ring is a symbol of authority. The lamb is a symbol of Jesus Christ, the sacrifice.

The other thing that's important about a symbol is that it shares characteristics and behavior with the thing it is said to represent. So consider the wind spoken of in John 3:8: "The wind blows wherever it wants. Just as you can hear the wind but can't tell where it comes from or where it is going, so you can't explain how people are born of the Spirit."

And Acts 2:2-4 speaks of the wind and the Holy Spirit,

> Suddenly, there was a sound from heaven like the roaring of a mighty windstorm, and it filled the house where they were sitting. Then, what looked like flames or tongues of fire appeared and settled on each of them. And everyone present was filled with the Holy Spirit and began speaking in other languages, as the Holy Spirit gave them this ability.

Notice Paul uses the words "like the roaring of a mighty windstorm.." He didn't say it was the wind, but like the wind in character and behavior. Later, he compares the Holy Spirit to the likeness of the wind.

The signet ring represented the King's authority. The King authorized Mordecai saying, "Now go ahead and send a message to the Jews in the king's name, telling them whatever you want, and seal it with the king's signet ring. But remember that whatever has already been written in the king's name and sealed with his signet ring can never be revoked."

And the lamb represents Jesus and what He would accomplish by death, burial, and resurrection for mankind. John 1:29 declares, "The next day John (the Baptist) saw Jesus coming toward him and said, "Look! **The Lamb of God** who takes away the sin **of** the world!" Revelation 7:17 reads, "For the Lamb on the throne will be their Shepherd. He will lead them to springs of life-giving water. And God will wipe every tear from their eyes."

These are just three of a myriad of examples in which symbols are used to illustrate and convey added meaning to spiritual realities. In the same manner, water is symbolic of God and the Holy Spirit. Water represents God and love both in character and behavior. A chart might make their similarities easily apparent. Diagram 8 compares water to love.

Diagram 8: Common Characteristics of Water and God's Love

CHARACTERISTIC	WATER	GOD'S LOVE
1. Make Up	3 molecules: 2 hydrogen, 1 oxygen	Three persons: Father, Son, Holy Spirit
2. Form: Can exist in three states	Solid, Liquid, or Gas	Solid – God, the Son Jesus, Liquid – God, the Holy Spirit, Gas – God, the Spirit
3. Capacity	Highest heat capacity of any substance, it's range of temperatures makes it virtually indestructible	Highest authority and power in the universe; its eternal nature make it virtually indestructible
4. Cohesive	Sticky, elastic, adheres to and climbs up materials like glass, and small tubular objects without breaking the molecule	God is One and thus inseparable **(Deuteronomy 6:4, Romans 3:30)**. And nothing can separate us from God's love **(Romans 8:35-39)**. God's love is a fountain springing up **(John 4:14)**.
5. Universal Solvent	Can dissolve more hydrophilic substances (as strong, or stronger than water's cohesive forces)	Dissolves sin, fear, and every other kind of evil rivaling mankind for supremacy **(John 3:16, I Peter 2:24)**.

Gives and Promotes Life

But not only do God's love and water share many characteristics, they also behave in a similar manner. Don't forget that God is Love. Water is largely responsible for getting life-giving oxygen to the cells of your body. Oxygen is carried in the blood. Blood is made up of about 55% plasma, which is 90% water, making our blood content about 50% water. Without water, our cells would die and our bodies would eventually stop functioning. Scripture teaches us that life is in the blood.[149] Moreover, Genesis 2:7 says that, "The Lord God formed man of the dust of the ground, and breathed into his nostrils the breath of life; and man became a living being."

The breath of love makes us come alive. The Holy Spirit, carries God's love to our soul and body. Romans 5:5 confirms this saying that it is the Holy Spirit that fills us with God's love. We need to come alive. We need this love.

Nourishment

Water nourishes the cells that make up the tissues and organs in our bodies. Taking all the vitamins and supplements in the world would be of no value if they were not delivered and absorbed by tissues and organs. Water aids in transporting these vital nutrients and makes it easy for tissues and organs to absorb them. Similarly, love works by feeding and distributing the graces of God throughout our soul and body. In Galatians 5:22 and 23, Paul writes of the graces as nine fruits of the Spirit. He begins with love and tells us that the Holy Spirit is responsible for nourishing and cultivating these fruits: "But the Holy Spirit produces this kind of fruit in our lives: love, joy, peace, patience, kindness, goodness, faithfulness, gentleness, and self-control. There is no law against these things!"

It is the love carried by the Holy Spirit that enables these to gain entrance to our soul and be absorbed throughout our being. We need this love.

Hydration

Water hydrates muscles and lubricates joints, thus facilitating movement. When the body does not get enough water, we experience muscle cramps and joint irritability that hinder our ability to move with ease. In the prolonged absence of water, we experience dehydration that ultimately can lead to death. Love works by validating our worth, communicating that we matter to God and those that truly know Him. The Holy Spirit uses our senses to convey God's love to us. Love tells us we are significant because of who we are and who we are becoming. Love makes us believe and feel that anything is possible.

When we are deprived of love, we wither away. We become hopeless. We don't believe or feel anything good is possible. We feel stuck and often shrink into the archives of despair. Lack of love can result in mental and emotional paralysis. Other indications that we need more of God's love include impatience, restlessness, blaming others, subtly or overtly controlling other's behavior, and isolating one's self. The list could easily go on. The encrusted underbelly to each of these is fear. Whether or not we are able to admit it, fear does not remove itself from your presence. Only love can do this.

Love hydrates us. It infuses us with a lubricant that massages the soul's muscles, improving our willingness to receive and respond to truth. Receiving the love of truth makes cooperating with God's will and His way easier, especially when choosing to do so results in an unpleasant experience. There is nothing forced about God's love. Rather, love inspires us to move with the rhythms of grace. We need this love.

Flushes Waste

Water flushes waste and toxins from the body through perspiration, mucus, urine, and our bowels. It also boosts our immune system. Love flushes fear from our soul and strengthens our immunity to it. Healthy relationships and communities are designed by God to help us get rid of behavior that is antichrist. Such relationships are "safe." We all need safe people and communities to learn, grow, receive, and give love. In the next chapter, we will identify the characteristics of safe people and communities.

Unlike most remedies that address the symptoms or surface, love tackles the root of the problem. Love eliminates the cause of our problems. Fear is one of the main reasons we do not experience deeper levels of intimacy in the relationships we say matter most to us. More so than money, time, or having the "right" relationships, fear prevents many of us from fulfilling our dreams. We need the love that conquers fear.

Regulates Temperature

Water regulates our body temperature so that we don't overheat or suffer from a lack of heat. Love regulates the climates of our soul so that we are able to respond most effectively to the demands of everyday reality. I remember one of the wives that sat with us during the period we prayed to receive love. I will call her Janice here. Janice told me that one of the things that characterized her reaction to her husband's shortcomings was explosive anger. She admitted feeling bad afterwards and often asked his forgiveness. For a couple of months, we had been sitting weekly to receive God's love with thanksgiving and limiting the remainder of our individual prayer lives to the same when Janice told me the following.

> I turned on the water to get a shower. After it had run for a few minutes, I realized that it wasn't getting hot. I started praying feverishly, but the water remained cold. I braved a cold shower instead of no shower at all. Occasionally, my husband is late paying bills. So typically, I raced pass the possibility that a power line could be down in the area. And this time it wasn't. About that time, my husband walked in the bathroom. A calm rose from within me. Calmly, spilling out of my mouth were the words, 'the water's cold. It isn't a power line. We must have forgotten to pay the bill. Is there anything I can do to help?' Immediately, my husband responded with, 'Sorry, thanks for letting me know. I'll take care of it.' And he did. I think my husband was as shocked by my response as I was. It was unplanned, effortless, and full of love and concern for his person.
>
> Janice ended by saying, Kim, receiving love and what it can do for you is real! I wasn't trying to conceal my frustration. Nor was I trying to speak politely. I was frustrated and I was polite. Therefore, I spoke politely. This has to be the result of love working through me.

I told Janice she was right. Love knows what it desires, and it knows how to get it without trying to manipulate or control others. God's love regulates the temperature of our emotions by cultivating the fruit of self-control. Zephaniah 3:17 (NLT) reads,

> For the LORD your God is living among you. He is a mighty savior. He will take delight in you with gladness. With his love, he will calm all your fears. He will rejoice over you with joyful songs.

Here's a summary of at least five tasks water shares with God's love,

Diagram 9: Summary of Shared Functions

WATER	GOD'S LOVE
1. **Delivers life-giving oxygen to blood and cells**	Gives us breath of life making us a living soul (**Genesis 2:7**)
2. **Nourishes the cells that make up tissues and organs**	Feeds the graces of God to our souls that enable us to reflect Christ (**Galatians 5:22, 23**)
3. **Hydrates muscles and lubricates joints, facilitating the body's movement**	Bathes us with a lubricant that massages the soul's muscles, improving our willingness to receive and respond to truth (**II Thessalonians 2:10**)
4. **Flushes harmful toxins and waste from our bodies.**	Flushes fear from our soul, improving its ability to engage its purpose.
5. **Regulates body temperature**	Manages the climate of our soul thoughts and feelings) (**Zephaniah 3:17**)

According to the Water Information Program,[150] the human body is about **60%** water. Blood is **92%** water, the brain and muscles are **75%** water, and bones are about **22%** water. A human can survive for a month or more without eating food, but only a week or so without drinking water. While the body itself is about 60% water, the amount of water making up the blood is enormous at 92%. And when we consider Leviticus 17:11 that states the life of the flesh is in the blood, it makes water essential to our physical human life.

Just as water is crucial to developing and performing necessary functions of the human body, God's love is critical to our spiritual, mental, and emotional development and performance as Christians. Love is not optional. Although we may survive for some time spiritually, mentally, and emotionally without study, prayer, and community, the affect of the absence of love is felt and expressed almost immediately. Outbursts of anger, irritability, strife, and intimidation are some immediate signs of a lack of love. As the health of our bodies largely depends on water, so the health of our soul largely depends on love—God's love. Jesus said that the thief's purpose was to drain us of life, but that He came to fill us with an abundance of life.[151] And that abundant life includes the fulfillment of our hopes and dreams.

Love Is Responsible

The very best part of all this is best posed in a question. Why take so much time to layout the similarities between water and the love of God? Because I hope that you will never view a bottle or glass of water the same way ever again. Now for my question:

Once you drink water, what more do you need to do for it to work within you? Do you tell it what cells need its nourishment most? Do you tell water which nutrients to absorb and which ones to forsake? Do you command water to hydrate certain muscles and lubricate certain joints? Do you officiate which toxins and waste that the water should remove? Do you tell water how to regulate your body's temperature and when to adjust for variances in temperature? Tell me, what is it you do to make water work? That's right, NOTHING! ABSOLUTELY NOTHING! Your body responds to water involuntarily. Your body understands the authority and role water plays in its wellbeing. And you taught your body none of these things. Water accomplishes for you what you cannot accomplish for your own body.

In the same way, God's love accomplishes for your soul what you cannot accomplish on your own. And your soul will rightly respond to God's love because built into it is the understanding of God's authority and role in its life. God's love has a natural response to fear and it is unlike our own!

Once ingested, love is responsible for carrying out the same functions water does, but within our souls. The more love we receive, the healthier our thoughts become, the more aligned our wills become with God's will, and the better our behavior reflects Christ's behavior. Our part is becoming intentional about receiving love from God. We can soak in love as we would a sauna or hot tub. We can drink copious amounts of love, as we would water. In fact, when I am in the shower, I often focus on thanking God for showering His love down upon me. Or, when

I am drinking water, whether in a bottle or glass, I thank God for liquefying His love that I may drink it in. Before you decide this to be a little much, consider that most Christians routinely receive elements symbolic of Jesus Christ's body and blood. We call it communion and we do it in remembrance of Him.

I learned something by receiving God's love as a regular part of my prayer life. It is this. When a man loves a woman, a woman loves a man, a parent loves a child, or a friend loves a friend, what is it that is needful that love withholds? Nothing. Therefore, if we have God's love in us, maturing us and working through us, we have everything we need. Receiving God's love has cut my requests of Him by more than half. Those things that are necessary for life and godliness have already been provided. "And this same God who takes care of me will supply all your needs from his glorious riches, which have been given to us in Christ Jesus."[152] II Peter 1:3 adds, "By His divine power, God has given us everything we need for living a godly life. We have received all of this by coming to know him, the one who called us to Himself by means of His marvelous glory and excellence."

By coming to know love, we find we have everything we need to live and be godly. If we find that we don't have what we need, then it could be we have misdiagnosed our need. Or it could be God has answered our need in an unexpected way so that we don't even notice. And it could be that the answer comes through a person with whom we are unfamiliar, or may even have disqualified as a possible carrier of God's message and love. Admittedly, sometimes it is hard to wait on God and see His answers, especially when we have found and are committed to our own.

Love Always Answers

This happened to me recently. I had a very hard decision to make. I agonized concerning letting go of something I equated with my life. To let go meant that I could place no stipulation on what was done with it, or how it was used. It meant giving up my right to make any determination concerning the thing. I sought counsel repeatedly. It wasn't wrong to fight for what I believed was at least in part mine. My time, my energy, and my resources—my life was tied up in this thing. I wanted this thing. A case easily could be made to fight to keep it or fight equally hard to let it go. What was clear is that I would fight. Whether this fight would be with another, or against myself is all that remained. In my heart, I knew what God said to me, but I had another idea in mind. There were those that I loved and trusted that supported my mind. Several times, I started down the road of implementing my mind. Still, I was unsettled. Praying had become my refuge. The last time I prayed, God shared with me Isaac's experience fighting over the wells his men had dug and Isaac's response. Twice Isaac's men dug wells and discovered water. Twice the Philistines' contended with him claiming the wells as their own. One well was named in Hebrew translated to mean, "Argument" and the other, "Hostility." Isaac abandoned both wells. He dug another well and this time there was no dispute.

> So Isaac named the place Rehoboth (which means "open space"), for he said, 'At last the LORD has created enough space for us to prosper in this land.' (NLT)

The entire account of Isaac's experience can be found in Genesis 26. A friend, while praying that God's will be done, later told me that what she received from God was the story of the two women that fought over a child.[153] Both claimed the living child was hers and the dead child belonged to the other. King Solomon expressed his intent to saw the child in two pieces and give one half to each woman. Then, the woman whose son *was* living spoke to the king, for she was filled with compassion for her son. She said, "O my lord, give her the living child, and by no means kill him!"

While my experience did not involve a living child, it was a baby of sorts to me. And giving it up for adoption accompanied by the loss of my parental rights was scary. Both Isaac and the real mother in this case, gave away what they labored for and valued without stipulations. God had indeed answered me. It was not the answer I desired, nor wanted to hear. But He answered. Now, like Isaac and the real mother, I would let go and walk away. Only love grants the courage to walk away from that which we have labored. And this kind of love comes from God alone. We need this love because when God answers, we need courage to respond.

Love is responsible for completing the work. Philippians 1:6 says that we can be confident that He that has begun a good work in us will complete it until Christ returns. And I say that love has begun a good work in each of us. And love will be careful to complete our transformation into the image of Christ, and at the same time, fulfill our dreams. Fulfillment of our dreams is on the other side of fear. Facing and overcoming that which we fear results in us looking and behaving increasingly like Christ. To face our fears is to fulfill our dreams. Only love provides the courage to conquer fear. First, each one of us must continuously receive this love from the Source: God. And then love must necessarily be cultivated in community. This is the stuff of which dreams are made.

face it *with Love*

CHAPTER 15

Community — The Game Changer

God has placed gifts, dreams, and desires within each of us. We have something to become and something to do. And we will spend the rest of our days either dreaming about it or living out our dreams. Fear is unavoidable. So is love. We will experience fear. However, we may or may not experience love. Believing that we are loved and experiencing love are not the same. That we are Christian does not guarantee that we have or will experience the full embodiment of God's love in this life. God's love is healthy and energetic; it leads us to personal and relational abundance. That's because like God, His love is organic and living. Love does not need to be forced in order to heal us, to set us free, or to empower us to overcome fear and fulfill our dreams. Love does all of these things because it is in love's nature to do so. Moreover, it's the pleasure of love to do so. Love's other name is Spirit. To Zerubbabel, whose dream it was to complete the second temple, the prophet Zechariah offered these words, "Not by might nor by power, but by My Spirit."[154]

God promised us a life of abundance in John 10:10. And it is Spirit's aim to bring us into this abundance. Many tend to associate this abundant life primarily with material wealth. Abundance can certainly include rich material blessings. But, I believe God had something much more in mind when He talks about abundance. Consider that God is life. Director Harold Cronk got it right when he named his movie, *God Is Not Dead* (2014). He is the living God. This living God is all about people. He inspired 66 books about people that we collectively call *The Bible*. There are 1,189 chapters making up *The Bible* that are written about all kinds of people and their relationships to Him and each other. And yet, there is one love story unfolding throughout the lives of many. Solomon writes, "There are sixty queens and eighty concubines, and virgins without number. My dove, my perfect one, is the only one . . ."[155]

It's the love story between a Man and the rest of humanity. That man's name is Jesus Christ to some and Messiah to others. We are His family. Perhaps no other book captures the dramatic, unrelenting, ravishing, and lavishing love between this God and man, than the Song of Songs—and yet there is no direct mention of God, the Messiah, or Jesus Christ within the text.

Love is about community. It's about being together, doing things together, and accomplishing things together. It's about experiencing joy and mutual fulfillment in relationship, rather than simply the accumulation of things. God intends for our hopes and dreams to be realized through relationships, just as He desired heaven to be realized on earth through Adam and Eve.

The abundant life is about community. It's about meaningful relationships beginning with God, His people, and others. Relationships are based on our ability to connect. We can communicate all day long, but at the end of the day if we do not connect, we remain impoverished. That's why we need Jesus. Without Jesus we would still be separated from God and living under the laws of Old Testament. Without Jesus, we would have no way of having a personal relationship with God. Paul's writing to Timothy makes this clear.

> For there is one God and one Mediator between God and men, the Man Christ Jesus,[156]

The deeper we are able to connect the more meaningful the relationship will be. Marriage between a man and a woman is the most meaningful human relationship of all. Unfortunately, for decades, the Church has focused on improving "communication" skills as the primary antidote to marital discord. Virtually every resource, sermon, seminar, or retreat emphasizes communication. Yet, we have not abated divorce. Communication skills that do not lead to connection, especially in marriage, fall short of the abundant life God promised.[157] Unless couples are taught how to connect (and then consciously *choose* to connect), they will continue to view separation and divorce as the answers to marital unhappiness.

Marriage is a community. It is exalted above every other human community because marriage offers connection on all levels. On one level, and the only level reserved for marriage, sexual connection produces more people that are able to connect deeply and meaningfully. Marriage is also the first community among human beings. That it produces offspring makes this community a game changer.

The abundant life is about knowing God and His Son through the Holy Spirit and experiencing this life with others. We call this *community* and accomplish this through community. To the Ephesians, Paul writes,

> For this reason I bow my knees to the Father of our Lord Jesus Christ, from whom the whole family in heaven and earth is named, that He would grant you, according to the riches of His glory, to be strengthened with might through His Spirit in the inner man, that Christ may dwell in your hearts through faith; that you, being rooted and grounded in love, may be able to comprehend with all the saints what is the width and length and depth and height—to know the love of Christ which passes knowledge; that you may be filled with all the fullness of God.[158]

The abundant life is about experiencing love in community. Love has as much to do with our character as it does with enabling us to overcome fear and achieve great heroic feats. Community helps us become the people God intends us to become, while doing what He has given each of us to do. How well we live, how far we go, and how much we accomplish in this life are owed to the communities in which we participate. My hope is that many of us learn and practice the wisdom of the sages before we get old enough to be perceived a sage and dispense wisdom that we have not lived. Solomon, considered one of the wisest men that ever lived, writes, "There is *one* who scatters, yet increases more; and there is one who withholds more than is right, but it leads to poverty."[159]

I like the Message Bible's Translation of this verse: "The world of the generous gets larger and larger; the world of the stingy gets smaller and smaller." It's proof that true abundance isn't in how much we accumulate, but rather in how much we let go. And it makes sense because love is about giving and receiving and giving again. American writer Elbert Hubbard adds, "Life in abundance comes through great love."[160]

When we have a lot, we won't object to sharing, if when we have little, we give a lot. Communities offer us the possibilities for giving both when we have little and when we have much. Our relationships represent different kinds of communities. Besides communing with God and our families, there are church communities, business and professional communities, and sports and hobby communities. Our relationships with our doctors, dentists, mechanics, and cashiers at stores we frequent all represent communities. Communities are largely responsible for everything we possess and everything we accomplish.

Here's an example of the transformative power of community. I had been given a 1999 green Ford Explorer—*the green machine.* The paint was so faded on parts of it that it appeared two-toned. It had close to 300,000 miles on it. But the green machine ran and I was grateful for the transportation. It occasionally broke down, and when it did I called my auto and boat mechanic, Tom. He fixed the green machine so many times that I lost count. He knew I was separated and had very little money. He never charged me. Tom kept the green machine running until I could afford better. Additionally, Tom knew how therapeutic the lake is for me. So he made major repairs to my boat in advance of summer 2015. I was able to enjoy boating the entire summer! Without Tom, I would have had a far more difficult experience post-separation.

And then there is James. My parents and James informally adopted one another over 25 years ago. James has served extensively in the military and currently works for a consulting company in Afghanistan. Upon learning of my car situation, James helped research the reliability of SUV's I had an interest in. Aside from being presentable, and reliable, the vehicle had to be able to tow my boat. Once I had identified the vehicle and vetted it with James, Tom, and Phillip (my son-in-law), James gave me several thousand dollars for the down payment. James also told me that if I were ever at risk of missing a payment, to please let him know as he was committed to helping me rebuild my credit.

And how could I leave out my friend of 36 years, Pam an attorney in the Washington D.C. area. We met on the first day we arrived on campus at Howard University (1979). Instantly, we connected and have remained friends through the triumphs and tribulations that life dishes out to all of us. She has always been there for me. Pam helped me through my separation. She came and helped pack my house along with another friend Danny. She has often sent money as well.

These, along with those mentioned previously, and my family made up my community during one of the most challenging times in my life. They supported me and often acted my behalf! All of these became God's divine aid to me. This book is a result of Divine aid.

Eternal life is about relationship with God and Jesus Christ. It's about community and the opportunity to develop a real working understanding of love, truth, forgiveness, joy, peace, patience, power, and self-control. That we are not rich in these things may explain the poverty and pain many of us have experienced in marriage, family, our churches, and other communities. Perhaps the lack of these things also may be undermining our nation and nations around the world. John writes, "The thief does not come except to steal, to kill, and to destroy. I have come that they may have life, and that they may have it more abundantly."[161] The New Living Translation writes the same verse this way: "The thief's purpose is to steal, kill, and destroy. My purpose is to give them a rich and satisfying life." The thief comes to rob us of relationships and the communities they represent.

A Lie Many Have Been Prone to Believe

Some countries more than others promote brazen individualism. Perhaps this has been fueled by the erroneous idea of "self-made" men and women. One country in which this idea is deeply imbedded is America. The concept shuns the idea that relationships and favorable circumstances have anything to do with one's success. Frederick Douglas wrote, "Self-made men are the men who owe little or nothing to birth, relationship, [or] friendly surroundings; to wealth inherited or to early approved means of education; who are what they are, without the aid of any of the favoring conditions by which other men usually rise in the world and achieve great results."[162]

Since then, others have mistakenly referenced the term, "self-made." However, scripture suggests the opposite is true. Virtually everything that is born and happens in life occurs through relationship. Whether it's from babies, books, or brilliant ideas nearly everything comes into being through relationship. And that necessarily means community! We really do need each other to overcome fear and live a rich and satisfying life.

God, community, and our participation with each are what make us into the people we are. Whether a community of you and one other person or a large community, we are built up and empowered by the love found in our communities. To deny community is to deny our dreams—*yours and mine*. Thich Nhat Hahn, a Buddhist Monk, writes that a solitary rock, no matter how small, will sink in the lake. But a collection of rocks can stay afloat in a boat.[163]

John 10:10 not only speaks of the abundant life that we now know has to do with the quality of our character and relationships, but also he speaks of a thief. The first part of the verse reads, "The thief's purpose is to steal, kill, and destroy." Fear is a thief. Fear dismantles communities. It plans and implements strategies to steal what we have, kill what we do, and destroy who we are. That reads like a strategy to completely annihilate us. Still this scheme is stoppable. Recall John's words,

> There is no fear in love [dread does not exist]. But perfect (complete, full-grown) love drives out fear, because fear involves [the expectation of divine] punishment, so the one who is afraid [of God's judgment] is not perfected in love [has not grown into a sufficient understanding of God's love].[164]

Paul agrees in his second letter to Timothy, saying, "For God has not given us a spirit of fear, but of power and of love and of a sound mind."[165] The New Living Translation writes it this way, "For God has not given us a spirit of fear and timidity, but of power, love, and self-discipline." Expounding even further is the Amplified Version.

> For God did not give us a spirit of timidity, cowardice, or fear, but [He has given us a spirit] of power and of love and of sound judgment and personal discipline [abilities that result in a calm, well-balanced mind and self-control].

We need the strength that power grants us to receive love. We need love in order to develop sound, disciplined thinking that conquers fear. Communities empower, love, and affirm our identity. From the beginning of this book, one of the recurring themes has been "community." I spoke of the strength and love Moses received by becoming a part of Jethro and Zipporah's community and how this love inspired him to think differently about himself. He was open to God and able to look beyond a burning bush to see that it was not consumed. This encounter resulted in Moses facing many fears, the ultimate of which was confronting the fear of death. By doing so, Moses won the freedom of a nation of people.

I also shared Esther's story. After the death of her parents, she was welcomed into Mordecai's community where she received strong, generous love. She grew up in love and was disciplined in practicing the Jewish faith. Esther knew who she was and courageously confronted her fear of death. She risked her life by approaching the King, uninvited, hoping he would welcome her. He did. By taking a risk, Esther prevented the demise of her nation.

And I mentioned, those in Hebrews 11 that faced all kinds of fears. For some, the outcome was immediately favorable; for others, it was not. Yet, all were highly regarded. Hebrews 11:39 reads, "All these people earned a good reputation because of their faith, yet none of them received all that God had promised."

All entered the room of adversity and remained conscious. They stood facing all kinds of fear until love conquered it. All experienced what Paul calls the "confident hope" that follows being strengthened on the inside, flooded with love, and made resolute in thinking.[166] Perhaps they grew and understood that fulfilling destiny was not necessarily dependant on getting the results they desired. Rather, it was about getting in the room and facing that which they feared and trusting God with the outcome. Moses, Esther, and all these represent smaller communities to which they belonged. They also represent the larger community of faith to which we all belong. They won and we, too win and others benefit when we commune with others developing the kind of courage that defies fear. Speaking to the larger community, God offered these words in Deuteronomy 28:7 (NLT), "When you go out to fight your enemies and you face horses, chariots, and an army greater than your own, do not be afraid. The Lord your God, who brought you out of the land of Egypt, is with you!"

When we go and face what seems like insurmountable odds and every imaginable threat, it is God's power in us, His love working through us and right thinking about ourselves that causes us to prevail. Community is the soil in which these are cultivated. Community is the game changer. Regardless of the outcome, we are assured of this one thing: God is working through all things for the good of those who love Him. And we do love Him and His people. It is in the communities—those already near to Jesus, as well as those that are yet making their way to Jesus, that love matures. According to Romans 14:11 (NKJV), one day all will bow before Jesus Christ.

> For it is written: As I live, says the Lord, Every knee shall bow to Me, and every tongue shall confess to God."

This is why I include "those yet making their way to Jesus," in the sentence above. I believe that even those that do not share our faith in Christ will one day come before Him. Therefore, how we receive and relate to them is not only helpful to us, but also to them.

Communities Fulfill Dreams

Communities like The Make A Wish Foundation are making dreams come true. Of themselves they write,

> Tens of thousands of volunteers, donors, and supporters advance the Make-A-Wish® vision to grant the wish of every child diagnosed with a life-threatening medical condition. In the United States and its territories, on average, a wish is granted every 37 minutes. We believe a wish experience can be a game-changer. This one belief guides us and inspires us to grant wishes that change the lives of the kids we serve.[167]

Fear can be overcome and dreams really do come true. And communities are vital to making this happen. Communities are the best places to seed and cultivate love. Paul writes that God did not give us the spirit of fear; God gave us power, love, and a sound mind. That these would be placed side by side with fear elevates their significance. Fear's 3-pronged approach, that is to steal, kill, and destroy, is countered by a 3-pronged rebuttal, which is comprised of power, love, and sound thinking. Fear robs us of the sheer threatening force of community by isolating us so it can steal our power. Fear kills our desire to be present with others. When we are not present, we cannot love. Remember, God is love. But also, God is life. To love is to live and to live is to love. If we do not participate in love, we exist at best and die at worst. And if we do not intentionally engage community, then how can we love? Finally, fear attempts to destroy our beliefs about who we are and to whom we belong. And as if one of these is not enough, consider that all of these things are happening at the same time. We alone are no match for fear.

We conquer fear by exercising our power to receive love and develop Christ's way of thinking about others and ourselves. Though fearful of dental work, I exercised power when I made the decision to reach out to Dr. Richman and admit fear. I received love from Dr. Richman and his staff. They became a community to me. They did not judge me for being afraid. They did not laugh at me, nor minimize my fear. The community acknowledged fear by setting a calm, relaxed atmosphere. They were patient, reassuring, and supportive in helping me overcome anxiety. I never fully relaxed while the procedures occurred. But I remained. Love won out over fear. My teeth were fixed. And it was because of the love I experienced within this community.

Communities Surround Us

Communities surround us. All that is required for a community to develop is for one person to talk honestly and vulnerably with one or more other people. And they can form in the oddest of places.

Consider what happens when seven or eight people get stuck in an elevator, or any acute crisis in which people are put together involuntarily. Crisis exposes us to potential adverse outcomes that lure the spirit of fear. When we are together in crisis we all feel that we are at risk. When we feel threatened, we seek safety. And when the people stuck in the elevator with us are our only perceived safe haven, we are more inclined to talk to them. In these kinds of situations, people generally talk about what matters: how we will get out of the elevator, then our family, and then ourselves. Why? When we are forced together by crisis we have nothing to lose and everything to gain. Somehow we realize that vulnerability precedes victory. Our gender, culture, education, possessions, and resources are only worth what they can be traded for our freedom. Crisis produces rare opportunities for openness, honesty, and acceptance. Love grows when these are present and in generous supply. We all emerge from the elevator feeling closer to one another. The level of conversation has changed forever. Because in an instant, the people stuck in the elevator, or any shared crisis, became a viable, supportive, loving community by becoming vulnerable to one another.

Even When We Can't See Them

Communities form constantly, whether or not we are aware of them. I remember my youngest daughter preparing to go to college on the heels of her parents' separation. Her grades were negatively effected most of her junior year and the first part of her senior year of high school. Still, Jordan wanted to go to college and not just any college, but *Mercer University*. Mostly fearing she wouldn't get in and slightly hopeful she would, Jordan expressed her faint desire. Unbeknownst to Jordan, that dim desire, coupled with honesty, served as a catalyst for the formation of a community.

And in 2013, that's exactly what happened. Jordan's teachers were empathetic and supportive. They tutored and permitted her to make up missed tests, gave extra credit assignments, and provided recommendations she needed for college. The counselor maintained contact with Jordan. An outside counselor joined the community. Dr. Arvela Leslie-Cozart, educator and a long time family friend who we affectionately call Grandma V, helped Jordan remain on track with her ACT and SAT testing and submitting applications for early consideration. Jordan was initially unaware of all those helping her through a difficult time.

The community encouraged her with texts and calls and made it possible for her to complete assignments and meet college deadlines. The community provided resources and opportunities so that Jordan could succeed. What Jordan did not see was a community of many unrelated people with a common cause, all working on her behalf. What Jordan experienced in community was love and compassion. But also, Jordan got hands-on support in preparing for tests and completing applications. It was that love and support that gave Jordan the courage to take tests, complete college requirements, and submit applications to not knowing whether she would be accepted. Jordan was brave because she did these things despite the fear of not being accepted to college.

Two weeks after submitting her application, Jordan was accepted to Mercer University and received a partial scholarship! She is completing her first semester as I write. Recently, I asked whether she wanted to return to Mercer next year and she said, "Heck yeah! Is that even a real question?" Communities can form anywhere, for any purpose, and for any length of time. Some are goal driven, like Jordan's community. Other communities are event, incident, or seasonally driven. Team Moms and Dads are communities that occur during sports seasons. My dental community formed around an incident. My friends who helped me through my separation formed because of a crisis. The fact hat you are reading this book is a result a community of professionals including Ibi (a graphic designer), Nicole (an editor), Jennifer (a marketing consultant), and many others that have proofread, helped select a cover, or shared the book with their own communities. Together, we became a community for a project.

I have been a part of many communities. Some of these communities have endured, experiencing many seasons of trials and triumphs. Others have not. And some communities formed but for a few hours or days. I told you of the pastors' wives whose love provided the opportunity and empowerment to face my fear of rejection. At great length I spoke of the love I experienced in my Peru community and how it altered the trajectory of my life. Each of these represent communities of varying lengths from a couple hours in a dental chair, to nine days in Peru, to several years. Then, there are the communities like my local church, professional associations, friends that have become family, and of course my bio-family. These communities are long-term teams that help one another through all kinds of life experiences.

Still Needed Even Though They Can Hurt

Let's face it communities can hurt, sometimes more than they help. I have spoken to many that love Jesus Christ and seek to conform to His will for their lives. They are also highly disenchanted with the organized community called "Church." The very hands God has given in order to help them have instead hurt them. The very Word intended to build them up tears them down. The very ones God has given to love them have bred in them fear and contempt. Often the very ones that were to give have taken more than appropriate. It hurts. And if you have been a part of an organized community called church for any length of time, you have also likely experienced or witnessed such pain.

I know this hurt. As a minister in full time ministry, I have dispensed hurt and I have been a recipient of hurt. I heard one prominent minister say that wherever the Church is, in whatever state we find her—*we, the clergy have led her there*. We are responsible for the condition of the Church. Jesus, speaking to the multitudes and His disciples, had this to say in Matthew 23:2-4,

> The scribes and the Pharisees sit in Moses' seat. Therefore, whatever they tell you to observe, that observe and do, but

do not do according to their works; for they say, and do not do. For they bind heavy burdens, hard to bear, and lay them on men's shoulders; but they themselves will not move them with one of their fingers.

Loosely to some and more firmly to others, the scribes and Pharisees represent the organized Church. They were religious. They ruled by strict codes of conduct, rather than by love and compassion. The scribes and Pharisees were more concerned with finding and addressing sin than in loving and guiding the people to God. No wonder the people developed a sin and punishment consciousness, rather than awareness of love and forgiveness. Even still, Jesus said that they sit in a seat of authority. For that reason, He urged His disciples to obey them. However, that they say one thing and do another placed unnecessary hardship upon God's people. Moreover, the scribes and Pharisees did not seek to relieve any pain. Here's what Ezekiel, the Prophet spoke concerning thee shepherds.

> Therefore, you shepherds, hear the word of the Lord: As surely as I live, says the Sovereign Lord, you abandoned my flock and left them to be attacked by every wild animal. And though you were my shepherds, you didn't search for my sheep when they were lost. You took care of yourselves and left the sheep to starve.[168]

Much can be said of how we have mistreated and misled God's people then and now. We, the leadership of the church today, often have been similar to the scribes and Pharisees. Of money, we have said, "Give"; while we take. I met an individual brandishing a rubber bracelet that read, "My Church is debt free." I asked whether or not he was debt free to which he replied "No." Then I said, well then your church is not debt free. Such a bracelet brings no glory to God when the people wearing them are strapped for cash. Of sex we have said, "Wait for marriage," while we engage in fornication, adultery, and other kinds of sexual lewdness. While we encourage others to admit to their sins, we have justified our own. Or worse, we hide them—*often resulting in living double lives.* We build houses of cards that history proves will inevitably collapse. Yet, many continue.

We have hurt God's people immeasurably. As a minister of the gospel since 1982, I am asking you to please forgive us. We have sinned against God. We have misrepresented Him and as a result have mistreated and misled you. God have mercy on those of us that turn to Him now. Now and forevermore may our heart and mind adhere to His will concerning you. May the changes and course corrections He makes in us become increasingly apparent and beneficial to you. Finally, may God changing us be to the rejoicing of all.

I can tell you that the Church as we know it is in transition. God is inviting us to participate. Still change is difficult—*even good changes require adjustment.* I don't presume to know all of the changes that God has in store for His body. But I do know that if the Church is to be new and do new things, then we will have to see with new eyes. We will have to become new people. We must become individuals characterized by an uncompromising love—individuals abandoning themselves for the love of God and His people. Like when the Ark that symbolized the presence of God was brought into Jerusalem. II Samuel 6:14-16 says that David danced with all His might, with great enthusiasm, leaping before God.

Davids are coming forth, men, and women truly after the heart of God. They have been tending sheep. They look like sheep and smell like sheep. They are as wise as serpents, yet as harmless as doves. They are strong and gentle. They are uncompromising, yet kind. They are courageous and compassionate. You will know them not by how well they speak, nor how well they dress. Neither will you be able to distinguish them by their possessions. But you will know them by their love for one another, their commitment to living life with the communities God has given them, and exhibiting self-control in refusing gifts from the well to do when appropriate. Those God is sending forth, like Moses, have grown in faith. Of this maturity, Paul writes,

> It was by faith that Moses, when he grew up, refused to be called the son of Pharaoh's daughter. He chose to share the oppression of God's people instead of enjoying the fleeting pleasures of sin. He thought it was better to suffer for the sake of Christ than to own the treasures of Egypt, for he was looking ahead to his great reward.

I tell you some of these people are already among you. God has chosen them and has sent them among us. Ask Him to identify them to you. Look for them. You might even be surprised to find some of them in the very church with which you have become dissatisfied. And one of these might even be you! Yet, fear has prevented you from expressing the depth of your love for Christ and your fellow man. My hope for every reader is that you will discover these individuals, grow with them in community, and share your possessions with them as they share with you.

It's a new day in the Kingdom! It's God's day. And He made you to be a part of it. God gave you something to be and something to do. There is more to you and more God desires from you. Fear stands in the way. Communities strengthen, love, and affirm our identity in Christ. And love allows you to rise above the fear to live your fullest and most genuine life.

Even though communities sometimes hurt us, we still need them. The truth is that all communities have compost. But even the ugly, undesirable, and unlovable things each of us brings to a community can be used. Aside from being made up of organic waste, compost is also rich in nutrients. Farmers, gardeners, and landscapers use compost to fertilize the soil to enable crop and plant growth. Compost turns waste into food and gardens full of flowers. And food and beautiful flowers become next year's compost. Communities turn ugly, undesirable, unloving fearful people into beautiful, desirable, loving brave people. Life Coach Martha Beck asks and answers the question, "How can you keep yourself absolutely safe?" She says,

> You can't. Life is inherently uncertain. The way to cope with that reality is not to control and avoid your way into a rigid demi-life, but to develop. Doing what you to do, despite fear, will accomplish this.[169]

Communities are vital when cultivating the love that conquers fear. We need communities to help us thrive in relationships and fulfill our dreams. All of us are made better or worse by the people with whom we commune. Healthy communities are not perfect, just like the people that make them up are not perfect. However, there are some characteristics that all healthy communities have in common.

Healthy Communities vs. Unhealthy Communities

A healthy community, as described by the U.S. Department of Health and Human Services Healthy People 2010 report, is one that continuously creates and improves both its physical and social environments. It helps people to support one another in aspects of daily life and to develop to their fullest potential.[170] Communities that improve the quality of life and support their participants in making their own decisions tend to be healthier than those that encourage or require conformity and restrict the choices of the participants. Healthy communities produce outcomes that are beneficial to its members, as well as to others. This is important because unhealthy communities have some things in common with healthy communities. But only the results of truly healthy communities are beneficial for everyone.

ISIS' message is clear: "Convert to Islam or die." In December 2015, a letter from ISIS was sent to dozens of Swedish citizens containing the message: "Convert or die."[171] The outcome for those that decline to convert is fatal. ISIS' message seeks to polarize and operationalize the disgruntled and disenchanted; the outcome is unfavorable to many. Although held together by a strong message and willing warriors, ISIS can hardly be considered a healthy community. Healthy communities have a strong, convincing message and elated participants. But also, they have the benefit of all in mind.

Paul addresses this in Acts 2:41-47 (NKJV).

> Then those who gladly received his word were baptized; and
> that day about three thousand souls were added to them.
> And they continued steadfastly in the apostles' doctrine
> and fellowship, in the breaking of bread, and in prayers.
> Then fear came upon every soul, and many wonders and
> signs were done through the apostles. Now all who believed
> were together, and had all things in common, and sold
> their possessions and goods, and divided them among all,
> as anyone had need. So continuing daily with one accord in
> the temple, and breaking bread from house to house, they
> ate their food with gladness and simplicity of heart, praising
> God and having favor with all the people. And the Lord
> added to the church daily those who were being saved.

Whether we are speaking of marriage, a church, or a business, communities are made up of individuals. In the community described in Acts 2, the message was the gospel of Jesus Christ. Communities have different messages, but all participants buy into the message. The message of Nike is "Just Do It." Apple tells us to "Think Differently." The California Milk Processing Board asks if we've, "Got Milk?" And the State Farm Insurance Community wants us to know its, "Like A Good Neighbor, State Farm is there." Millions of us received these messages and bought their products. And we in the FACEIT Community want you to know that you can, "Be Fearless. Be Free." Healthy communities have simple, easy to remember messages that appeal to a want or desire. Large and small communities have clear concise messages. My Peru Community's aim was to "Set People Free." While my Joy Church Community "Brings Hope. Restores Joy. Makes Disciples." My dental community wanted to "Give (Me) A Better Smile."

Secondly, it wasn't receiving the message alone that contributed to the outcomes in Acts 2:41. They accepted the message with gladness and did something in response. They were joyful, willing, and grateful to participate. Moses was delighted at best and appreciative at least to participate with Jethro and his family. An orphan, Esther was likely relieved and thankful to join Mordecai's family. And what about the joy Ruth (and Naomi) must have experienced in becoming a part of Boaz's family. There was my own happiness in participating with the various communities during my journey in facing fear. We all felt something and that something was good. Even in unhealthy communities, participants express a feeling of jubilation upon receiving the message. In a 2014, NBC aired a recruitment video portraying five ISIS fighters, sitting in front of a black and white flag. During the video, one fighter remarks,

> All my brothers, come to jihad. Feel the honor we are feeling, feel the happiness that we are feeling.[172]

In Acts 2, those that joyfully received the gospel responded by becoming baptized, continuing to discuss and follow the instructions of the apostles, and interacting daily with one another through meals and prayers. The individuals spoken of in Acts 2 bought into the community with both their words and actions. Each had their "skin in the game."

ISIS Community members, like the community in Acts 2, did something about what they happily heard and received. The fighters have and continue to commit terrorists' attacks like the one in Paris (November 2015) in which 130 people were killed and many more injured. And like San Bernardino (December

2015), in which ISIS sympathizers killed 14 people and injured 22 others.. Like the community in Acts 2, ISIS Community members and sympathizers followed instructions and interacted with one another through meals and perhaps prayers. And they also had their skin in the game—*they all died.* Despite the horrific outcome for scores of innocent people, a sense of community is apparent within ISIS.

In community, there is a regularity of interaction. Acts 2:46 and 47 (NKJV) reads,

> Day after day they met in the temple [area] continuing with one mind, and breaking bread in various private homes. They were eating their meals together with joy and generous hearts, praising God *continually*, and having favor with all the people.

Sometimes a community's regularity might look like constant togetherness for a short period of time. Consider the community of Shadrach, Meshach, and Abed-Nego and their short, albeit intense, stay in the fiery furnace. Or, how about the brief community assembled at the first wedding in John 2. That community experience resulted the first recorded miracle of water being changed to wine. And then there is the brief community experience between Jesus and the woman at the well recorded in John 4. And what about the community that formed between Jesus and the woman caught in adultery. In the presence of her accusers, Jesus affirms her, acquits her, and releases her. This community lasted all of eleven verses.

It is love that heals, not time. It is love that overthrows fear. And this kind of love is practiced and matures in healthy communities. Healthy individuals and their communities exhibit joy over the message, respond to the message with action, and interact regularly by learning together, eating together, and praying together.

Healthy Communities Are Private

Love protects the privacy of others. Everyone in a community does not need to know the details of the life of each member. However, in community someone or ones do need to know. In any relationship, some information is secret and some is private. Private information is not for mass consumption. Secret information goes beyond private to the intent that it hides information from others. Typically, we hide out of fear. Secret information generally reflects negatively on the person hiding it. Guilt, shame, and fear accompany secrets. The fear of undesirable consequences fuels the secret-keeper to hide and withhold information. The truth is all have kept information and activity about themselves secret. For communities to be effective they must be private, protecting information about its members that is not needful, nor helpful to those outside.

Healthy communities are places where people willingly divulge secrets and receive love, rather than judgment. To be fearless and free, we need love to inspire us to release our grip on that which frightens and imprisons us. For years, I was ashamed of the quality of my marriage considering I had helped so many others in their marriages. I called this private what I actually regarded as a secret. I told no one the extent of our shared unhappiness. Inadvertently, we taught our girls to lie by telling them our separation was a private matter even though we stood in public light. People were respectful. No one pried because of our position and our influence.

Not even those in our alleged community pressed. Perhaps we were just that skillful in hiding the truth and did not appear to need help. Or maybe they were just too busy to notice. In either case, we did not reflect the community in Acts 2. There is no way we can be interacting with others regularly through various activities and not sense when something is wrong. Healthy communities not only sense when something is wrong, they do something about it.

Healthy Communities' Members Act On Each Other's Behalf

When God approaches Cain concerning his brothers whereabouts, Cain angrily countered by saying, "I do not know. Am I my brother's keeper?" Love acts on others behalf. In healthy communities, participants accept a certain level of responsibility for each other. Paul agrees and instructs the Galatian Community accordingly, saying that they should share one another's burdens.[173] In Romans 15:1, Paul also advises the mature that they ought to support others in their weakness. James joins the cause with the following example.

> If a brother or sister is naked and destitute of daily food, and one of you says to them, "Depart in peace, be warmed and filled," but you do not give them the things which are needed for the body, what does it profit?

A person without clothes may fear humiliation and imprisonment for public nudity. A person without food may eventually fear hunger. And a person without a community might fear being alone. Healthy communities clothe and nourish those in need. In Acts 2:44 and 45 (AMP), we get an idea of a healthy community in action.

And all those who had believed [in Jesus as Savior] were together and had all things in common [considering their possessions to belong to the group as a whole]. And they began selling their property and possessions and were sharing the proceeds with all [the other believers], as anyone had need.

It is easy to meet the needs we can see. But what is the case when the need is mental, emotional, or spiritual in nature? What happens when the needs are not readily observable? And by the way, when it comes to conquering fear this is primarily the case. It is also the reason fear looms large in the Church. One of my favorite writers is Watchman Nee. He writes in "Release of the Spirit,"

We must emphasize it again: Every worker must learn before the Lord how to know man. How many lives were spoiled after passing through the hands of zealous brothers who have not learned this? They vainly and impulsively give their subjective opinions to meet simple objective needs! People are not necessarily afflicted with the ailments that we imagine. Our responsibility is to discern their true spiritual condition.[174]

That's why love is so vital to healthy communities. Love draws out weaknesses, discrepancies in thinking, and impurities to the surface of relationships and seeks to replace these with power, love, and a disciplined mind—*sound familiar?* It should because Paul reminded us that God has not give us a spirit of fear, but one of power love and sound thinking.[175] And it is love's power working through right thinking that conquers fear. Revisit Zechariah's words to Zerubbabel, after work on finishing the second temple stalled due to lack of resources. The Message Bible Translation expounds.

"You can't force these things. They only come about through my Spirit," says God-of-the-Angel-Armies. "So, big mountain, who do you think you are? Next to Zerubbabel you're nothing but a molehill. He'll proceed to set the Cornerstone in place, accompanied by cheers: Yes! Yes! Do it!"[176]

It's God's love, that is, Spirit, that is responsible for conquering fear. And love cannot be forced. Next to God's love, the mountain of fear we face is but a molehill. What seemed impossible to us, love makes possible. Love requires open, available hearts with which to work through. When love is working as God intends, needs are met, hope is revived, joy is restored, fear is defeated, and dreams are fulfilled.

Healthy communities not only see and address the physical well-being of the community as a whole, but also the spiritual, mental, and emotional well-being of its members. It is worth repeating that a healthy community can accomplish this in a few days or even a few hours. We can expect to experience different kinds of communities in our quest to overcome fear and fulfill our destinies. The lessons to be learned and the value we assign the community, whether we experience healing or hurt, hope or harm, depends almost entirely on our intent to grow in love.

Healthy Communities Are Affirming

Love is affirming. Communities that help people overcome fear are affirming. They confirm and reassure people about who they are and what they can do. That's what love does. Healthy communities constantly remind their members who they are in Christ. We can do this because everything Christ was then, we are now.177 I love how my Pastor upholds and repeats who we are in Christ. He constantly says, "I am talking to the YOU in you." What he means is this. There is the 'you' that everyone sees whether behaving well or poorly, rightly or sinfully. And then there is the 'YOU' that you became upon receiving Christ. That 'YOU' is on the inside of 'you." Colossians 1:27 reads,

> To them God willed to make known what are the riches of the glory of this mystery among the Gentiles: which is Christ in you, the hope of glory.

That 'YOU" is sinless because Christ is sinless. Earlier, I stated that before coming to Joy Christian Center Church, I was treated as rebellious. So often, and in so many ways, both directly and indirectly, I heard that I was not submitted or supportive of authority. I was convinced that these people were all right about me. On more than one occasion, church leadership disciplined me by sitting me down and forbidding me to minister. Then I was left to figure it out for myself. At no time did anyone discern or examine my heart to know my intention to submit to authority. I became a problem.

For two years now, I have been a member of the Joy Church Community. From the very outset, Pastors Michael and Michelle Leavell lavished me with affirming words. They spoke to the person God made me to be—the 'Me' on the inside. If they have experienced me as rebellious, they have not said so. Instead, they continuously assert that I am submitted and rightly relating to those in authority. They also tell me that God calls and qualifies men and women and that I have no need for man's approval. And you know what? I have an even greater desire to honor those in authority and bring things I am doing to the light of their love and counsel. It's not that I am required. I want to. They do not tell me what to do, but share scripture and insight so that I may make wise choices. Instead of focusing on rebellion and what I could do to be more submissive, the Leavell's have and continue to emphasize that I am submitted in Christ and encourage me to do all that God has placed in my heart to do. Love adds strength to bruised reeds and smoking flaxes. We need strength in order to get in the room with fear. I need courage to get in the room with those in authority that look and/or behave like those that have mistreated me in the past.

It's not that the Leavell's overlook areas in which I need a change of mind. I remember when Kimberly Taylor, a well-respected prophet, came to our church to minister for a few days. I did not go initially. Pastor Michelle informed me that Kimberly inquired concerning me. Still, I did not go to the following service. Pastor Michelle texted and said that if a prophet had called her out by name, then she would make every effort to be present. She was kind and encouraged me to make an effort to attend the final service. I did. Pastor Michelle did not call me unsubmitted, rebellious, or dishonoring. I felt the warmth of God's love and guidance in how to respond to the authority of this prophet. I felt convicted and invited all at the same time.

Healthy communities succeed in enabling people to face that which they fear. I know that placing so much emphasis on the importance of love in healthy communities will invite criticism.

Anytime one thing is stressed over another, it is easy for some to think that this opposes the other thing or excludes it entirely. It happens often. This tendency leads to much misunderstanding and division in the Church. A current and notable example of this in the Church are those that vehemently argue the significance of the law and equally as vehement are those that argue the importance of grace. It has resulted in division among people that equally love God. While I do not consider myself an expert or either, what I do know is that God is not at war with His Word. We need law and grace. We need love and truth. And healthy communities will inevitably have opportunity to engage both.

Sin is real. When we are tempted and it results in sin, we need to admit what we have done, accept forgiveness, and return to being whom God intends. Hopefully, then we can offer a different response to future temptation. Healthy communities do not focus on sin or shaming it members. They understand sin has been judged finally. Therefore, they do not dwell on sin. Sin does have consequences that a community may not be able to prevent, nor may God want them to. Consider Ananias in Acts 5:1-6. The community was flourishing. All were engaged in selling their possessions and bringing the proceeds to the apostles. Read what Ananias (and his wife) did.

> But a certain man named Ananias, with Sapphira his wife,
> sold a possession. And he kept back part of the proceeds, his
> wife also being aware of it, and brought a certain part and
> laid it at the apostles' feet. But Peter said, "Ananias, why has
> Satan filled your heart to lie to the Holy Spirit and keep back
> part of the price of the land for yourself? While it remained,
> was it not your own? And after it was sold, was it not in your

own control? Why have you conceived this thing in your heart? You have not lied to men but to God." Then Ananias, hearing these words, fell down and breathed his last. So great fear came upon all those who heard these things. And the young men arose and wrapped him up, carried him out, and buried him.

A few hours later Ananias' wife came in and she too lied. Instantly, she fell to the ground and died.

I realize that there are situations in which sin does need to be named and people given the opportunity and support to change. And this is not only necessary in church communities. Sometimes an employer must point out performance problems and offer a plan for improvement. In sports communities of all sorts, feedback is important to the overall health and vitality of the team. In marriage, behaviors that undermine the relationship like drugs and abuse must be confronted openly. Yet and still, it is love that draws the unlovely stuff to the surface and inspires us to let it go.

Healthy communities focus on the end game. When it comes to fear the endgame is whether we are conquering or cowering to fear? What communities choose to focus on contributes greatly to how their members will respond. Each of us has fear to conquer. Former Colorado State Senator (2009-2015), Mark Udall, said,

> You don't climb mountains without a team, you don't climb mountains without being fit, you don't climb mountains without being prepared, and you don't climb mountains without balancing the risks and rewards. And you never climb a mountain on accident - it has to be intentional.[178]

We will not conquer fear without developing love. And community is the best place to grow and mature in love.

Healthy Communities Love

Like the community in Acts 2, healthy communities specialize in love. Love is the foundation and strength of healthy communities. Love is about commitment. Dedication to a community may vary in duration. No matter the length of time a community exists, when love is a prominent feature, there is no limit to what it can accomplish individually and collectively.

For the time such a community is together, its members obligate themselves to one another. Commitment is not a feeling. Interestingly, Darryl a divorced man in his forties suggests that commitment is a skill that must be learned and developed.[179] Healthy communities have members that are learning and growing in commitment. They are routinely challenged and overcoming conditions that tempt them to forsake others. Commitment is a decision that once made will be tested severely and again and again. Practicing commitment results in maturing unconditional love. Perhaps such repetitiveness brings each of us to the place where we too can say that we love others as a sovereign act of our will. True love depends on no one and no thing. Love is and does as it wills for its own pleasure. In your vilest thought or worst act, hear God saying, "It is still my pleasure to love you." That's the kind of love healthy communities offer. Jethro's family loved Moses in his crisis of failure. It was their pleasure. It was Mordecai's pleasure to love Esther after her parents died unexpectedly. It was Ruth's pleasure to love Naomi when she was bitter and had nothing to offer. Ruth's own words convey the strength of her love and commitment to Naomi. After the death of their husbands, twice Naomi insisted that Ruth return to her family of origin. Ruth answered this way,

> Don't ask me to leave you and turn back. Wherever you go, I will go; wherever you live, I will live. Your people will be my people, and your God will be my God. Wherever you die, I will die, and there I will be buried. May the Lord punish me severely if I allow anything but death to separate us![180]

Ruth and Naomi were a community. Today, the depth of love and commitment between these two women might be easy for some to misinterpret. However, there is no indication that their love was maligned. In fact, we have every reason to believe that it was pure and holy. Boaz told Ruth that everybody knew she was a "virtuous" woman. To Boaz's credit, he loved God and was a man of integrity.[181] In time, they married, had children and Ruth became the great grandmother of Jesus. Community offered Ruth love and acceptance. Boaz speaks to Ruth,

> And now, my daughter, do not fear. I will do for you all that you request, for all the people of my town know that you are a virtuous woman.

Healthy communities love, provide, and care for their members. When we use words like love, care for, and provide we are most inclined to think of our more intimate relationships like marriage, or parenting. Seldom do we consider shorter-term communities in this manner. But just think about all the caring communities that arise and provide triage after tragedies, like the Columbine Massacre (1999), September 11 (2001), and more recently Sandy Hook Elementary School (2012). And then there are the communities like the Red Cross that converge and provide disaster relief to victims. But also, we can include those communities that come together to conduct short-term mission trips, or to plan a wedding, a baby shower, a family, or high school reunion. All these represent communities with different objectives, different durations, and differing results.

We are in these communities not only to fulfill the purpose, for which we have joined, but also to give and receive opportunities to practice love. The more love there is working in us and through us the more willing we will be to face fear and fulfill our dreams. And in route, we have the opportunity to become the people that God intends for us to become. Moreover, we get to experience some of the most wonderful relationships imaginable. These are relationships based on love, honesty, and truth that result from individuals taking personal responsibility for their thoughts and actions contributing to the quality of their lives.

Be fearless. Be free.

Listen my friend. No one, absolutely nobody, can tell you how to be you. No one knows more deeply than you the dreams God has placed within you. No one can give you permission to be who God meant you to be. No one can prevent you from becoming all that God desires and accomplishing what He expects. No book, including this one, can make you fearless or set you free.

Only you know how to be you. That's why you are you! Go be you! You already have permission to be you. God granted you permission when He created you and then made you. At best, others can only confirm or condemn you. But as surely as you breathe and your eyes land on these words, you are here, now. You are here on purpose, if only to read the words, "*You are acceptable to God, if to no other."* Whatever is wrong with you, God will take it up with you and in the community He has assigned to love you. In the meantime, dream you must.

Some stir up your God given dreams. Others try to snuff them out. But God does not lie. Whatever He has placed in you to do, whatever He has promised you, He is more than capable of doing it. And He is able to do even more than you can imagine. Becoming fearless is a process. And that process begins now.

Stop asking when it will be your turn. Stop asking when it will be your time, your season, and your opportunity. NOW IS YOUR TURN. NOW IS YOUR TIME. Your season isn't coming; it's here! Right now. It doesn't matter what your situation looks like or what it feels like. You have a desire, a dream, and a purpose. And God gave you the assignment to fulfill each. Stop asking whether or not you have what it takes. You don't. You can't figure it, plan it out, or work it out well enough to accomplish your dreams. Your resources may be slight, but God's are not. God is not depending on you to have enough knowledge, intellect, or money to do what He desires. No one goes to war at his own expense or with his own intelligence and neither will you.

Finally, stop wondering when you will be brave enough to defy fear. As long as you do, fear is your focus. When you become afraid, you are really asking for love. Love happens in community. But loves requires vulnerability. Before there is victory, there must be vulnerability. And before we can be vulnerable, we need love. So, start uploading love from the Server and allow it to become your new operating system. Start drinking love from the fountain and allow rivers of living waters to flow from you. Start inhaling and exhaling love that all those around you may live. Do it intentionally. Do it now. Do it again. Do it often. And watch and see what God will do for you! Fear doesn't stand a chance!

face it *with Love*

NOTES

1. Romans 5:5
2. Eleanor Roosevelt, "You Learn By Living: Eleven Keys For A More Fulfilling Life", Harper-Collins Publishers, New York, NY (1960)
3. Sarah Dressen, "Lock and Key"
4. Romans 7:21 (CEB)
5. Apostle Michael Leavell, Joy Christian Center Church, Buford, GA
6. John 10:10 (NLT)
7. Exodus 2:14
8. Exodus 2:15
9. Exodus 3:10 (NLT)
10. Galatians 1:4 (NLT)
11. Exodus 4:24 (NLT)
12. Exodus 2:22 (NLT)
13. Dr. Henry Cloud, "Necessary Endings: The Employees, Businesses, and Relationships that All of Us Have to Give Up in Order to Move Forward, HarperCollins Publishers, New York, NY 2011
14. Henry Cloud, "Necessary Endings", Harper-Collins Publishers, New York, NY (2010)
15. Genesis 4:6-8 (NLT)
16. Hebrews 4:13 (NKJV)
17. I Samuel 16:7 (MSG)
18. Daniel 3:28 and 29 (NKJV)
19. Philippians 1:21 (NKJV)
20. Daniel and Esther are two examples of people God used to influence the system from within.
21. Genesis 1:26-28 (NLT)
22. I John 4:18
23. Exodus 7:3, 4 (NLT)
24. Exodus 8:8
25. Exodus 13:17 (NKJV)
26. According to Megillah 13a, a scroll read during the Feast of Purim. (http://jwa.org/encyclopedia/glossary/megillah)
27. Esther 2:7 (NLT)
28. Esther 2:15, 17 (AMP)
29. Esther 2:20 (AMP)
30. Esther 4:1-3 (NLT)

31. Esther 8:7, 8 (NLT)

32. Job 3:25 (NKJV)

33. Mark 6:12, 13 and John 4:2 (NKJV)

34. I Peter 2:21, 4:1, 5:8-10; II Timothy 3:12

35. John 15:13

36. Isaiah 9:6 (NLT)

37. Romans 7:21

38. Luke 22:40, 46

39. Luke 22:44

40. Luke 22:43

41. Hebrews 12:3, 4

42. John 19:8 (NKJV

43. John 19:10 (NKJV)

44. I Corinthians 4:17

45. Romans 8:18 (AMP)

46. Psalm 56:1-4 (MSG)

47. Stormie Omartin, "The Power Of A Praying Wife", Harvest House Publishers (1997), Eugene, Oregon

48. USA Today, "Renewed Calls for Gun Control Laws Spur Sales" by Kevin Johnson, September 5, 2015

49. For a list of other industries check out: http://www.businesspundit.com/25-people-and-industries-that-profit-from-fear/

50. Job 3:24-26 (AMP)

51. Henry Wright, "Be In Excellent Health", Whitaker House Publishing (2009), New Kensington, PA

52. http://www.cdc.gov/violenceprevention/acestudy/

53. https://www.psychologytoday.com/blog/the-last-best-cure/201508/7-ways-childhood-adversity-changes-your-brain

54. Tahereh Mafi, "Ignite Me", Harper Collins (2014), New York, NY.

55. Matthew 26:42 (NKJV)

56. Matthew 27:46 (NKJV)

57. Wikipedia offers that Gil Bailie in his book, "Violence Unveiled" (p. xv) attributed the quote to Howard Thurman during a personal conversation.

58. James 1:2-4 (AMP)

59. Exodus 3:11 and 4:10

60. Exodus 3:13 and 4:1

61. Esther 4:11

62. Numbers 13:33 (NKJV)

63. Numbers 13:30 (NKJV)

64. Mark 6:11 (NKJV)

65. Song of Solomon 8:6-8 (MSG)

66. Galatians 5:22

67. Ephesians 4:4-6

68. I Corinthians 12:12 (NKJV)

69. Dvorsky and Hughes, "Postgenderism: Beyond Gender Binary", http://ieet.org/archive/IEET-03-PostGender.pdf

70. http://time.com/3918308/miley-cyrus-transgender-rights-instapride/

71. Instagram Post (April 2015)

72. James 4:7 (NKJV)

73. John 13:34 and 35 (NKJV)

74. I Corinthians 13:4-7 (NLT)

75. http://forums.philosophyforums.com/threads/all-we-do-is-avoid-pain-54699.html (June 2012)

76. Luke 22:44 (NLT)

77. Matthew 27:46 (NLT)

78. John 19:28-30 (NLT)

79. I John 4:18, 19 (AMP)

80. http://www.theguardian.com/world/2015/feb/02/meriam-ibrahim-pregnant-death-row-sudan-your-questions

81. http://www.queerty.com/county-clerk-kim-davis-says-this-isnt-a-gay-or-lesbian-issue-its-about-heaven-or-hell-20150901

82. I John 4:18 (NKJV)

83. I Kings 4:29-31 (NLT)

84. http://www.dailymail.co.uk/news/article-2840460/Life-Kardashians-d-stay-poverty-Thailand-13-year-old-orphan-girl-Kim-desperate-adopt-says-NO.html#ixzz3mr81ygGe

85. http://www.today.com/parents/pronounced-dead-revived-moms-hug-miracle-baby-turning-2-366375

86. I Corinthians 13:8 (NKJV)

87. Philippians 4:6, 7 (NLT)

88. Jacqueline Howard, "Nine Ways Falling In Love Makes Us Do Strange Things", http://www.huffingtonpost.com/2013/12/02/falling-in-love-strange-things_n_4340958.html

89. Arthur C. Brooks, "Taking Risks In Love", http://www.nytimes.com/2015/02/14/opinion/arthur-c-brooks-taking-risks-in-love.html

90. http://med.stanford.edu/news/all-news/2010/10/love-takes-up-where-pain-leaves-off-brain-study-shows.html#sthash.RdhuvZu5.dpuf

91. http://med.stanford.edu/news/all-news/2010/10/love-takes-up-where-pain-leaves-off-brain-study-shows.html

92. I Corinthians 13:4-6 (AMP)

93. Romans 5:1 and 2 (NKJV)

94. I Peter 2:23 (NKJV)

95. Ephesians 3:17-19 (NLT)

96. Romans 12:3

97. Philippians 4:19 (NLT)

98. Philippians 4:11, 12 (NLT)

99. Colossians 1:15 and 16 (NLT)

100. Galatians 5:23

101. Luke 12:11, 12 (NLT)

102. Gissendaner, http://www.nbcnews.com/storyline/lethal-injection/pope-urges-halt-execution-georgia-woman-kelly-gissendaner-n435566

103. I John 2:8

104. Genesis 1:28 (AMP)

105. Acts 11:30, I Thessalonians 5:12, I Timothy 5:17

106. Luke 19:41 (NLJV)

107. I John 1:1-3 (NKJV)

108. Roman 15:1, 2 (NKJV)

109. I John 4:17 (NKJV)

110. Philippians 2:17 (AMP

111. II Timothy 4:6 (AMP)

112. John 4:16-19 (NKJV)

113. John 4:18

114. John 4:25

115. John 4:12

116. John 4:20

117. Isaiah 29:13 (AMP)

118. Luke 6:45 (NKJV)

119. Galatians 6:7 (NKJV)

120. Titus 1:16 (NLT)

121. Matthew 23:27 (NKJV)

122. Romans 5:20

123. I John 4:18 (NLT)

124. Psalm 32:1 (NLT)

125. http://www.brainyquote.com/quotes/quotes/t/thomasaed132683.html

126. http://www.baseball-reference.com/players/a/aaronha01.shtml

127. III John 1:2

128. "Sex In the City" - a 6-week scriptural study of sexual immorality.

129. Proverbs 15:1 (NLT)

130. Matthew 11:29 (NKJV)

131. Dr. Elaine Aron, "The Highly Sensitive Person", Broadway Books (Division of Random House), New York, NY 1996

132. I Corinthians 12:8-10, Galatians 5:22, 23

133. Job 33:28-30 (NLT)

134. Job 33:6, 7 (NLT)

135. See Chapter 16

136. Romans 8:28

137. Philippians 2:5 (NKJV)

138. I Corinthians 4:6-9 (NKJV)

139. II Corinthians 12:9 (NLT)

140. Hannah Hurnard, "Hind's Feet In High Places", Wilder Publications, Blacksburg, VA (2010)

141. I Thessalonians 5:18

142. I John 4:10 (NLT)

143. I Timothy 4:1-3 (NKJV)

144. II Thessalonians 2:10

145. http://jejusauna.com/korean-bathing-house-in-atlanta/

146. Psalm 46:10 (NLT)

147. Job 33:14-18 (NKJV)

148. James 3:10-12 (NLT)

149. Leviticus 17:11

150. http://www.waterinfo.org/resources/water-facts

151. John 10:10

152. Philippians 4:19

153. I Kings 3:16-28

154. Zechariah 4:6 (NKJV)

155. Song of Solomon 6:8, 9 (NKJV)

156. I Timothy 2:5

157. "Your Spouse Is Not Your Problem!" Amazon.com (http://tinyurl.com/oon6nmb)

158. Ephesians 3:14-19 (NKJV)

159. Proverbs 11:24 (NKJV)

160. http://www.brainyquote.com/quotes/keywords/abundance.html

161. John 10:10 (NKJV)

162. http://www.monadnock.net/douglass/self-made-men.html

163. The Thich Nhat Hanh Collection: Peace is Every Step; Teachings on Love; The Stone Boy and Other Stories, Bookspan (2004)

164. I John 4:18 (AMP)

165. II Timothy 1:7 (NKJV)

166. Ephesians 1:18 (NLT)

167. http://wish.org/about-us

168. Ezekiel 34:7, 8 (NLT)

169. http://www.oprah.com/shiftyourlife/Questions-That-Could-Change-Your-Life

170. http://www.cdc.gov/healthyplaces/about.htm

171. http://www.raymondibrahim.com/2015/12/13/swedish-government-in-state-of-panic-after-isis-letters-give-dozens-of-citizens-three-days-to-convert-to-islam-or-be-decapitated/

172. http://www.nbcnews.com/storyline/iraq-turmoil/isis-jihadists-send-video-message-english-speakers-join-us-n137281

173. Galatians 6:2 (NLT)

174. Watchman Nee, "Release of the Spirit", Christian Fellowship Publishers, Inc., New York 2000

175. II Timothy 1:7

176. Zechariah 4:6, 7 (MSG)

177. I John 4:7

178. http://www.brainyquote.com/quotes/keywords/intentional.html

179. Catherine Gibson McCauley, "The Esquire Life" (Show #9 Aired 12/05/15), http://www.1690wmlb.com

180. Ruth 1:16 and 17 (NLT)

181. Ruth 3:12 and 13 (NKJV)

face it *with Love*